Learning Android Application Development

Build Android N applications using modern techniques and libraries to get your own high-quality apps published on Google Play in no time

Raimon Ràfols Montané
Laurence Dawson

BIRMINGHAM - MUMBAI

Learning Android Application Development

First published: August 2016

Production reference: 1190816

Published by Packt Publishing Ltd.

Livery Place

35 Livery Street

Birmingham B3 2PB, UK.

ISBN 978-1-78528-611-7

www.packtpub.com

Credits

Authors

Raimon Ràfols Montané
Laurence Dawson

Reviewers

Vincent Brison
Pablo Pera
Karim Varela

Commissioning Editor

Veena Pagare

Acquisition Editor

Reshma Raman

Content Development Editor

Zeeyan Pinheiro

Technical Editors

Vivek Pala

Copy Editor

Gladson Monteiro

Project Coordinator

Suzanne Coutinho

Proofreader

Safis Editing

Indexer

Rekha Nair

Production Coordinator

Aparna Bhagat

Cover Work

Aparna Bhagat

About the Author

Raimon Ràfols Montané is a software engineer currently living in the Barcelona area. He has been working on mobile devices since the early stages, ranging from monochrome devices to the current smartphones. In all these years, he has worked in several areas: B2C/B2E/B2B apps, portals, and mobile gaming. Due to this broad experience, he has expertise in many technologies and, especially in UI, build systems, and client-server communications.

He is currently working as an engineering manager at AXA Group Solutions in Barcelona, taking care of all the engineering and development processes, mobile application quality, and leading a small R&D team. In the past, he has worked abroad for Imagination Technologies near London and for Service2Media in the Netherlands.

In his spare time, he enjoys taking part in hackathons, photography, and speaking at conferences. Raimon has won more than 40 international awards, including AngelHack Barcelona 2015, Facebook World Hack Barcelona, and he has secured second place at js1k 2016. He has been speaking about Java/Android performance and bytecode, Android custom views, and entrepreneurship in several conferences around the world.

I would like to thank my girlfriend for her support and understanding during the late night and lengthy writing weekends. Also, I would like to thank my parents and Rafa, my cousin, as without their support and encouragement, I would not be doing what I do today.

Last, but not least, I would like to thank everyone who challenged me and helped me grow in my professional career, people such as Carlos Carrasco, Alfred Ferrer, Pau Vivancos, Miquel Barceló, David Domingo, Marcel Roorda, Diego Morales, Alberto Chamorro, Teun van Run, Tom van Wietmarschen, Josep Cedó, Joanne Pupo, Jordi Valldaura, Mathieu Sivade, Chris Jakob, Tomas Kustrzynski, Bartłomiej Żarnowski, Radosław Holewa, and all those who I have forgotten to mention here.

Laurence Dawson is a software developer and an academic focused on mobile development.

He received a PhD in 2015 from Durham University, developing efficient parallel implementations of algorithms for GPUs using NVIDIA CUDA with an emphasis on metaheuristics and image processing.

Laurence currently runs his own mobile software development company and is also a guest lecturer at King's College London, teach software engineering modules.

You can follow his projects on his GitHub page at `https://github.com/laurencedawson`.

About the Reviewers

Vincent Brison is a veteran Android software craftsman. With 4 years of Android development experience, he successfully lead the development of reference banking applications as the lead Android developer. He specializes in application architecture around Clean Code, code quality and testing on Android, and cutting edge graphical implementations for Android. As an open source enthusiast, Vincent is sharing some of his work on GitHub (`https://github.com/vincentbrison`), on his personal website (`https://vincentbrison.com`), and in events like Droidcon.

I personally would like to thank Thomas B. for showing me the right way of crafting Android applications.

Pablo Pera is an entrepreneur and engineer who has built and launched Android apps that have reached more than 30 million users worldwide. He started his professional career at Google, right about the time Android was born, and worked for large organizations such as CERN and tech startups, where he has been leading various engineering teams.

Karim Varela is an entrepreneur and mobile enthusiast at heart. He is currently involved in a couple of mobile start-ups, Coffee Meets Bagel and Tastemates. At Coffee Meets Bagel, he leads the engineering team and he advises Tastemates and Proxloop on strategy, product, and technology. Previously, he built the Android app for the world-famous Tinder app.

He earned an MBA from the University of Florida and a bachelor's degree in computer science from the University of California. He also contributed as a technical reviewer on the book *Pro Android 4* and coauthored the book *Instant GSON*.

www.PacktPub.com

For support files and downloads related to your book, please visit www.PacktPub.com.

eBooks, discount offers, and more

Did you know that Packt offers eBook versions of every book published, with PDF and ePub files available? You can upgrade to the eBook version at www.PacktPub.com and as a print book customer, you are entitled to a discount on the eBook copy. Get in touch with us at customercare@packtpub.com for more details.

At www.PacktPub.com, you can also read a collection of free technical articles, sign up for a range of free newsletters and receive exclusive discounts and offers on Packt books and eBooks.

https://www2.packtpub.com/books/subscription/packtlib

Do you need instant solutions to your IT questions? PacktLib is Packt's online digital book library. Here, you can search, access, and read Packt's entire library of books.

Why subscribe?

- Fully searchable across every book published by Packt
- Copy and paste, print, and bookmark content
- On demand and accessible via a web browser

Free access for Packt account holders

Get notified! Find out when new books are published by following @PacktEnterprise on Twitter or the Packt Enterprise Facebook page.

Table of Contents

Preface

Mobile development has been a market with huge potential since the very beginning, but there have been some issues in the past, ranging from content discovery, where to download apps and games, to the prohibitive costs of data in some countries. With the launch of iPhone and the App Store, the whole market skyrocketed. Google followed up and introduced Android and the Google Play Store. Today, we all know where we can find applications for our smartphone and flat data rates or, at least, very accessible data plans are more common in many countries. In addition, many companies transformed their operating model to become mobile first and, nowadays, it is very strange not to find a mobile application of a service or business that has direct interaction with consumers that provides services to their employees and, obviously, those companies whose whole business model is based on a mobile application.

The aim of this book is to introduce newcomers to Android development and, for those that are already experienced, to brush up on some concepts and maybe add some final touches to their applications. We will cover several aspects of Android development, ranging from the very basics to the more advanced subjects. We will briefly explain the foundations, as it is important to understand how everything works, but we will focus more on open source and broadly used third-party libraries. Android has a very rich, open source, and extensively tested library ecosystem, and it will be a mistake not to take advantage of it. These libraries are widely used by many of the most downloaded apps in Google Play and knowing how they work is becoming crucial, both to speed up the development time and to perform well in job interviews. Do not forget to contribute back to the community!

What this book covers

Chapter 1, *Getting Started with Android Development*, will explain how to install Android Studio, create a sample project, and run it on an Android emulator, and finally provide an introduction to the Gradle build system.

Chapter 2, *Activities and Fragments – The Backbone of Your App*, will demonstrate how to create activities and fragments and understand their lifecycle.

Chapter 3, *Working with Views – Interacting with Your App*, will show the most common Views and ViewGroups and how to create custom Views.

Chapter 4, *Lists and Adapters*, will explore how to add lists to our application, ranging from the good old ListView to the new RecyclerView. We will also cover the possible performance issues we might run into.

`Chapter 5`, *Remote Data*, will explain how to retrieve data from the network using Android standard classes and then some third-party open source libraries.

`Chapter 6`, *Image Management*, will describe how to load images, cache them efficiently, and use different libraries to hide all the complexity.

`Chapter 7`, *Permanent Data*, will teach you how to store information on the local device, ranging from temporary files to an SQLite database.

`Chapter 8`, *Testing Your Application*, will demonstrate how to automatically test our application and add unit and UI tests.

`Chapter 9`, *Publishing Your Application*, will describe how to publish our application to Google Play.

`Chapter 10`, *Monetization – Make Money with Your App*, will explain how to add in-app purchases, set the price of our application, and add in-app advertisements.

What you need for this book

To start developing for Android, you will need a version of Android Studio. In this book, we will cover how to download and install the latest stable version and, for the brave, how to install a development or beta version. The development version will contain all the latest features but they might not be as stable as they should be.

Who this book is for

Want to get started with Android development? Start here.

Conventions

In this book, you will find a number of text styles that distinguish between different kinds of information. Here are some examples of these styles and an explanation of their meaning.

Code words in text, database table names, folder names, filenames, file extensions, pathnames, dummy URLs, user input, and Twitter handles are shown as follows: "To edit your app manifest, open the folder `manifests` and double-click on the `AndroidManifest.xml` file."

A block of code is set as follows:

```
public class SampleActivity extends Activity {

  @Override
  protected void onCreate(Bundle savedInstanceState) {
    super.onCreate(savedInstanceState);

    // Called when the activity is first created
  }
}
```

New terms and important words are shown in bold. Words that you see on the screen, for example, in menus or dialog boxes, appear in the text like this: "Click on this tab and select **Android** from the top drop-down menu."

 Warnings or important notes appear in a box like this.

 Tips and tricks appear like this.

Reader feedback

Feedback from our readers is always welcome. Let us know what you think about this book—what you liked or disliked. Reader feedback is important for us as it helps us develop titles that you will really get the most out of.

To send us general feedback, simply e-mail `feedback@packtpub.com`, and mention the book's title in the subject of your message.

If there is a topic that you have expertise in and you are interested in either writing or contributing to a book, see our author guide at `www.packtpub.com/authors`.

Customer support

Now that you are the proud owner of a Packt book, we have a number of things to help you to get the most from your purchase.

Downloading the example code

You can download the example code files for this book from your account at `http://www.packtpub.com`. If you purchased this book elsewhere, you can visit `http://www.packtpub.com/support` and register to have the files e-mailed directly to you.

You can download the code files by following these steps:

1. Log in or register to our website using your e-mail address and password.
2. Hover the mouse pointer on the **SUPPORT** tab at the top.
3. Click on **Code Downloads & Errata**.
4. Enter the name of the book in the **Search** box.
5. Select the book for which you're looking to download the code files.
6. Choose from the drop-down menu where you purchased this book from.
7. Click on **Code Download**.

You can also download the code files by clicking on the **Code Files** button on the book's webpage at the Packt Publishing website. This page can be accessed by entering the book's name in the Search box. Please note that you need to be logged in to your Packt account.

Once the file is downloaded, please make sure that you unzip or extract the folder using the latest version of:

- WinRAR / 7-Zip for Windows
- Zipeg / iZip / UnRarX for Mac
- 7-Zip / PeaZip for Linux

The code bundle for the book is also hosted on GitHub at `https://github.com/PacktPublishing/learningandroidapplicationdevelopment`. We also have other code bundles from our rich catalog of books and videos available at `https://github.com/PacktPublishing/`. Check them out!

Errata

Although we have taken every care to ensure the accuracy of our content, mistakes do happen. If you find a mistake in one of our books—maybe a mistake in the text or the code—we would be grateful if you could report this to us. By doing so, you can save other readers from frustration and help us improve subsequent versions of this book. If you find any errata, please report them by visiting http://www.packtpub.com/submit-errata, selecting your book, clicking on the Errata Submission Form link, and entering the details of your errata. Once your errata are verified, your submission will be accepted and the errata will be uploaded to our website or added to any list of existing errata under the Errata section of that title.

To view the previously submitted errata, go to https://www.packtpub.com/books/content/support and enter the name of the book in the search field. The required information will appear under the Errata section.

Piracy

Piracy of copyrighted material on the Internet is an ongoing problem across all media. At Packt, we take the protection of our copyright and licenses very seriously. If you come across any illegal copies of our works in any form on the Internet, please provide us with the location address or website name immediately so that we can pursue a remedy.

Please contact us at copyright@packtpub.com with a link to the suspected pirated material.

We appreciate your help in protecting our authors and our ability to bring you valuable content.

Questions

If you have a problem with any aspect of this book, you can contact us at questions@packtpub.com, and we will do our best to address the problem.

1
Getting Started with Android Development

In this chapter, we will go through all the steps required to start developing Android devices. We have to be aware that Android is an evolving platform and so are its development tools. We will show how to download and install Android Studio and how to create a new project and run it on either an emulator or a real device. We will spend some time going through some additional components that we will use in later chapters.

- Installing Android Studio
- Creating a sample project
- Additional components

Setting up Android Studio

Before being able to build an Android application, we have to download and install Android Studio on our computer. It is still possible to download and use Eclipse with the **Android Development Tools (ADT)** plugin, but Google no longer supports it and they recommend that we migrate to Android Studio. In order to be aligned with this, we will only focus on Android Studio in this book. For more information on this, visit `http://android-developers.blogspot.com.es/215/6/an-update-on-eclipse-android-developer.html`.

Getting the right version of Android Studio

The latest stable version of Android Studio can be found at `http://developer.android.com/sdk/index.html`.

If you are among the bravest developers, and you are not afraid of bugs, you can always go to the Canary channel and download the latest version. The Canary channel is one of the preview channels available on the Android tools download page (available at `http://tools.android.com/download/studio`) and contains weekly builds.

The following are other preview channels available at that URL:

- The **Canary** channel contains weekly builds. These builds are tested but they might contain some issues. Just use a build from this channel if you need or want to see the latest features.
- The **Dev** channel contains selected Canary builds.
- The **Beta** channel contains the beta milestones for the next version of Android Studio.
- The **Stable** channel contains the most recent stable builds of Android Studio.

The following screenshot illustrates the Android Tools download page:

 It is not recommended to use an unstable version for production. To be on the safe side, always use the latest stable version. In this book, we will use the 2.2 preview version. Although it is a beta version at this moment, we will have the main version quite soon.

Installing Android Studio

Android Studio requires JDK 6 or higher: JDK 7 is required as a minimum if you aim to develop for Android 5.0 and higher. You can easily check which version you have installed by running this on your command line:

```
javac -version
```

If you don't have any version of the JDK or you have an unsupported version, please install or update your JDK before proceeding to install Android Studio.

Refer to the official documentation for a more comprehensive installation guide and details on all platforms (Windows, Linux, and Mac OSX) at `http://developer.android.com/sdk/` `installing/index.html?pkg=studio`.

Once you have JDK installed, unpack the package you have just downloaded from the Internet and proceed with the installation. For example, let's use Mac OSX. If you download the latest stable version, you will get a `.dmg` file that can be mounted on your filesystem. Once mounted, a new Finder window will appear and will ask us to drag the Android Studio icon to the `Applications` folder. Just doing this simple step will complete the basic installation.

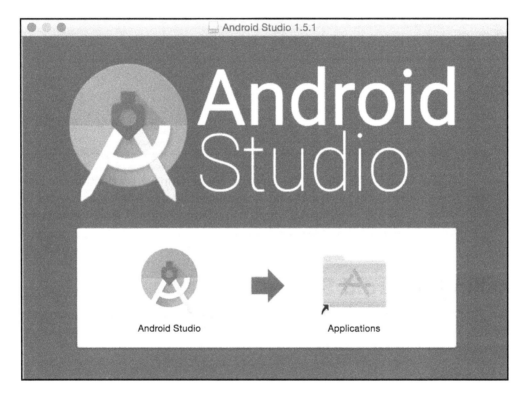

If you have downloaded a preview version, you will have a ZIP file that once unpacked will contain the Android Studio Application directly (it can be just dragged to the `Applications` folder using Finder).

For other platforms, refer to the official installation guide provided by Google at the web address mentioned earlier.

First run

Once you have finished installing Android Studio, it is time to run it for the first time. On the first execution (at least if you have downloaded version 2.2), it will let you configure some options and install some SDK components if you choose the custom installation type. Otherwise, both these settings and SDK components can be configured or installed later.

The first option you will be able to choose is the UI theme. We have the default UI theme or the Darcula theme, which basically is a choice of light or dark backgrounds, respectively.

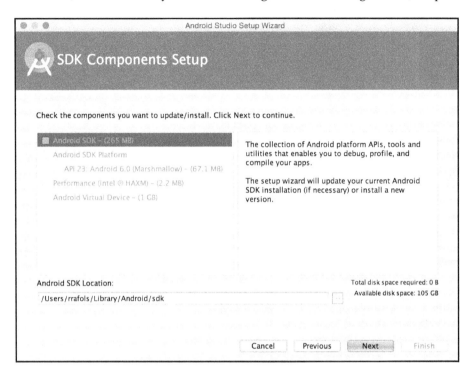

After this step, the next window will show the **SDK Components Setup** where the installation process will let you choose some components to automatically download and install. On Mac OS, there is a bug in some versions of Android Studio 2.0 that sometimes does not allow selecting any option if the target folder does not exist. If that happens, follow these steps for a quick fix:

1. Copy the contents of the **Android SDK Location** field, just the path or something like /Users/<username>/Library/Android/sdk, to the clipboard.
2. Open the terminal application.
3. Create the folder manually as
   mkdir /Users/<username>/Library/Android/sdk.

4. Go back to Android Studio, press the **Previous** button, and then the **Next** button to come back to this screen. Now, you will be able to select the components that you would like to install.

5. If that still does not work, cancel the installation process, ensuring that you checked the option to rerun the setup on the next installation. Quit Android Studio and rerun it.

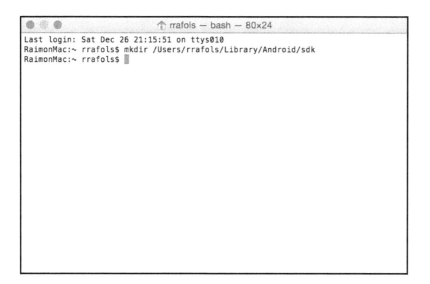

Creating a sample project

We will introduce some of the most common elements in Android Studio by creating a sample project, building it, and running it on an Android emulator or on a real android device. It is better to display those elements when you need them rather than just enumerate a long list without a real use behind.

Starting a new project

Just press the **Start a new Android Studio project** button to start a project from scratch. Android Studio will ask you to make some project configuration settings, and you will be able to launch your project. If you have an already existing project and would like to import it to Android Studio, you could do it now as well. Any projects based on Eclipse, Ant, or Gradle build can be easily imported into Android Studio. Projects can be also checked out from Version Control software such as Subversion or Git directly from Android Studio.

When creating a new project, it will ask for the application name and the company domain name, which will be reversed into the application package name.

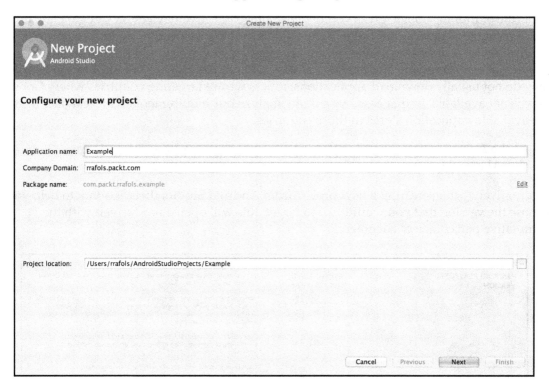

Once this information is filled in, Android Studio will ask the type of device or form factors your application will target. This includes not only phones and tablets, but also Android Wear, Android TV, Android Auto, or Google Glass. In this example, we will target only phones and tablets and require a minimum SDK API level of 14 (Android 4.0 or Ice Cream Sandwich). By setting the minimum required level to 14, we make sure that the app will run on approximately 96.2% of devices accessing Google Play Store, which is good enough. If we set 23 as the minimum API level (Android 6.0 Marshmallow), our application will only run on Android Marshmallow devices, which is fewer than 1% of active devices on Google Play right now.

Unless we require a very specific feature available on a specific API level, we should use common sense and try to aim for as many devices as we can. Having said that, we should not waste time supporting very old devices (or very old versions of Android), as they might be, for example, only 5% of the active devices but may imply lots and lots of work to make your application support them. In addition to the minimum SDK version, there is also the target SDK version. The target SDK version should be, ideally, set to the latest stable version of Android available to allow your application to take advantage of all the new features, styles, and behaviors from newer versions.

As a rule of thumb, Google gives you the percentage of active devices on Google Play, not the percentage of devices out there in the wild. So, unless we need to build an enterprise application for a closed set of devices and installed ad hoc, we should not mind those people not even accessing Google Play, as they will not the users of our application because they do not usually download applications, unless we are targeting countries where Google Play is not available. In that case, we should analyze our requirements with real data from the available application stores in those countries.

To see the Android OS version distribution, always check the Android developer dashboard at `http://developer.android.com/about/dashboards/index.html`.

Alternatively, when creating a new project from Android Studio, there is a link to help you choose the version that you would like to target; this will open a new screen with the cumulative percentage of coverage.

If you click on each version, it will give you more details about that Android OS version and the features that were introduced, as shown in the following screenshot:

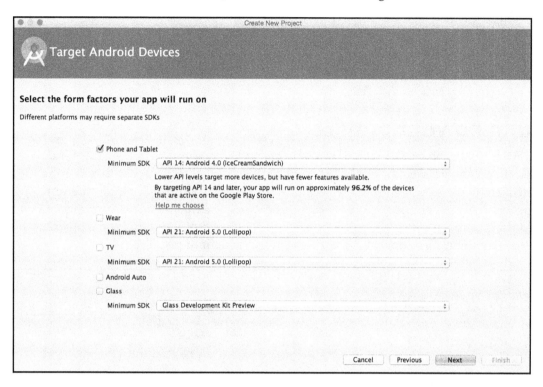

After this step, and to simplify our application creation process, Android Studio will allow us to add an `Activity` class to the project from some templates. In this case, we can add an empty `Activity` class for the time being. Let's not worry about the name of the `Activity` class and layout file at this moment; we can safely proceed with the prefilled values.

> As defined by Android developer documentation an: `Activity` *is a single, focused thing that the user can do.*
> (*Source:* `http://developer.android.com/reference/android/app/Activity.html`)

To simplify further, we can consider an `Activity` class as every single screen of our application where the user can interact with it. If we take into consideration the MVC pattern, we can assume the `Activity` class to be the Controller, as it will receive all the user inputs and events from the views, and the layout XML and UI widgets to be the views.

To know more about the MVC pattern, check out the following page: `https://en.wikipedia.org/wiki/Model%E2%8%93view%E2%8%93control ler`.

So, we have just added one `Activity` class to our application; let's see what else the Android Studio wizard created for us.

Running your project

The Android Studio project wizard not only created an empty `Activity` class for us, but it also created an `AndroidManifest`, a layout file (`activity_main.xml`) defining the View controlled by the `Activity` class, an application icon placed carefully into different mipmaps (`https://en.wikipedia.org/wiki/Mipmap`) so that the most appropriate will be used depending on the screen resolution, some Gradle scripts, and and some other `.xml` files containing colors, dimensions, strings, and style definitions.

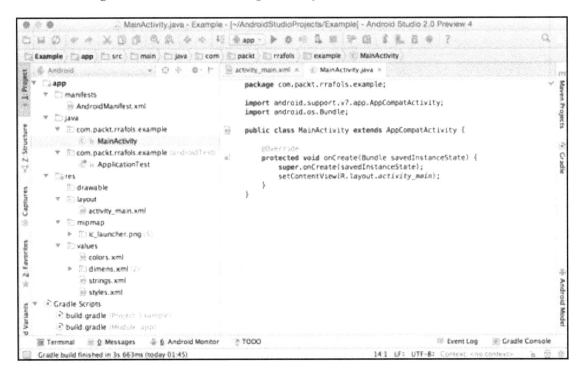

We can have multiple resources, and even repeated resources, depending on screen resolution, screen orientation, night mode, layout direction, or even the mobile country code of the SIM card. Take a look at the next topic to understand how to add qualifiers and filters to resources. For the time being, let's just try to run this example by pressing the Play button next to our build configuration named app at the top of the screen.

Android Studio will show us a small window where we can select the deployment target: a real device or emulator where our application will be installed and launched. If we have not connected any device or created any emulator, we can do it from the following screen. Let's press the **Create New Emulator** button.

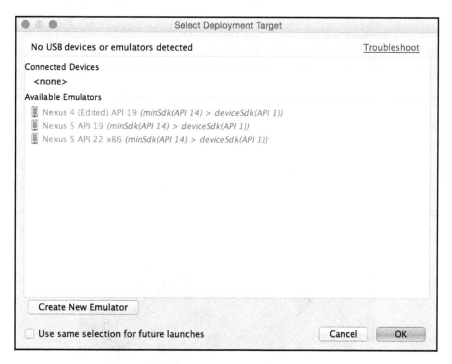

From this new screen, we can easily select a device and create an emulator that looks like that device. A Nexus 5X will suit us. After choosing the device, we can choose which version of the Android OS and architecture the platform will run on. For instance, if we want to select Android Marshmallow (API level 23), we can choose from armeabi-v7a, x86 (Intel processors) and x86_64 (Intel 64bit processors). As we previously installed HAXM during our first run (https://software.intel.com/en-us/android/articles/intel-har

`dware-accelerated-execution-manager`), we should install an Intel image, so the emulator will be a lot faster than having to emulate an ARM processor. If we do not have the Android OS image downloaded to our computer, we can do it from this screen as well. Note that you can have an image of the OS with Google APIs or without them. We will use one image or another depending on whether the application uses any Google-specific libraries (Google Play Services) or only the Android core libraries.

Once the image is selected (and downloaded and installed, if needed), we can proceed to finish the **Android Virtual Device** (**AVD**) configuration. On the last configuration screen, we can fine-tune some elements of our emulator, such as the default orientation (portrait or landscape), the screen scale, the SD card (if we enable the advanced settings), the amount of physical RAM, network latency, and we can use the webcam in our computer as the emulator's camera.

You are now ready to run your application on the Android emulator that you just created. Just select it as the deployment target and wait for it to load and install the app. If everything goes as it should, you should see this screen on the Android emulator:

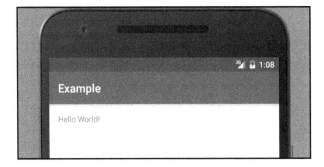

If you want to use a real device instead of an emulator, make sure that your device has the developer options enabled and it is connected to your computer using a USB cable. To enable development mode on your device or get information on how to develop and debugapplications over the network, instead of having the device connected through an USB, check out the following links:

- `http://developer.android.com/tools/help/adb.html`
- `http://developer.android.com/tools/device.html`

If these steps are performed correctly, your device will appear as a connected device on the deployment target selection window.

Resource configuration qualifiers

As we introduced in the previous section, we can have multiple resources depending on the screen resolution or any other device configuration, and Android will choose the most appropriate resource at runtime. In order to do that, we have to use what is called configuration qualifiers. These qualifiers are only strings appended to the resource folder. Consider the following example:

```
drawable
drawable-hdpi
drawable-mdpi
drawable-en-rUS-land
layout
layout-en
layout-sw600dp
layout-v7
```

Qualifiers can be combined, but they must always follow the order specified by Google in the *Providing Resource* documentation, available at `http://developer.android.com/guide/topics/resources/providing-resources.html`.

This allows us, for instance, to target multiple resolutions and have the best experience for each of them. It can be also used to have different images based on the country in which the application is executed, or the language.

We have to be aware that putting in too many resources (basically, images or any other media) will make our application grow in size. It is always good to apply common sense. And, in the event of having too many different resources or configurations, do not bloat the application and produce different binaries that can be deployed selectively to different devices on Google Play. We will briefly explain in the Gradle build system topic in this chapter, how to produce different binaries from one single source code. It will add some complexity on our development but will make our application smaller and more convenient for end users. For more information on multiple APK support, visit `http://developer.and roid.com/google/play/publishing/multiple-apks.html`.

Additional elements

Now that we have already introduced some of the elements involved in the process of building mobile applications for Android devices, we will dive deep into some of them.

Resources

To build an application we do not only need source code, we also need some additional files such as images, text, layout description files, or others. Those additional files are what we call resources. Our project will contain a res directory together with our `src` directory. Inside this directory, we can find resources needed by our application.

To make our application as easy as possible to maintain and add new features to we should externalize resources such as application images and texts from the source code. It will keep our application code simple and we can easily add support for new countries or new languages for example. As explained earlier, we can have multiple resources and, thanks to the resource qualifiers, the Android device will pick the proper resource based on its properties in runtime.

For static files that need to be included without any kind of filter, you can use the assets folder. Everything there will be included into the final application. To access these assets, we will have to use the `AssetManager` class, but we will cover this later. Visit `http://deve loper.android.com/reference/android/content/res/AssetManager.html` for more information on the `AssetManager` class.

Modules

In order to keep the code of the application tidy and uncoupled, we can identify parts of the application, which might be even reused later in some other applications, that can be completely decoupled and exposed as a module. Gradle, the build system, allows us to have several modules and establish dependencies between the main application and those modules. To make it more interesting, these modules can be extracted as independent projects and have an independent release cycle as though we are using a third-party library. Modules can be considered as Android libraries or Android library projects. Instead of having third-party dependencies pulled from remote repositories, we have them inside our project. Visit `https://developer.android.com/studio/projects/add-app-module.html` for more information on modules.

Android Manifest

The Android Manifest file is our application descriptor. Here, we can find all the activities, services, content providers, and broadcast receivers defined in our application, the list of permissions required, which icon to use on the `Application` menu, and a lot of other configurations. For an exhaustive list of configurations, check the official documentation at `http://developer.android.com/guide/topics/manifest/manifest-intro.html`.

When the application is compiled, the manifest is transformed into a binary format. In order to see the manifest of a compiled APK, we can use the following tool, included with the Android SDK:

```
<Android SDK path>/build-tools/23.0.2/aapt dump badging <apk file>
```

On Mac OS, Android SDK will be installed inside your local `Library` directory, as `~/Library/Android/sdk/`.

Gradle build system

Gradle(`http://gradle.org`) is the new build system recommended by Google. On previous versions, and before the introduction of Android Studio, Ant was the default build system used. Gradle is a DSL, or domain-specific language, that allows scripting for more complex build processes or configurations. You can do lots of things with it, but some of the most used parts of the Gradle build system are dependency management and the option to build different flavors (or configurations) of your application.

Dependency management is not only useful for managing internal modules, but also for managing external third-party libraries that we will use in our application.

If, for instance, we want to include Retrofit (HTTP client, http://square.github.io/retrofit/) and Picasso (the image downloading library, http://square.github.io/picasso/), we will have to add the two dependencies to our build.gradle file under the dependencies keyword:

```
dependencies {
    compile fileTree(dir: 'libs', include: ['*.jar'])
    testCompile 'junit:junit:4.12'
    compile 'com.android.support:appcompat-v7:23.1.1'
    compile 'com.squareup.retrofit2:retrofit:2.0.0-beta3'
    compile 'com.squareup.picasso:picasso:2.5.2'
}
```

We have just added the last two lines to the dependencies that Android Studio puts in by default.

Let's now discuss flavors, a very powerful way to build multiple configurations out of the same source code. If we take a look at Google Play, we will notice that there are many apps and games with a free version, usually limited or with ads, and a full or pro version.

Instead of duplicating all the code and having to build two different applications, adding two different flavors to your application allows you to have two or more different builds out of almost the same source code. Each flavor can have a specific source code and resources that will differentiate it from the other flavors, but at the same time each flavor will share the common source code and resources with all the others.

Let's modify our test application, the one created by the Android Studio Wizard, to add two flavors.

First, we need to add the two flavors to our build.gradle file. Here is the resulting file with the two flavors and the dependencies we introduced in the previous topic.

```
apply plugin: 'com.android.application'
android {
    compileSdkVersion 23
    buildToolsVersion "23.0.2"
    defaultConfig {
    applicationId "com.packt.rrafols.example"
    minSdkVersion 14
    targetSdkVersion 23
    versionCode 1
    versionName "1.0"
    }
```

```
productFlavors {
  free {
    applicationId "com.packt.rrafols.example.free"
  }
  pro {
    applicationId "com.packt.rrafols.example.pro"
  }
}
buildTypes {
  release {
    minifyEnabled false
    proguardFiles getDefaultProguardFile('proguard-
    android.txt'),'proguard-rules.pro'
  }
}
}
dependencies {
  compile fileTree(dir: 'libs', include: ['*.jar'])
  testCompile 'junit:junit:4.12'
  compile 'com.android.support:appcompat-v7:23.1.1'
  compile 'com.squareup.retrofit2:retrofit:2.0.0-beta3'
  compile 'com.squareup.picasso:picasso:2.5.2'
}
```

As you can see, there are two different flavors, free and pro, with different applicationId objects, so we can have both installed on any device at the same time.

Now, we go to Android Studio and create these directories:

- app/src/free/java/com/packt/rrafols
- app/src/pro/java/com/packt/rrafols

The shared part of the code will remain in app/src/java and the specific code for each flavor will go into its own directory. Let's create a dummy class named ApplicationName inside the directory we created for the free flavor with the following content:

```
package com.packt.rrafols;
public class ApplicationName {
  public static final String APPLICATION_FLAVOR = "free";
}
```

We will do the same for the pro flavor:

```
package com.packt.rrafols;
public class ApplicationName {
  public static final String APPLICATION_FLAVOR = "pro";
}
```

Now, we will have two classes with the same name but, no need to worry, only one of them will be included in our build, depending on which flavor we are building.

To show that this is working, let's modify the `MainActivity` class to change the title to the `APPLICATION_FLAVOR` value:

```
package com.packt.rrafols.example;
import android.support.v7.app.AppCompatActivity;
import android.os.Bundle;
import com.packt.rrafols.ApplicationName;
public class MainActivity extends AppCompatActivity {
  @Override
  protected void onCreate(Bundle savedInstanceState) {
    super.onCreate(savedInstanceState);
    setContentView(R.layout.activity_main);
    getSupportActionBar()
    .setTitle(ApplicationName.APPLICATION_FLAVOR);
  }
}
```

We can choose which flavor to build from the **Build Variants** tab in Android Studio.

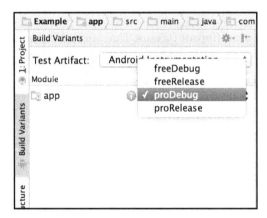

We can also achieve the same effect by having different resources in each flavor. Let's change our `MainActivity` layout, as follows:

```
<?xml version="1.0" encoding="utf-8"?>
<RelativeLayout xmlns:android="http://schemas.android.com/apk/res/android"
  xmlns:tools="http://schemas.android.com/tools"
  android:layout_width="match_parent"
  android:layout_height="match_parent"
  android:paddingBottom="@dimen/activity_vertical_margin"
  android:paddingLeft="@dimen/activity_horizontal_margin"
```

```
android:paddingRight="@dimen/activity_horizontal_margin"
android:paddingTop="@dimen/activity_vertical_margin"
tools:context="com.packt.rrafols.example.MainActivity">
<TextView
  android:layout_width="wrap_content"
  android:layout_height="wrap_content"
  android:text="@string/app_flavor" />
</RelativeLayout>
```

Next, let's create the property in the `res/values/strings.xml` directory:

```
<string name="app_flavor">No flavor specified</string>
```

To customize this message, we will have to create two resource folders, one for each flavor like we did before for the source code:

- `app/src/free/res/values`
- `app/src/pro/res/values`

In the free flavor resource folder, we will create a new `strings.xml` file with the following content:

```
<resources>
<string name="app_flavor">Application flavor: free</string>
</resources>
```

Also, we will do the same for the pro flavor:

```
<resources>
<string name="app_flavor">Application flavor: pro</string>
</resources>
```

Properties from our flavor will be merged with the default properties. Those that are equal will be overwritten by the flavor-specific value and the application will show the selected flavor message.

As an alternative to Gradle, if you have a very big application and the build time is one of your bottlenecks, you might even try Buck. Buck (`https://buckbuild.com`) is the build system developed by Facebook. It highly focused on build performance although the latest versions of Gradle are improving on performance, and Gradle is the tool selected by Google.

ProGuard

ProGuard is a code obfuscation tool. The Java compiler does not do a good job of optimizing the resulting class files when compiled from Java sources. By default, it preserves all the variable names, method names and code is quite easy, not to say straightforward, to decompile to high-level code once again. There are many tools out there that allow us to do that, for example, smali (`https://github.com/JesusFreke/smali`) or dedexer (`http://dedexer.sourceforge.net/`). To make it difficult for anyone else to peek into our code, it is always recommended that we run ProGuard to obfuscate (or minify) the compiled version of our application. Not only will it replace all our class names, methods, and variables with single-letter strings (`a`, `b`, `..`), but it will also slightly optimize the compiled bytecode and make it more complex (although not impossible) for hackers to hack our application. We should not rely only on ProGuard for the security of our application, but we can say that ProGuard is an additional barrier that we add to our application.

To enable ProGuard, we have to make a small change to our `build.gradle` file in our app folder:

```
release {
  minifyEnabled false
  proguardFiles getDefaultProGuardFile('proguard-android.txt'),
  'proGuard-rules.pro'}
```

By just changing minifyEnabled to `true`, we are telling Gradle that it has to run ProGuard on the release build.

ProGuard needs to be configured properly to do a good job; we cannot just obfuscate the whole enchilada. The ProGuard configuration file tells ProGuard, among other things, which classes or methods need to be preserved. There are some methods that need to be retained as Android expects them to be there and, when using third-party libraries, always double-check the ProGuard requirements of those libraries, as they might come with their own set of rules. As an example, if we use retrofit, which will be introduced in Chapter 5, *Remote Data*, we will have to add the following set of rules:

```
-dontwarn retrofit2.**
-keep class retrofit2.** { *; }
-keepattributes Signature
-keepattributes Exceptions
```

For more information about rules and how to configure ProGuard properly, check out its official website and documentation at `http://proguard.sourceforge.net/manual/introduction.html`.

We can add these rules to the `proguard-rules.pro` file, as it is specified in the `build.gradle` section that we modified before enabling ProGuard.

Even though Android does not use the bytecode produced by the Java compiler directly, prior to Android 5.0, we had the DALVIK VM, which converted the java bytecode to DALVIK (DEX) bytecode, and now, with the introduction of ART, bytecode is compiled into native code for the sake of performance. So, to sum this up, all the resulting code, either DEX or native, is produced from the original Java bytecode, so optimizing it will definitely make a small improvement to the final code that will be run by the Android device. For more information, check out what I discussed at the talk in Droidcon, Amsterdam in late 2014 (`http://blog.rafols.org/wp-content/uploads/droidcon_nl_android.pdf`).

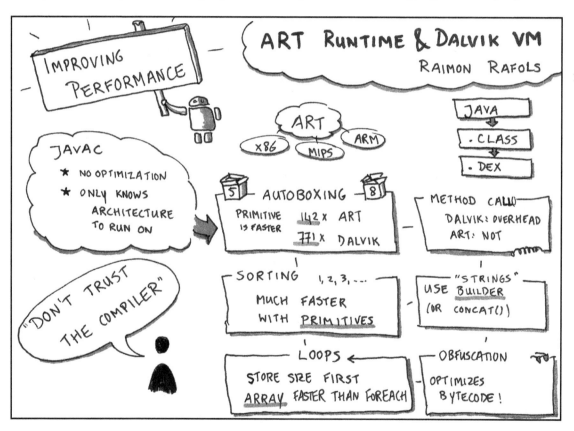

Another issue where ProGuard might help is with the 64k method limit. There is a design flaw on the DEX file specification that only allows 65536 methods to be referenced on each DEX file (`http://developer.android.com/tools/building/multidex.html`).

This is much of a problem for a simple application, but if we start adding lots of third-party libraries or our application is relatively complex, it can be a problem. For example, if we have to include the whole Google Play Services, it will already add 38k methods to our application. Now, Google Play Services is split into several smaller packages, and we can include only the parts that we require. Nevertheless, if we enable minification or, basically, ProGuard, it will remove all unused methods from both our application and the libraries we include, drastically reducing the total number of methods we will end up having in our application.

If you are concerned about security and would like to go the extra mile, I suggest that you go for DexGuard (`https://www.guardsquare.com/dexguard`); it is not free, but has more features than ProGuard and it is developed and maintained by the same company as ProGuard.

Summary

In this chapter, we covered how to install Android Studio and get started with it. We also briefly covered some of the additional parts or components that we will use in addition to the source code to build our application resources, Gradle build system, obfuscation, and Android Manifest.

2

Activities and Fragments - The Backbone of Your App

Activities and fragments are two of the most important concepts for an Android developer to master. In fact, in just about any Android-related programming interview, a common starting question is to ask a candidate to describe and outline activities, fragments, and their respective life cycles!

Broadly speaking, most Android apps consist of a series of connected screens that a user is able to navigate through. Obviously, more complex apps can be offered additional functionality such as background services, cloud messaging, broadcast receivers, and so on. However, the core UI will usually be centered around navigating through a series of connected activities or fragments nested within an activity.

A simple example of this basic UI in, for instance, a cooking-recipe application, would be a screen displaying a list of available recipes (**Recipe List Activity**) and another screen displaying details of each recipe (**Recipe Detail Activity**). These screens can be mapped easily to activities and managed by the system as an activity stack. In the earlier example, if a user navigates from the recipe list activity (by clicking on a recipe in the list), a new instance of the recipe detail activity is added to the stack. When a user navigates back, the current recipe detail activity is popped off the top of the stack and the user is taken back to the recipe list activity. On tablets, this pattern can be simplified by displaying both the recipe list and recipe details view within a single activity. This allows more information to be presented to users at once and to utilize the available screen space more efficiently.

In this chapter, we will introduce the following:

- Activities and fragments
- Practical examples on how activities and fragments make the backbone of any Android app
- How to create activities and fragments
- How to create custom activities and fragments
- How to allow your user to navigate through your application moving between fragments and activities

 If you are more of a practical learner, I would suggest skipping straight to the *Creating Activities* section.

Activities

Google describes an activity as an application component that provides a screen for a user to interact with. An Activity can be used to display information, call someone, or to even play a game. As mentioned earlier, a typical Android app consists of multiple activities and allows a user to navigate through them (an example of this is shown in the following screenshot). These Activities represent the basic building blocks of an application and knowing how to create and manage activities is fundamental to Android development. The following screenshot shows an example of navigating from a list activity to detail activity on an Android device. For more information, visit

`http://developer.android.com/guide/components/activities.html`.

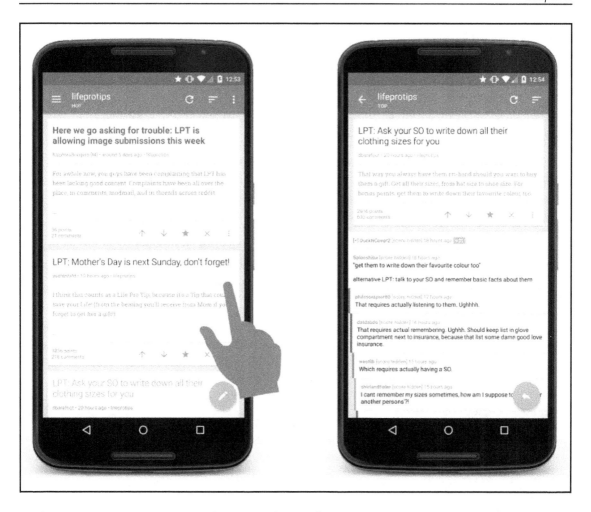

Each activity can contain a set of views and even fragments presenting information to users and to allow users to interact with the application. The preceding list-detail pattern is common among Android apps and can be seen in the stock apps provided by Google, such as Gmail and Google Play. It is crucial as an Android Developer to follow these patterns recommended by Google (`https://developer.android.com/training/implementing-na vigation/index.html`) to help your user understand your app.

Android design guidelines

Following the design guidelines and patterns can help your app stand out in a sea of lazy iOS ports and provide the experience that your users expect. Personally, if I see an app with an iOS style bottom tab bar, I will immediately uninstall the app as either the designers were too lazy to create a native Android design or the app was likely built in a rush with no consideration for the Android guidelines!

Google places particular emphasis on following the design guidelines and, since the introduction of *Material Design* (`http://www.google.com/design/spec/material-design/introduction.html`), your users will come to expect a certain look and feel along with following the set of standard navigation patterns. Google also provides a great playlist of *Android Design in Action* (`https://www.youtube.com/playlist?list=PLWz5rJ2EKKc8j2B95zGMb8muZvrIy-wcF`) videos that I strongly recommend to any budding Android developer before trying their hand at design. Alternatively, if you are working with a team of designers, encourage them to watch the whole playlist so that they will have an understanding of the specific design needs for Android.

Patterns and guidelines are great, but that does not say that you cannot experiment with app design and navigation. However, at this early stage, it is best to follow the guidelines and *do as Google does*. It worked for me personally and has helped my apps become the successes they are today. But, be aware that Google likes to change their mind often and a good app developer should be quick to implement these changes in their apps to keep their users happy; also, do not expect designs to last longer than 6 months!

The Activity context and scope

Now that we have introduced activities, it is important to understand what an activity can do. For many essential operations in Android, a `Context` object is often required as part of the method parameters. The `Context` objects (`http://developer.android.com/reference/android/content/Context.html`) are necessary for many essential tasks such as loading resources, starting an activity, and even creating views. Basically, if you are going to load anything or navigate to anywhere, chances are you will need a reference to a `Context` object.

There are different types of context, however for now we will concentrate on the `Activity` context. The `Activity` class inherits from `ContextWrapper` (`http://possiblemobile.com/213/6/context/`) and keeps an internal reference to a context instance. An `Application` context is able to start services, send broadcasts (system-wide interprocess communication messages), and load resource values; however, it cannot interact or instantiate UI components. An `Activity` context allows the developer to start activities, load layouts into those activities and even show popups known as dialogs. As all activities inherit from `ContextWrapper`, the activity itself can be passed when a context is required that touches the UI. An Activity also has access to the application context if required.

Activity lifecycle

As a user interacts with your app, the Android system will call various life cycle callback methods on your activities. We refer to this process as the activity lifecycle and it is important to be aware of and understand this life cycle before using many activities and interacting with them. This is something you will need to feel comfortable early on in order to progress further, so take your time to get to know the life cycle inside out. Additional advanced resources can be found on the Android Developer site (`http://developer.andro id.com/training/basics/activity-lifecycle/index.html`).

A good understanding of the life cycle is likely to be something that you will need to demonstrate in any Android development interview. Often, you will be asked to explain what an activity is, what are the common life cycle events and when are these called. Be prepared and do not say I did not warn you!

Activity states

As mentioned earlier, activities are managed and placed on an `Activity` stack. On this stack, an activity can be in one of the following four states:

- If an activity is fully displayed, it means that the activity is running and is at the top of the `Activity` stack
- If an activity is displayed but is partially covered by something else, for instance, a dialog or another activity with transparent regions, it will be in the paused state
- When an activity is no longer visible and there is another activity running, the previous activity is stopped and is not active any more
- When an activity is stopped, it can be killed by the system in order to recover system memory, in which case the activity is finished

For more information on activity states, visit `http://developer.android .com/reference/android/app/Activity.html`.

As an activity moves through any of the four main states, the `Activity` class receives a callback to signify that the activity state has changed. At this point, code can be added to execute at any of the state changes. For example, when using any of the popular in-app analytic monitoring tools, it is often required to manually start and stop the monitoring as the activity is resumed and paused in order to accurately monitor the journey of the user through your app. Only one activity can be in the resumed state at once, all previous activities will be paused or stopped when new activities are started, and they can be killed either by the system or by explicitly requesting the activity to finish.

Activity lifecycle callbacks

In the following code example, we will show the main callback methods in an example custom activity (named `SampleActivity`). We have annotated these methods; however, additional information can be found on the official Android developer site (`http://developer.android.com/reference/android/app/Activity.html`):

```
public class SampleActivity extends Activity {

  @Override
  protected void onCreate(Bundle savedInstanceState) {
    super.onCreate(savedInstanceState);

    // Called when the activity is first created
  }

  @Override
  protected void onStart() {
    super.onStart();

    // Called when the activity is becoming visible
  }

  @Override
  protected void onResume() {
    super.onResume();

    // Called when the activity will start interacting with the user
  }

  @Override
  protected void onPause() {
    super.onPause();

    // Called when an activity is being paused
  }
```

```
@Override
protected void onStop() {
  super.onStop();

  // Called when an activity is being stopped and is no
  // longer visible to the user
}

@Override
protected void onDestroy() {
  super.onDestroy();

  // Called when an activity being destroyed
}

}
```

Activity states and callbacks

The entire life cycle of an activity spans from onCreate() to onDestroy(). An activity is visible to the user after it passes from onStart() to onStop(). And finally, the activity is in the foreground between onResume() and onPause().This is illustrated in the following diagram. It is not required for any of the lifecycle callback events to be overridden and used; however, this is often the case.

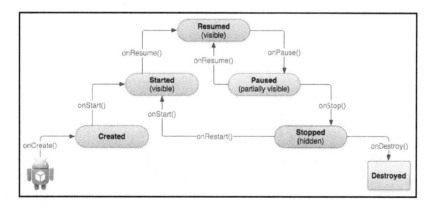

This diagram shows an overview of the activity lifecycle as the app moves from being created to subsequently being destroyed (http://developer.android.com/training/basics/activity-lifecycle/starting.html). The callbacks previously described are shown as the app transitions through the various states.

The activity stack

In Android, we can refer to a collection or series of activities as a task, and these activities are arranged in a stack, otherwise known as a back stack. When a user moves from activity to activity, these activities are placed on the stack in the order in which they are visited.

For example, if the user moves from activity A to activity B to activity C, the back stack would be A > B > C (where C is at the top of stack). If a user navigates away from a particular activity to a previous activity, for example, from C back to B, this activity is then stopped, destroyed, and popped from the top of the back stack. In this example, the stack after navigating back to the previous activity would be A > B, where B is at the top of the stack. When a previous activity in the stack is resumed, its previous state is resumed and the corresponding callbacks are triggered.

When a new activity replaces the current top of the stack, the current activity is pushed down into the stack and is stopped. The activity stack is a standard **LIFO** (**Last In First Out**) stack, although the Android SDK allows the application developer to implement a custom behavior as needed.

Creating activities

Now that we have gone through the essentials and covered the activity boilerplate introduction, we can actually begin to have some fun and create our first activities! In this simple example, we will cover how to launch an activity and show how to extend the `Activity` super class to create an instance of our own activity. This will be a very simple introductory example and should not take more than 20-25 minutes to complete. So grab a coffee and let's get started!

Defining your activity

In the previous chapter, we introduced the *Android App Manifest* (`AndroidManifest.xml`) that contains essential information such as the package name and components of an application. For each activity in your application, you must create a corresponding entry in the app manifest along with additional information such as theme of the activity.

Creating an entry in the manifest is easy and you will only need the name of your activity in this example. You also need to add your activities to the manifest file always, so bookmark this page for future reference!

 If you ever forget to create an entry, your app will crash as soon as that activity starts, so your mistake will not go unnoticed for long! As an alternative, using the **File** | **New** | **Activity** from Android Studio, will add it automatically.

Editing the app manifest

1. To begin, open Android Studio.
2. Once you have created a project or opened an already existing one, you will be able to see an editor tab called **Project** on the left-hand side of the screen.
3. Click on this tab and select **Android** from the top drop-down menu. The following screenshot shows the Android Studio project tab:

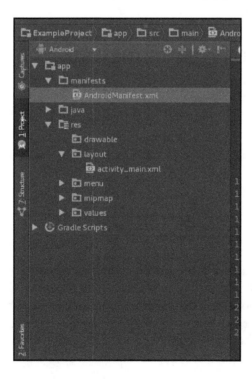

4. To edit your app manifest, open the folder `manifests` and double-click on the `AndroidManifest.xml` file.

If you have a large project with multiple modules (more information on projects can be found at `https://developer.android.com/sdk/installing/create-project.html`), then multiple app manifests will show under `manifests` folder. But luckily, as we are just starting, there is only one to choose from!

In our example from the previous chapter, the Android Studio new project wizard automatically created the project structure and the manifest file, but we did not check in details:

```xml
<?xml version="1.0" encoding="utf-8"?>
<manifest xmlns:android="http://schemas.android.com/apk/res/android"
    package="com.packt.rrafols.example">

    <application
        android:allowBackup="true"
        android:icon="@drawable/ic_launcher"
        android:label="@string/app_name"
        android:theme="@style/AppTheme" >
        <activity
            android:name=".MainActivity">

            <intent-filter>
                <action
                    android:name="android.intent.action.MAIN" />

                <category
                    android:name="android.intent.category.LAUNCHER" />
            </intent-filter>

        </activity>
    </application>

</manifest>
```

Declaring an `Activity` class only requires its name. However, in the preceding case, we have also included an intent filter that tells the system to launch this `Activity` by default when the app starts. Without this, the system would not know which `Activity` to start when a user clicks on your app icon and, actually, there won't even be an icon, as Android Launcher will not know that there is an `Activity` that can be launched. To know more about intent filters, visit `http://developer.android.com/guide/components/intents-filters.html`.

Creating our Activity class

All Activities within an application extend the `Activity` class. So, let's create a sample Activity called `SampleActivity`, as shown in the following code:

```
public class SampleActivity extends Activity {

  @Override
  protected void onCreate(Bundle savedInstanceState) {
    super.onCreate(savedInstanceState);

    // Set the Activity background to red
    getWindow().getDecorView().setBackgroundColor(Color.RED);
  }

}
```

In the previously mentioned `onCreate()` callback, insert an additional line to change the color of the background of the activity to red. At this stage, it does not matter what `getWindow()` or `getDecorView()` do, we will use this to change the color of our activity to a lovely bright `#ff000` red for the sole purpose of testing.

Building the sample application

So, we created a bared tiny activity, and Android Studio added an entry for it in the application manifest. Before going any further, it is time to test our activity and execute it on an Android device. In the previous chapter, we showed how to configure an Android emulator, but let's see how to connect a real Android device.

Setting up your device for debugging

Personally, I prefer to develop directly with a real Android device as you can get a good feel of the app as you are developing it and get to see how your design looks on a physical device.

Follow these steps to enable debugging on your Android device:

1. Navigate to **Settings | About Phone | Build number**.
2. Tap the **Build Number** times until you see the popup **You are now a developer (hurrah!)**.
3. Once you have enabled the developer options, navigate to **Settings | Developer Options | enable USB debugging**.

4. Once you have enabled USB debugging, connect your Android device to your computer.
5. The Android device will ask for permission to debug from that computer.
6. You will now be able to use this device to test and execute your code directly without any painful certificate process (as compared to Xcode).

Running the application

Once your Android device is set up and connected, perform these steps:

1. Like we did while running on an emulator, click on the green arrow in the menu bar at the top in Android Studio (you can also go to **Run | Run**). This will build your app and popup a dialog box asking you how you would like to run the application.
2. Select choose a running device.
3. Select your phone from the first box and click on **OK** to push the newly built application to your phone directly.

The result should be a lovely bright red screen on your device from our newly created custom activity, which is as shown in the following image:

Fragments

Informally, fragments are UI building blocks and are analogous to activities. They can be treated as **subactivities** and multiple fragments can be placed in a single activity. Fragments can represent screens within an application and are typically associated with a particular task such as a map fragment. Fragments can also exist within fragments to allow module portions of activities to be easily reused. Google formally defines a fragment as a piece of an application's user interface that can be placed in an activity (`http://developer.android.com/reference/android/app/Fragment.html`). Like activities, fragments have their own life cycles complete with similar callback events to use when implementing custom fragments. Fragments can also be placed on a stack for activity-like navigation through an app, complete with back button support.

Definitions and introductions aside, fragments are one of the most useful concepts to master in Android and they will make your life much easier when developing complex user interfaces, reusing code, and developing for tablets or large displays. The following figure shows a simple example of using multiple fragments within a single activity to create a multi-pane tablet experience or spread the two fragments over two activities to adapt the interface for smaller devices such as phones:

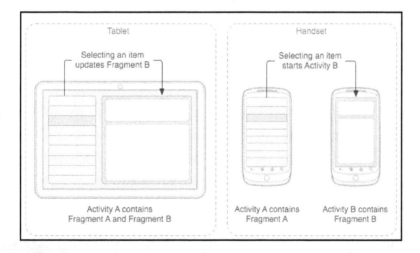

When to use fragments

The use of fragments is slightly contentious in the Android development community. Some developers will always suggest using fragments and, thus, minimize the use of activities; whereas, other developers will completely go against fragments favoring activities. At this point, there is no right answer and it is completely up to you to decide whether to use fragments in your application.

Personally, I will move most of my activity code and into fragments or code straight into fragments at the beginning of a project. You never know how or where you would like to reuse a component! So having the ability to drop the UI code into one or more places without additional work is a no brainer! For example, if you have a fragment that displays a gallery of images, there is a good chance that you will likely use this exact component elsewhere in your app, making this a great use case for using fragments. If you suspect that you will develop a tablet user interface, then fragments are almost always necessary, as they can greatly simplify this process and allow you to use multiple fragments within a single activity and create a multi-pane user interface. The following image shows an example of the official Google Gmail application running on a Nexus 7 utilizing a multi-pane user interface. Two columns of information are displayed using fragments within a single activity. On the left-hand side, we have a list containing the users incoming emails and a detailed view of the selected e-mail on the right-hand side.

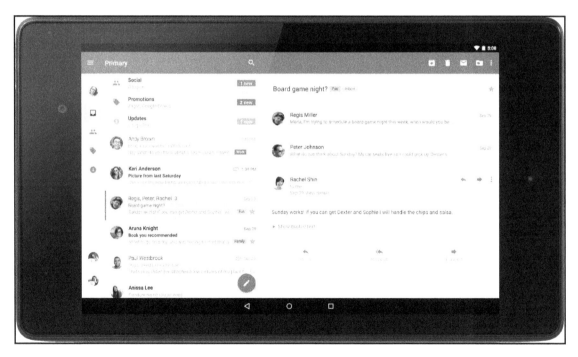

Fragment lifecycle

Just like activities, fragments have their own life cycles and corresponding lifecycle event callbacks. A fragment contains the same four basic callbacks an activity uses: onCreate(), onStart(), onPause(), and onStop(). Due to this similarity, Google found that it is pretty simple to port your existing activity code into a custom fragment instance without too much modification or effort.

Unlike an activity, a fragment does not provide a default root view for the UI. As your fragment will be most likely used for interacting with your users, you will need to provide the default root view for the fragment. Fragments allow you to easily provide this as part of the fragment lifecycle by overriding the onCreateView() callback method. This callback method is executed straight after the fragment is created. After this method is executed, the root view is set and you can easily access this view by calling getView() from anywhere else in the custom fragment. However, providing a root view is not required and it is permitted for the onCreateView() method to return null if no root view is needed.

Unlike activities, fragments are only placed on the back stack if explicitly requested. When using activities, this is the default behavior. However, this can also be explicitly disabled if you do not wish to record a user's journey history. This can be especially useful if you wish to move through multiple fragments within a single activity and allow a user to go back like with activities using the physical button on their device.

Fragment context

A fragment does not have its own instance of a Context object; however, once the fragment is added to the parent activity, it can call getActivity() to get access to the parent activity and, thus, use the context of the parent activity. Google found that this operation must be used with caution as this can only be performed after the fragment has attached to the parent activity. If the fragment is not attached this will result in a null reference being returned:

http://developer.android.com/guide/components/fragments.html#Lifecycle

Activity – fragment lifecycles

The lifecycle of the parent activity is closely coupled with the lifecycle of the child fragment. For example, when the parent activity is paused, the child fragment will in turn be paused and receive the onPause() lifecycle event. As a result, the lifecycle of the fragment and issuing of callback methods is highly dependent on the parent activity. An activity can only create and attach fragments when it is active and has entered the resumed state. When an activity leaves the resumed state, the child fragments go through their respective lifecycle events.

Fragment lifecycle callbacks

In addition to the callbacks mentioned earlier shared with the Activity class (onCreate(), onStart(), onPause(), and onStop() and so on), a fragment exposes additional fragment-specific callbacks and these, just like the activity callbacks, can be overridden. In the following code example, we will show the main callback methods in an example custom fragment (named SampleFragment). We have annotated these methods; however, additional information can be found on the official Android Developer site at htt p://developer.android.com/reference/android/app/Fragment.html.

```
public class SampleFragment extends Fragment {

  @Override
  public void onAttach(Activity activity) {
    super.onAttach(activity);

    // Called when the Fragment is attached to an Activity
  }

  @Override
  public View onCreateView(LayoutInflater inflater,
      ViewGroup container, Bundle savedInstanceState) {

    // Override this method and return a default root UI
  }

  @Override
  public void onActivityCreated(Bundle savedInstanceState) {
    super.onActivityCreated(savedInstanceState);

    // Called when the parent Activity has called onCreated
  }

  @Override
```

```
public void onDestroyView() {
  super.onDestroyView();

  // Called when the root UI is destroyed
}

@Override
public void onDetach() {
  super.onDetach();

  // Called when the Fragment is detached from the parent Activity,
  // after this point the Fragment is no longer associated with the
  // parent Activity
}

}
```

Creating fragments

As with activities, now that we have covered the same old dry introduction to fragments, we can actually begin to use them! In the following sections, we will cover how to create fragments, create a static `Fragment` constructor, and instantiate a fragment that binds one or several fragments into a single parent activity.

Creating our own fragment

As we did in the activity example, perform the following steps:

1. Open the **Project** tab on the right-hand side of the screen.
2. Right-click on the `com.example` folder.
3. Go to **New** | **Java Class** and name the class `SampleFragment`.

As all custom activities extend the class `Activity`, all custom fragments extend the class `Fragment`.

> If you are using the support library, you can choose to either use the `Fragment` class built into Android as of Honeycomb (API v11) or the `android.support.v4.app.Fragment` class bundled as part of the support library. If you are planning on supporting devices pre-ICS (API v14), you must use the support library version; otherwise, I tend to just use the stock instance built into the framework.

On the next page, we define a simple instance of a fragment. As with our activity example, to see the results of creating our fragment, we set the background color to a nice bright blue `#0000ff`. To do this, we must override the `onCreateView` lifecycle callback (refer to the fragment lifecycle). In this method, you can either inflate the layout from a layout resource file (covered in `Chapter 3`, *Working with Views – Interacting with Your App*) or create and return a view programmatically.

In this example, we will create a new instance of a `FrameLayout`, a simple `ViewGroup` designed to display a single item. In the constructor of the `FrameLayout`, you can see that we pass in the `Activity` context using the `getActivity()` method. As `onCreateView` method is called after the fragment is attached to the parent activity, it is safe to call this method.

Before returning the instance of the `FrameLayout`, we set the background of the view using the `setBackgroundColor()` method. This is the same process as the previous activity example; however, in the activity example, there was a default root view provided by the `Activity` class:

```
import android.app.Fragment;

public class SampleFragment extends Fragment {

  @Override
  public View onCreateView(LayoutInflater inflater,
      ViewGroup container, Bundle savedInstanceState) {
    FrameLayout frameLayout = new FrameLayout(getActivity());
    frameLayout.setBackgroundColor(Color.BLUE);
    return frameLayout;
  }

}
```

Creating a static fragment constructor

When creating a fragment, it is considered best practice to use a static constructor to pass the input variables in a bundle. The reason for this is that if the system needs to recreate your fragments at a later time, when restoring the activity state, it will call the default empty constructor for your custom fragment. Even if you overload the constructor, the default empty constructor will be called and your input variables will be lost.

For more information on `Fragment` constructor, visit `https://developer`
`.android.com/reference/android/app/Fragment.html#Fragment()`.

One common solution to avoid this problem is to use the static factory pattern and create a
static method, usually called `newInstance`, to create a new instance of the fragment (`http:`
`//www.androiddesignpatterns.com/212/5/using-newinstance-to-instantiate.html`).
In the following code example, we will see how to use the `newInstance` pattern to create
an instance of our fragment and add a variable to a bundle that we can later retrieve:

```
public class SampleFragment extends Fragment {

  private static final String COLOR = "color";

  public static SampleFragment newInstance(int color){
    SampleFragment fragment = new SampleFragment();
    Bundle bundle = new Bundle();
    bundle.putInt(COLOR, color);
    fragment.setArguments(bundle);
    return fragment;
  }

  ...

}
```

In the preceding example, we created an instance of our `SampleFragment` with a `Bundle`
class containing a color. This color is added to the bundle using the static `COLOR` key. This
value can be set to whatever you want but you will need to use the same key to later
retrieve the color value out of the `Bundle` class. Each key must also be unique to avoid
overriding values in the bundle.

Using values from the static factory implementation

Once we have passed the color integer value into the `newInstance` method, this is added
to a `Bundle` class and this bundle is then linked to the fragment. At any of the lifecycle
events for a fragment we can then access this bundle by calling the `getArguments()`
method. The `Bundle` class contains all of the variables set in the static constructor that are
accessible using the previously set key (in this case, the key was `COLOR`).

In the following code, we give a complete example of how to create a fragment, implement a static factory pattern, and pass through variables using the `Bundle`:

```
import android.graphics.Color;
import android.os.Bundle;
import android.view.LayoutInflater;
import android.view.View;
import android.view.ViewGroup;
import android.widget.FrameLayout;

import android.app.Fragment;

public class SampleFragment extends Fragment {

  private static final String COLOR = "color";

  public static SampleFragment newInstance(int color){
    SampleFragment fragment = new SampleFragment();
    Bundle bundle = new Bundle();
    bundle.putInt(COLOR, color);
    fragment.setArguments(bundle);
    return fragment;
  }

  @Override
  public View onCreateView(LayoutInflater inflater,
      ViewGroup container, Bundle savedInstanceState) {

    // Grab the color from the bundle
    int color = getArguments().getInt(COLOR, Color.RED);

    // Create the root view
    FrameLayout frameLayout = new FrameLayout(getActivity());

    // Set the background color of the root view using the value
    // passed through from the static constructor
    frameLayout.setBackgroundColor(color);

    // Return the root view
    return frameLayout;
  }

}
```

Adding a fragment to an activity

As previously mentioned, unlike activities, fragments do not have to be declared in your Android app manifest file. Fragments can either be added to your UI as part of a layout file (covered in Chapter 3, *Working with Views – Interacting with Your App*) or programmatically using what is known as a FragmentTransaction, visit http://developer.android.com/reference/android/app/FragmentTransaction.html for more information.

In the code following example, we will see how to add a fragment to the default root view of our custom Activity (SampleActivity):

```
public class SampleActivity extends Activity {

  @Override
  protected void onCreate(Bundle savedInstanceState) {
    super.onCreate(savedInstanceState);

    if(savedInstanceState == null){

      // We're going to be using blue as the background of
      // our custom Fragment
      int color = Color.BLUE;

      // Create a new instance of our Fragment
      SampleFragment fragment = SampleFragment.newInstance(color);

      // Grab the FragmentManager
      getFragmentManager()
        // Begin a FragmentTransaction
        .beginTransaction()
        // Add the fragment to the default root view
        .add(android.R.id.content, fragment)
        // Finish the FragmentTransaction
        .commit();
    }

  }

}
```

If we would like to preserve the state of our activity if the system recreates it, we can do so by implementing the onSaveStateInstance method. If we store something in the savedInstanceState bundle on the onSaveStateInstance, we will get it back on the onRestoreStateInstance and as a parameter in the onCreate method as well. Most implementations will simply use the onCreate method, but it might be convenient to do it on the onRestoreStateInstance depending on the logic we would like to implement.

For more information, visit `https://developer.android.com/training/basics/activity-lifecycle/recreating.html`.

In this example, we first check whether the bundle `savedInstanceState` is null. If the bundle is null, we can rest assured that this is the first time the activity has been created and has not been rotated or stopped previously. The reason for this check is that we do not want to recreate our fragment each time the activity is recreated as this would result in multiple instances of the same fragment being attached to the same parent activity, leading to poor performance and redundancy. Once we have performed this check, we then create an instance of our `SampleFragment` using the static `newInstance` constructor and pass in the color value `blue`. To attach the fragment to the parent activity, we grab an instance of the `FragmentManager` to bind the fragment to a particular view using a `FragmentTransaction`. In this case, we have bound the fragment to the default root view of the activity, which has an ID of `android.R.id.content`. Once we have instructed the fragment to be bound to the view ID provided, we then finish the `FragmentTransaction` using the `commit()` method.

Running the application

As with the activity example, click on the green arrow in the top menu bar in Android Studio (you can also go to **Run** | **Run**). The result should be a bright blue screen on your device from our newly created custom activity and custom fragment. The following figure shows our super simple custom activity with a blue background:

Adding multiple fragments to a single activity

One of the main benefits of using fragments is that multiple fragments can be added to a single activity (and even fragments within fragments!). In the preceding example, we attached our simple `SampleFragment` to the default view of our `SampleActivity`. In the following example, we will update our `SampleActivity` to contain two views and then attach a fragment to each one of these views with different colors (blue and red) for testing. This is still all pretty simple but is designed to show off how powerful fragments are.

Adding multiple fragments to an activity

As discussed, one of the main benefits of using fragments is creating reusable components that can be easily rearranged to form both phone and tablet user interfaces. In the following example, we will show how we can reuse our simple colored fragment and include two instances of the fragment in a single activity.

To start, we will need to create a new root layout in our activity file. To do this, we will use a layout file. We will cover these in much more detail in Chapter 3, *Working with Views – Interacting with Your App*, but for now, copy the following file into the `layout` folder in `res` with the filename `activity_sample.xml`:

```
<LinearLayout
    xmlns:android="http://schemas.android.com/apk/res/android"
    android:layout_width="match_parent"
    android:layout_height="match_parent"
    android:orientation="vertical">

    <FrameLayout
        android:id="@+id/sample_one"
        android:layout_weight="1"
        android:layout_width="match_parent"
        android:layout_height="match_parent"/>

    <FrameLayout
        android:id="@+id/sample_two"
        android:layout_weight="1"
        android:layout_width="match_parent"
        android:layout_height="match_parent"/>

</LinearLayout>
```

In the preceding code sample, we created a `LinearLayout` (http://developer.android.com/reference/android/widget/LinearLayout.html) with two `FrameLayout`s within it. Each of the views are set to fill the height of the `LinearLayout` and have a weight of 1. This means that as there are two views, each of the views will occupy half of the screen. We set the orientation of the `LinearLayout` to vertical so that the views will occupy the top and bottom halves of the screen. To set the new root, we amend our `SampleActivity` `onCreate` method to the following:

```
@Override
  protected void onCreate(Bundle savedInstanceState) {
    super.onCreate(savedInstanceState);

    // Set the root view to the newly created activity_sample.xml
    setContentView(R.layout.activity_sample);

    ...
  }
```

Adding two fragments in a single FragmentTransaction

In our previous `FragmentTransaction` example, we added a single fragment to the default root view of the activity. In the following code example, we will now add two fragments to the newly created custom layout containing two vertically stacked `FrameLayout`s. To do this, we can simply chain an additional add method to the existing `FragmentTransaction` and modify the layout IDs to match those specified in the layout file `activity_sample.xml`:

```
if(savedInstanceState == null){

  // Create our Fragments
  SampleFragment fragmentTop =
    SampleFragment.newInstance(Color.BLUE);
  SampleFragment fragmentBottom =
    SampleFragment.newInstance(Color.RED);

  // Add the two fragments
  getFragmentManager()
    .beginTransaction()
    .add(R.id.sample_one, fragmentTop)
    .add(R.id.sample_two, fragmentBottom)
    .commit();
}
```

Running the application

Once again, click on the green arrow in the top menu bar in Android Studio (you can also navigate to **Run | Run**). All going well, you should be able to see two fragments stacked vertically in bright blue and red. The following figure shows two fragments added to single activity stacked vertically in a `LinearLayout`:

Navigating through an app

In this section, we will cover how to navigate between fragments in your app. To keep things simple for the chapter, we will build upon our existing `SampleActivity` example and show how to add simple navigation to our application.

Activity navigation

Navigating between activities is one of the simplest actions that you can perform and is very commonly used. In the following example, we will show how to move from one instance of our `SampleActivity` (which we will refer to as activity A) to another instance of `SampleActivity` (which we will refer to as activity B). As we have already added the `SampleActivity` to our Android app manifest, we do not need to add an additional entry.

First, we will start by modifying the layout file to add an extra view. This view is a `Button`, and we will hook up this button to perform the activity navigation. The updated layout file should look like this:

```
<LinearLayout
    xmlns:android="http://schemas.android.com/apk/res/android"
    android:layout_width="match_parent"
    android:layout_height="match_parent"
    android:orientation="vertical">

    <Button
        android:id="@+id/button"
        android:text="Click me!"
        android:layout_width="match_parent"
        android:layout_height="wrap_content" />

    <FrameLayout
        android:id="@+id/sample_one"
        android:layout_weight="1"
        android:layout_width="match_parent"
        android:layout_height="match_parent"/>

    <FrameLayout
        android:id="@+id/sample_two"
        android:layout_weight="1"
        android:layout_width="match_parent"
        android:layout_height="match_parent"/>

</LinearLayout>
```

In the preceding code, you can now see that before the first `FrameLayout` for the top fragment, we have added a `Button` object with the ID `button`. We will now hook up this button.

In the following code, we find the `Button` object in our `SampleActivity` and set an action to perform when the button is clicked using an implementation of the`OnClickListener` interface. When the button is clicked, we create an `Intent`. An `Intent` describes to the system an action to perform. In this case, we tell the system that we would like to navigate from the current activity to a new instance of `SampleActivity`.

For more information on intents visit `http://developer.android.com/re`
`ference/android/content/Intent.html`.

```java
public class SampleActivity extends Activity {

  @Override
  protected void onCreate(Bundle savedInstanceState) {
    super.onCreate(savedInstanceState);

    setContentView(R.layout.activity_sample);

    // Hook up the button
    findViewById(R.id.button).setOnClickListener(
        new View.OnClickListener() {
          @Override
          public void onClick(View v) {
          Intent intent = new
              Intent(SampleActivity.this, SampleActivity.class);
          startActivity(intent);
          }
    });

    // The Fragment code remains unchanged in this example
    if(savedInstanceState==null){

        SampleFragment fragmentTop =
            SampleFragment.newInstance(Color.BLUE);
        SampleFragment fragmentBottom =
            SampleFragment.newInstance(Color.RED);

      getFragmentManager()
        .beginTransaction()
        .add(R.id.sample_one, fragmentTop)
        .add(R.id.sample_two, fragmentBottom)
        .commit();
    }
  }

}
```

Once you have updated the `SampleActivity` code and hooked up the button, click on the green run arrow and give it a try! Clicking on the **Click me!** button on the screen will launch a new instance of the `SampleActivity`. Clicking back will navigate back to the previous instance and will pop off the current instance off of the activity back stack.

Summary

In this chapter, we introduced activities and fragments. Activities represent screens within your app and moving from activity to activity allows your user to navigate through your application.

Fragments are analogous to subactivities and encapsulate much of the actions and code from an activity. This allows you to easily reuse the activity logic and add multiple instances of a fragment to a single activity allowing for richer user experiences, including designing for larger screens and tablet devices. The next chapter we will focus on how to add views to our activities and fragments to make them more useful.

3
Working with Views – Interacting with Your App

In the previous chapter, we introduced activities and fragments, which represent the backbone of an Android application. As activities are analogous to screens, we can easily link multiple activities together to create an application. In this chapter, we will go one step further and add content to those connected screens and will explore how to use common user interface components to build a rich touch-friendly experience for our user.

The Android SDK provides a set of pre-built user interface components to help you create a great app without having to reinvent the wheel. The interface components are split into two groups: views (all of which extend the class `View`) and `ViewGroups` (otherwise known as layouts). Simply put, `ViewGroups` hold views, and views display content to a user. For example, a `TextView` allows you to display text to a user and a `LinearLayout` allows you to show multiple `TextViews` on one screen (either horizontally or vertically). By building up these `View` and `ViewGroup` components, we can easily create rich graphical user interfaces with minimal effort.

In this chapter, we will cover the following topics:

- Types of views and `ViewGroups`; what they are used for, and what they look like.
- How to use these views and `ViewGroups` programmatically and via layout files, and how we can perform actions when a user interacts with them.
- How to extend the basic `View` components to create custom views, build practical examples of how to add extra drawing code to our custom `View`, and how to handle user interface events directly.

- Additional user interface components, including Toasts and Dialogs. We will show how to use them in our applications and under what circumstances each component should be used.

By the end of this chapter, we will have covered the basics of building a user interface.

Views and ViewGroups

In this section, we will review the main views and `ViewGroups` you will use as an Android developer. You'll simply be able to use many of these components over and over and never have to worry about what goes on behind the scenes. In time, you might even begin to dabble with developing your own versions.

We will start by covering the main views in Android and then move on to `ViewGroups`. For each component, we will give a description, a screenshot of the view in action, and an overview of the most common view operations. As this section will largely act as a reference, if you have had prior experience of dealing with Android views you can skip to the next section, where we will show how to use these views both programmatically and through layout files.

 In this section, we will cover some of the most common view types used in Android development; however, by visiting the Javadoc for view, you can refer to all the known direct and indirect subclasses (`http://developer.a ndroid.com/reference/android/view/View.html`).

Common views

These might be the most widely used Android components, or widgets. With just the elements introduced here, we can have the core of many popular applications. Additionally, combining them with layouts, which will be introduced later, we will be able to build pretty rich UIs for our own applications.

TextView

`TextView` is one of the most commonly used views, and as the name would suggest, it is used to display text to the user.

The font size, weight, and typeface can all be configured either in the layout file or programmatically. By default, a `TextView` does not allow a user to edit the text; `EditText` must be used if editing is required. The following screenshot is an example of `TextView`:

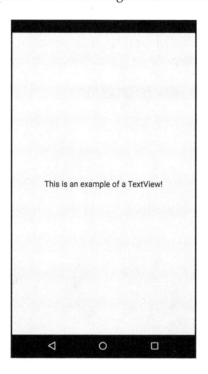

Common operations

As you would expect, with a `TextView` you can set the text displayed, configure the font and typeface, configure how many lines should be shown, allow a user to copy the text, and finally automatically enable URLs to open in browsers when detected and clicked.

More information on `TextView` is available at `https://developer.andro id.com/reference/android/widget/TextView.html`.

EditText

As previously mentioned, if you need to allow a user to edit the text in a TextView, EditText should be used. EditText is a subclass of TextView, so it maintains the core functionality of TextView, but adds extra functionality to it. Clicking on an EditText will automatically open a user's keyboard on the screen and allow them to modify the content of the EditText. The following image is an example of EditText:

Common operations

As with a TextView, you can set the default text displayed on the view. With an EditText, you can grab the current content of the view and use it elsewhere in your app. For example, you might have an EditText to set the name of a playlist in a music application. You can also set a "hint" that displays text that will be removed automatically as a user enters new text.

More information on `EditText` is available at `https://developer.andro id.com/reference/android/widget/EditText.html`.

ImageView

Along with `TextView`, `ImageView` is one of the most basic and fundamental views in Android. Quite simply, `ImageView` allows you to draw an image in a View and will take care of all the nasty scaling and aspect ratio issues for you.

In `Chapter 6`, *Image Management*, we will discuss how to efficiently display remote images in an `ImageView` using image management libraries. The following image is an example of `ImageView`:

Common operations

Again, as you would expect, with `ImageView` you can set the current image being shown and change how the image is scaled to fit the view.

 More information on `ImageView` is available at `https://developer.andr oid.com/reference/android/widget/ImageView.html`.

Button

Even though what we will explain here can apply to any view, we will focus on the `Button` widget for simplicity. `Button` is a simple view that, as Google searches represents, is a `push-button` widget. It handles all the states and styling out-of-the-box. For example, whenever the user presses a `Button`, it will change its state to `state_pressed` and adjust the drawing of the `Button` accordingly.

Having said this the default style of a `Button` can be overridden if a valid `StateListDrawable` is provided. This drawable contains a different drawable for each state the button is in, for example, clicked and not clicked. We will use a `StateListDrawable` class to provide this list of drawables for each state we would like to change.

 More information on `StateListDrawable` is available at `https://devel oper.android.com/reference/android/graphics/drawable/StateList Drawable.html`.

The following image is an example of `Button`:

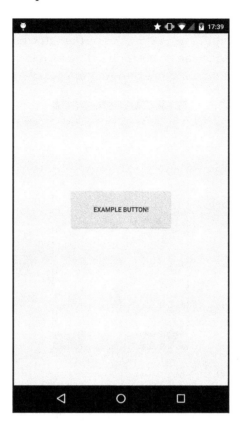

Common operations

As with `TextView`, you can set the text displayed in `Button`. More importantly though, you can add a listener to any view to detect when a user has pressed it, and this is one of the main functionalities of having a `Button` in our application UI.

 More information on `Button` is available at `https://developer.android.com/reference/android/widget/Button.html`.

ImageButton

`ImageButton` is a simple extension of the default `ImageView` that shows a button with an image instead of text. By default, `ImageButton` has the same background as that of a regular button, although this too can be customized by providing a custom `StateListDrawable`. The following image is an example of `ImageButton`:

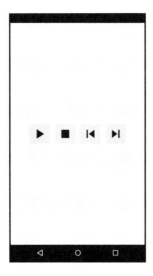

Common operations

The most commonly used method in `ImageButton` is setting the `Button` image. As we can see in the preceding image, we arranged four `ImageButtons` side by side to create a simple media player controller interface using generic media player icons.

 More information on `ImageButton` is available at `https://developer.an droid.com/reference/android/widget/ImageButton.html`.

Switch and CheckBox

A `Switch` view is a common view you will commonly find in places such as **Settings**. It has two states: on and off. You can even add a little text label to the side of Switch. A `CheckBox` view is a button with two states as well: checked and unchecked. The following image is an example of `Switch`:

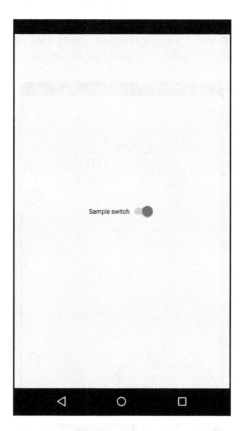

Common operations

With a `Switch` view, you can get its current state to determine whether the switch is enabled/disabled in your user interface code and act accordingly. Similarly, with `CheckBox`, you can check whether it is checked or not.

More information on `Switch` and `CheckBox` is available at `https://deve loper.android.com/reference/android/widget/Switch.html` and `http s://developer.android.com/reference/android/widget/CheckBox.ht ml`.

WebView

WebView is exactly what the name describes. It allows you to embed a limited web browser within your application. WebView has the ability to use a local cache and cookies, and can even handle downloads.

Try not to include WebView in your application unless it is absolutely essential. The content will feel non-native to your users and may result in a reduced application user experience. Having a different navigation and UI widgets than those that Android provides might be confusing for some users. The following image is an example of WebView:

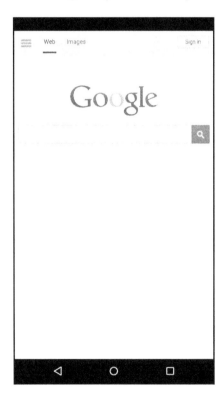

Common operations

WebView allows you to perform many operations you would expect from a browser, such as navigating to a URL, going backward and forward through pages, and even loading local HTML content.

 More information about WebView is available at https://developer.and roid.com/reference/android/webkit/WebView.html.

Common ViewGroups

Until now, we have seen a few basic widgets that allow us to show text, let users input data, trigger an action when the button is pressed, and so on. However, we have not mentioned any mechanism that will help us place them properly on the screen. To do so, we will introduce some ViewGroups that will allow us to define how elements are put on the screen relative to one another. For example, we can have elements one below the other, one on top of the other (imagine text on top of an image), or one widget in one corner of the screen and another in the opposite corner.

FrameLayout

FrameLayout is one of the simplest layout classes. It is typically used to hold a single view; however, multiple child views can be added by using the Gravity attribute. If the Gravity attribute is not used, views will be stacked one on top of an other. This might be a desirable effect though, depending on the design and widgets we stack.

Both the foreground and background of `FrameLayout` can be customized, which is handy for drawing over child views. The following image is an example of `FrameLayout`:

Common operations

Child views can be added to `FrameLayout` using the `addView` method. Views are drawn in a stack with the first view added being the first to be drawn and the view added last being the last to be drawn.

 More information on `FrameLayout` is available at `https://developer.an droid.com/reference/android/widget/FrameLayout.html`.

CardView

CardView is a relatively new Android view and is included in the support library. If you have used Google Now or Google Play, you will be used to the beautiful rich card UI, which is powered by CardView.

The CardView class extends from the FrameLayout class; however, it draws a beautiful card layout by default. The following image is an example of CardView:

Common operations

The background color of the card can be changed along with the corner radius of the rounded corners. By default, the card also casts a shadow, giving the feeling that the card is elevated in the UI.

 More information on CardView is available at https://developer.andro id.com/reference/android/support/v7/widget/CardView.html.

LinearLayout

As we have seen in the previous chapter, `LinearLayout` is a view that allows us to easily add and arrange multiple child views either vertically, as shown in the following screenshot, or horizontally. This layout is great if you want to share the available space between multiple views. The following screenshot is an example of `LinearLayout`:

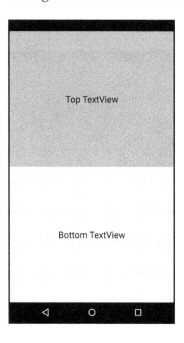

Common operations

As with all layouts, you can add child views to `LinearLayout`. However, you can also specify how the views should be arranged and the weights of child views. Views with a larger weight will occupy more of the parent `LinearLayout`. This is a great way to set child views to occupy fractions of the parent layout.

 More information on `LinearLayout` is available at `https://developer.a ndroid.com/reference/android/widget/LinearLayout.html`.

RelativeLayout

`RelativeLayout` is a powerful layout that allows child views, which have positions described in relation to each other and to the layout itself, to be added. For example, in the following screenshot, we have two views. One of these aligns to the top left of the parent and the other aligns to the bottom right of the parent layout:

Common operations

Child views can again be added, but additional layout operations, such as aligning to the parent layout or aligning to other views in the layout, are available when you add child views.

 More information on `RelativeLayout` is available at `https://developer` `.android.com/reference/android/widget/RelativeLayout.html`.

ScrollView

ScrollView provides an easy way to scroll through a child view, or ViewGroup, that is taller than the available screen size. In the following example, we include a TextView in a ScrollView. The ScrollView automatically allows a user to scroll up and down through the content and shows a scrollbar on the right-hand side of the content as an indicator. The following image is an example of ScrollView:

Common operations

ScrollView extends FrameLayout and allows you to add a single child view. It only allows vertical scrolling; HorizontalScrollView should be used to provide horizontal scrolling. Scrollbar indicators, as with any other View that scrolls its content, can be controlled using the android:scrollbars property in the XML layout file. Views that handle scrolling by themselves should not be added to ScrollView, for example, WebView or ListView.

More information on `ScrollView` is available at `https://developer.and` `roid.com/reference/android/widget/ScrollView.html`.

ListView

`ListView` is a powerful component that allows you to show sets of data in a scrollable container. Each item will appear as a row in `ListView`. It will continually recycle the rows allowing very large datasets to be presented only using a small number of views, thus improving performance. We will cover how to use `ListView` in `Chapter 4`, *Lists and Adapters*. The following image is an example of `ListView`:

Common operations

Broadly speaking, `ListView` creates views for each row of your input data and presents this to a user. You can specify how many rows should be shown and UI customizations are required, such as the color of the dividers in between rows.

 More information on `ListView` is available at `https://developer.andro` `id.com/reference/android/widget/ListView.html`.

GridView

GridView is very similar to ListView, but it allows you to have multiple columns as well as multiple rows of data. This can be very useful in e-commerce apps where a user is browsing a list of products.

A common pattern used when designing for both phones and tablets is to simply increase the number of columns as the screen size increases in order to show more information on the screen at once, thereby utilizing the available space. The following image is an example of GridView:

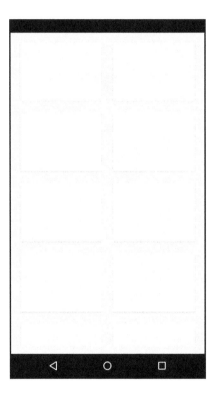

Common operations

As with ListView, GridView allows you to specify the number of rows and also set the number of columns.

More information on GridView is available at `https://developer.andro id.com/reference/android/widget/GridView.html`.

RecyclerView

`RecyclerView`, one of the latest and greatest layouts, allows you to have a much higher level of control over the older `ListView` and `GridView` components. `RecyclerView`, in order to be as compatible as possible with older Android versions, is included in the Android support library. `RecyclerView` needs to be be given a layout manager that specifies how the child views will be arranged. For example, the views should be vertically or horizontally scrollable. The following image is an example of `RecyclerView`:

Common operations

RecyclerView is a complex component, and we will cover this in detail in Chapter 4, *Lists and Adapters*. But again, broadly speaking, you can set how the child views are displayed and how many child views should be shown.

 More information on RecyclerView is available at https://developer.android.com/reference/android/support/v7/widget/RecyclerView.html.

ConstraintLayout

ConstraintLayout is a new type of layout introduced together with Android Studio 2.2. The aim of ConstraintLayout is to reduce the number of layouts inside other layouts and improve performance. In complex applications, it was very common to find LinearLayout components embedded inside other
LinearLayout components, which at the same time were embedded inside other LinearLayout components, for example. ConstraintLayout works by defining a set of constraints and anchors between the widgets. To simplify the design of screens using ConstraintLayout, in Android Studio 2.2 Google included a new layout editor tailored to ConstraintLayout. This new layout editor has been written from scratch and it is way more usable than the older one.

To make it as compatible as possible, ConstraintLayout is part of the support library and needs to be downloaded as an external dependency. We have to download the support library from the Android SDK Manager if we have not done so yet and add the following line to our build.gradle file inside the app folder:

```
dependencies {
    compile 'com.android.support.constraint:constraint-layout:1.0.0-alpha4'
}
```

At the time of writing this book, the latest version available is 1.0.0-alpha4; it might be a different version right now.

We can create a new layout file now by right-clicking on the layout folder, navigating to **New | XML | Layout XML**, and then setting android.support.constraint.ConstraintLayout as the root tag.

As soon as the editor opens, we can start dragging elements and creating constraints between the widgets. To become familiar with how `ConstraintLayout` works, there is a Codelab by Google that shows how to use it and build an example layout step by step; refer to `https://codelabs.developers.google.com/codelabs/constraint-layout/index.html` for more information.

The following image is an example of the new layout editor with a `ConstraintLayout` in action:

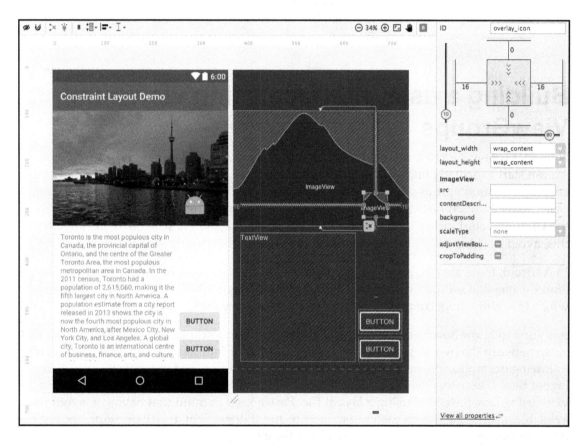

Common operations

As with other layouts, the main operation we will perform is adding views to this layout. Even if it is possible to do so, the generated XML might be a bit cumbersome, so it is highly recommended that you use the graphic editor when using `ConstraintLayout`.

 For the time being, there is no API reference documentation available until the component is made more stable. Anyway, more information about `ConstraintLayout` can be found at the technical document page for Android tooling, which is available at `http://tools.android.com/te ch-docs/layout-editor`.

Building a user interface using views and ViewGroups

Now that we have introduced the most commonly used Android views and `ViewGroups`, we can start to actually build a user interface using them. One recommendation would be to keep layouts as simple as possible in order to avoid performance issues and to make them easier to maintain. If possible, stick to `LinearLayout` components and, as the complexity of the UI grows, start including `RelativeLayout`, `FrameLayout`, and so on. In addition to this, avoid stacking multiple layouts inside each other; do this only when required.

In Android, there are two main ways to create a UI. The first, and by far the simplest way (and the one you should use in most cases), is to use a layout XML file. The second way, which is slightly more complicated, is to handcode all of your UI using Java.

It is good to know how to make a UI using both methods, as there is a good chance you will swap between the two, depending on how complex your interface is. As you will see in the following examples, it is much easier to create large, complex, and reusable layouts using layout files. Likewise, when you just need one view, it is sometimes easier just to create a view using Java instead of using a layout file. Please keep in mind that having a layout file available most of the time is easier to maintain, and if done right, it will decouple the logic from the process where you lay out the UI for the elements.

 It is not a one-size-fits-all scenario with Android. Sometimes it is best to lay out files, and at other times it is easier to programmatically create your views.

Creating interfaces using layout files

The basic gist of using XML layout files is that you specify how you want your interface to be constructed using simple XML tags from an Android XML vocabulary. In this vocabulary, the view and ViewGroup names easily correspond to XML tags. For example, TextView would look like <TextView ... />.

Each layout file must contain exactly one root element, which can be either a view or ViewGroup. The root element must specify the Android namespace. If you want to have multiple views in your layout, then the root node must be a ViewGroup, as this can hold multiple views. If you add a ViewGroup, child nodes can be added to XML in order to add the views as children of the ViewGroup.

> The root node in a layout must specify the Android namespace. This attribute must always be set to xmlns:android="http://schemas.android.com/apk/res/android".

Once a layout has been defined, the interface is later "inflated" by the system and the views are created for you. You can then search for your views and access them in activities and fragments. If all of this sounds complex, do not worry; we will go through examples now. In the following example, we will show you where to keep your layout files, how to create a simple interface, and how to access the views in your activity.

Creating a basic layout

All layout files are kept in the application resources folder under layout. In the following example, we will create a new layout file named "example." Open Android Studio, and using the same project as in the previous chapter, open the **Project** tab on the left-hand side.

Ensure you have the Android view selected as shown in the following screenshot:

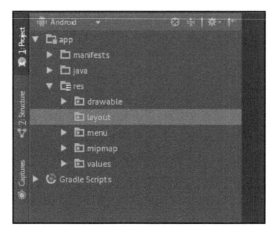

Right-click on the **layout** folder and navigate to **New | Layout resource file**. This will display the new resource file shown in the following image, and allow us to easily create new resource files:

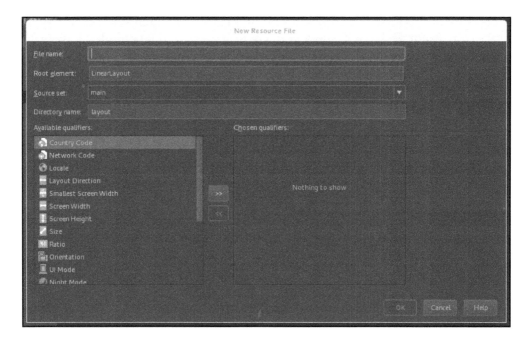

In the new resource file popup, enter example next to **File name** and set **Root element** to **LinearLayout**. Then click on **OK** in the bottom right-hand corner of the popup. This will create a new layout file for us called example in the `layout` folder with a single root element that is a `LinearLayout`. If you double-click on the newly created example layout, it should look something like the following:

```
<?xml version="1.0" encoding="utf-8"?>
<LinearLayout
    xmlns:android="http://schemas.android.com/apk/res/android"
    android:orientation="vertical"
    android:layout_width="match_parent"
    android:layout_height="match_parent">
</LinearLayout>
```

As you can see, a single `LinearLayout` was added to the example layout. The namespace was automatically set for us. You will also notice three additional elements: `layout_width`, `layout_height`, and `orientation`. Each view or `ViewGroup` you add to a layout file must have a `width` and `height`. You can either set these to an exact size, for example 10 dp, or use relative sizing. Please be aware we used dp instead of pixels. We have to be aware that there are many different devices that run Android, and these devices have different screen sizes. In order to make things work and adapt to most of the screens, we should not use pixels but dp instead. A dp is, as Google defines it, a density-independent pixel and the system, internally, adjusts the size to fit the device density. One dp is equivalent to one pixel on a 160 dpi screen, so the conversion is the following:

*px = dp * (dpi / 160)*

Although we should not really worry about this at this point, just be aware that, if we use dp, it will automatically adjust to the device screen where our application is running.

By default, our LinearLayout was set to `match_parent`, which means the ViewGroup will stretch to fill the entire parent size, or in this specific case the entire screen. By setting `width`/size to `wrap_content`, the `LinearLayout` would only take up as much room as its children. The `LinearLayout` ViewGroup also has the notion of orientation. This element will denote how the children will be added, top to bottom (vertical) or left to right (horizontal).

Adding a TextView

We will now modify our simple `LinearLayout` to have a single `TextView` as a child view. As previously mentioned, to add a child view to a ViewGroup, you can simply add the child within the parent tag. We will also add an ID for the "`@+id/textview`" view. This will allow us to access the view from our activity:

```xml
<?xml version="1.0" encoding="utf-8"?>
<LinearLayout
    xmlns:android="http://schemas.android.com/apk/res/android"
    android:orientation="vertical"
    android:layout_width="match_parent"
    android:layout_height="match_parent">

    <TextView
        android:id="@+id/textview"
        android:layout_width="match_parent"
        android:layout_height="match_parent"/>

</LinearLayout>
```

Previewing the layout

Android Studio has a pretty nifty feature in the layout editor. At the bottom of the editor, you will see two tabs: **Design** and **Text**, as shown in the following screenshot. So far, we have been looking at **Text**, but if we switch to **Design**, we will be able to see what our new view will look like without building and deploying our application; pretty good, right? It gets even better. While having the **Text** tab enabled, we can enable the **Preview** panel on our right-hand side panel tab (and view the XML and how it would look) at the same time.

The **Design** tab allows us to preview and edit the layout without deploying the app to our test device for speedy development.

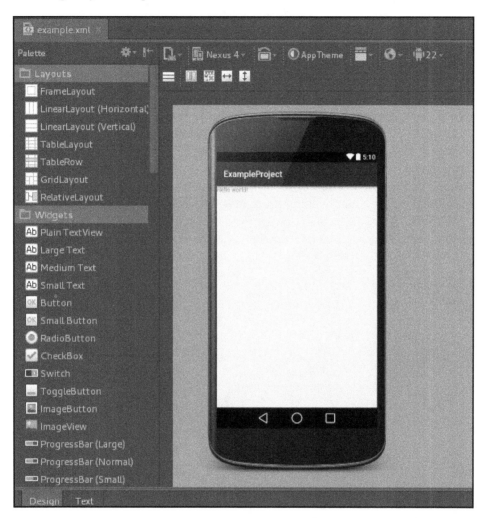

Using your layout file

Now that we have created our simple layout file, we can use it in our activity and access the `TextView`. In the following code sample, we call `setContentView` to inflate our example layout. This will create the actual view objects out of the layout file and set them into the view hierarchy of the activity. We can then grab our `TextView` using the ID we defined in the preceding XML.

As a `View` attribute, this ID is accessible to other elements in the layout and to our code through the R class. **Android Asset Packaging Tool** (**AAPT**) will automatically generate a `R.java` class that will contain all the IDs from our resources. We can reference the ID in Java by calling `R.id.id_name` (where `id_name` is any ID we have specified in our application). In our example, we will be able to access the `TextView` we created by using ID `R.id.textview`. Using this ID, we call `findViewById` and cast the result to `TextView`. The `findViewById` fragment traverses the View hierarchy until it finds the specified ID, then it either returns a View or `null` if it could not find it. We will need to cast the returned view to the specific view subclass we already know, as we previously assigned the ID to it. To avoid potential cast issues, do not reuse the same ID for different widgets.

Once we have grabbed the `TextView`, we can call `setText()` to change the text displayed. In this case, we will set `Hello World!` as our text:

```
public class SampleActivity extends Activity {

  @Override
  protected void onCreate(Bundle savedInstanceState) {
    super.onCreate(savedInstanceState);
    setContentView(R.layout.example);

    TextView textView = (TextView) findViewById(R.id.textView);
    textView.setText("Hello World!");
  }
}
```

It is as simple as that! If you add additional child views to the `LinearLayout` with IDs, you will be able to grab them in your code too. Now, this was a simple example and it might seem unnecessary to keep the view layout in a separate file. However, for larger projects, as mentioned earlier in this chapter, you will find the clear separation, and decoupling, beneficial. This is because it makes updating your layout much easier, as you do not have to touch the Java code.

Be careful when searching for views by ID when you want to determine that your view is accessible in the current activity or fragment. IDs defined in a layout file are accessible anywhere in your project.

In the preceding example, if we remove `setContentView()`, the code will still compile but will result in `NullPointerException` when we try to call `setText` on a `null` object. This is because the `TextView` will not have been found!

 Fortunately, some of the newer Android lint tools will look out of this, but it is good practice to name your IDs after where they should be expected. For example, our ID could be renamed `@+id/activity_sample_textview`.

Styling the TextView

Before testing our implementation, let's make the `TextView` a little prettier. The default text size in Android is pretty small, so let's increase this to 22 sp (scale-independent pixels) to actually see the text. Scale-independent pixels share the same base unit as density-independent pixels, but are scaled by the value set in **Settings** as the preferred text size. For this reason, for text, we should always use sp instead of dp.

Let's also place the text at the center of the screen by changing the gravity of the `TextView`. Changing a view's gravity allows us to change the placement of a child view within a parent ViewGroup.

 As always, a complete reference to any Android class is available in the Android developer docs. For more on `TextView`, visit `https://developer.android.com/reference/android/widget/TextView.html`.

The completed styled `TextView` code will look like the following:

```
TextView textView = (TextView) findViewById(R.id.textView);
textView.setText("Hello World!");
textView.setTextSize(TypedValue.COMPLEX_UNIT_SP, 22);
textView.setGravity(Gravity.CENTER);
```

Testing the layout

Now that we have inflated our example layout and set the text in our `TextView`, it is time to connect to your Android device, hit **Run** and your output should look like the following screenshot:

Creating user interfaces programmatically

In the following section, we will cover how to create the same user interface in the previous example but programmatically. And this time we will only use Java. Each view and ViewGroup in Android has three default constructors. To create a view programmatically, we will use the first basic constructor, which only requires a context to instantiate the view. In our case of `SampleActivity`, we can pass the activity itself as the context. Remember that all activities inherit from `ContextWrapper`, which in turn is inherited from context.

To begin, let's clean up our `SampleActivity` class and strip out all of the layout code from the last example. Your `SampleActivity` should look like the following:

```
public class SampleActivity extends Activity {

    @Override
    protected void onCreate(Bundle savedInstanceState) {
        super.onCreate(savedInstanceState);
    }
}
```

Now that we have a blank canvas, let's create the `TextView` programmatically, passing in the `SampleActivity` as the context. After creating the `TextView`, we can also apply the same styling as we did in our previous example:

```
TextView childTextView = new TextView(this);
childTextView.setText("Hello World!");
childTextView.setTextSize(TypedValue.COMPLEX_UNIT_SP, 22);
childTextView.setGravity(Gravity.CENTER);
```

If we were to deploy this example to our test device now, we would not see anything. This is because we have not added the child `TextView` to the root view of the activity, and as a result, it is not part of the view hierarchy. At this stage, we could simply add the `TextView` to the root view of the activity using `setContentView`; however, to match the previous example, we will create a parent `ViewGroup`, in this case a `LinearLayout`, as we did in our previous example using a layout file. We will again pass the `SampleActivity` to the `LinearLayout` constructor to instantiate the view:

```
LinearLayout parentLayout = new LinearLayout(this);
parentLayout.setOrientation(LinearLayout.VERTICAL);
```

To match the previous example, we will also set the orientation of `LinearLayout` using the `setOrientation` method. We will again set the orientation to vertical.

 XML element attributes often have a very similar-sounding Java implementation. For our `LinearLayout`, we used `android:orientation` when defining the layout using XML; for our Java version, we called `setOrientation`.

Next, we will add our `TextView` to our `LinearLayout`. In the previous example, we simply included the `TextView` in the `LinearLayout`, and this adds the `TextView` as a child to the `LinearLayout`. In our Java example, we can call `addView` to achieve the same result.

However, we must also set the width and height of the child `TextView`. If we do not set the width and height, the view will not, by default, fill the parent `LinearLayout`. We can set the width and height using the `LayoutParameter` components. Each `ViewGroup` has its own layout parameters, and in this case we will use `LinearLayout.LayoutParameters`. We will use the `match_parent` size for the width and height, as we used in the previous example. Once we create an instance of the `LayoutParameters`, we will call `setLayoutParameters` to set the `LayoutParameters` of the `TextView`.

In the following code, we show all the examples we have just walked through. If you deploy and run the `SampleActivity` example, you should see the exact same screen with a `TextView` centered with the words **Hello World!** in a nice large font:

```java
public class SampleActivity extends Activity {

    @Override
    protected void onCreate(Bundle savedInstanceState) {
        super.onCreate(savedInstanceState);

        TextView childTextView = new TextView(this);
        childTextView.setText("Hello World!");
        childTextView.setTextSize(TypedValue.COMPLEX_UNIT_DIP, 22);
        childTextView.setGravity(Gravity.CENTER);

        LinearLayout.LayoutParams layoutParams =
            new LinearLayout.LayoutParams(
                LinearLayout.LayoutParams.MATCH_PARENT,
                LinearLayout.LayoutParams.MATCH_PARENT
        );
        childTextView.setLayoutParams(layoutParams);

        LinearLayout parentLayout = new LinearLayout(this);
        parentLayout.setOrientation(LinearLayout.VERTICAL);
        parentLayout.addView(childTextView);
        setContentView(parentLayout);
    }

}
```

As you can see in the preceding example, even for small user interfaces, writing everything by hand in Java can be kind of cumbersome.

Creating custom views

Now that we have created a simple user interface using views and ViewGroups, both using a layout resource and programmatically using Java, we will now have a go at creating our own custom views. Although the Android SDK provides many useful views, as we reviewed at the start of this chapter, sometimes you will find yourself extending the View class and making your own to add additional functionality. Luckily, this is all supported out of the box and is pretty simple.

The first custom view example

In our first custom view example, we will extend the View class and add some basic additional drawing code to the view. To begin, add a new Java class named CustomView to your sample project. To add a new Java class, right-click on the com.example folder located under app/java, where SampleActivity is currently located, and navigate to **New** | **Java Class**. This will show the new class pop up as shown in the following screenshot:

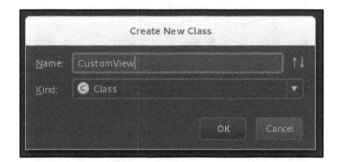

Once you have created your class, open it and change your CustomView to extend view, shown in the following code sample:

```
import android.view.View;
  public class CustomView extends View {

}
```

At this point, your code will not compile and Android Studio will complain that there is no default constructor available for the class View. To fix this, we will have to add our own default constructors to the CustomView.

Luckily for us, Android Studio has a built-in handy generate constructor function, so we do not have to memorize the parent `View` class constructors. Right-click on the **CustomView** editor pane and navigate to **Generate**… | **Constructor**. This will pop up the generate constructor window, as shown in the following image. Select the first two constructors and click on **OK**:

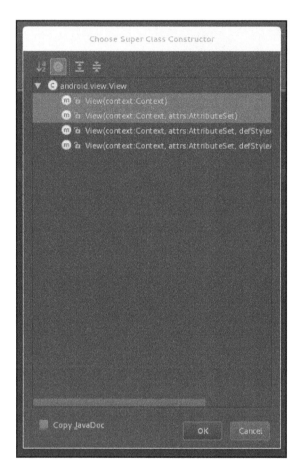

Once the constructors have been generated, your class should now look something like the following code example and Android Studio will stop complaining:

```
public class CustomView extends View {

  public CustomView(Context context, AttributeSet attrs) {
    super(context, attrs);
  }

  public CustomView(Context context) {
    super(context);
  }

}
```

We have chosen these two constructors for some specific reasons. We chose a constructor with only the context so we can easily instantiate it from code, and we selected the constructor with the `AttributeSet` so we can inflate it from XML. While inflating from XML, we will get the attributes defined in the XML file in the `AttributeSet` parameter.

 More information on `AttributeSet` is available at `https://developer.android.com/reference/android/util/AttributeSet.html`.

Custom drawing

With our custom view all set up, we can now add some custom drawing code. To override what is drawn by the custom view, we can simply extend the `onDraw` method. In fact, it is rather exhaustively described in the Google Javadoc, *Implement this to do your drawing*.

To override the `onDraw` method, we can again use the built-in generate method in Android Studio. Simply right-click on the `CustomView` editor pane, and navigate to **Generate** | `Override Methods`. This will popup the override method dialog, shown in the following screenshot. Scroll down and select `onDraw`, followed by **OK**.

Once you hit **OK**, the `onDraw` method will be automatically generated, including the `@Override` annotation:

```
@Override
protected void onDraw(Canvas canvas) {
  super.onDraw(canvas);
}
```

Drawing on a Canvas

In the signature of the onDraw method, you can see that it passes to a Canvas object. To add custom drawing to our custom view, we will be drawing directly on this Canvas object. If you look up the Canvas Javadocs on developer.android.com, you will be able to check the methods available. If you scroll down to the draw method, you'll see that you can draw bitmaps, lines, colors, rectangles, text, and much more.

 If in doubt, do not forget to check the official Javadocs for any Android class at http://developer.android.com/reference/android/graphics /Canvas.html.

For this example, we will draw a rectangle that fills exactly half of the view's available space. To draw a rectangle on a Canvas, we will need to instantiate a Paint object. The Paint class allows us to specify color and style information for when we draw on a Canvas. We have to be aware that instantiating new objects in the onDraw method is considered bad practice. The onDraw method will be called every time the view needs to be painted, and this will lead to unnecessary object creation and in turn garbage collection. Imagine, for example, that we are animating a view; it will be drawn lots of times! To avoid this, we will initialize an instance of the Paint class in our constructor, as shown in the following code. As you can see, we used a method called init in both constructors to perform the setup of our Paint object. After we create a new instance of the Paint class, we can then set the color of the Paint object to solid black using the Color class:

```
public class CustomView extends View {

  private Paint mPaint;

  public CustomView(Context context, AttributeSet attrs) {
    super(context, attrs);
    init();
  }

  public CustomView(Context context) {
    super(context);
    init();
  }

  private void init(){
    mPaint = new Paint();
    mPaint.setColor(Color.BLACK);
  }

  @Override
```

```
protected void onDraw(Canvas canvas) {
   super.onDraw(canvas);
}

}
```

 If you've been observant, you will notice that we have called our private instance of the Paint class mPaint. This is compliant with the Android open source contributors' style guidelines (https://source.android.com /source/code-style.html).

Once we set up the Paint class, we can easily modify the onDraw method to draw a rectangle using the mPaint variable. As we want to draw a rectangle to fit half of the screen, we can grab the size of the view using getWidth and getHeight. In our example, we will draw a rectangle that fits half of the screen horizontally. The following code sample shows the completed drawing code for our custom view:

```
public class CustomView extends View {

   private Paint mPaint;

   public CustomView(Context context, AttributeSet attrs) {
      super(context, attrs);
      init();
   }

   public CustomView(Context context) {
      super(context);
      init();
   }

   private void init(){
      mPaint = new Paint();
      mPaint.setColor(Color.BLACK);
   }

   @Override
   protected void onDraw(Canvas canvas) {
      super.onDraw(canvas);

      canvas.drawRect(0, 0, getWidth()/2, getHeight(), mPaint);
   }

}
```

Drawing directly on the Canvas is easy and will be refreshed each time the view is invalidated. If you need to manually force the View to update, say if you were drawing the text of the current system time for example, you can call `invalidate()` on the view to trigger a redraw. Try to keep your `onDraw` method light and avoid any heavy lifting, as you need this to do the drawing process as quickly as possible to keep a smooth buttery UI. For example, do not load Bitmaps in your `onDraw` method as this will block the drawing process and result in a super slow UI. We will cover how to efficiently draw images in `Chapter 6`, *Image Management*.

Hooking up the CustomView

To test our custom view, we will hook it into the previously created `SampleActivity`, first programmatically and then using a layout file.

Adding the custom view programmatically

To add the view programmatically, we can simply call `setContentView` in our `SampleActivity` with a new instance of our `CustomView`. We will use the first constructor, which only takes an instance of context, as shown in the following code example:

```
public class SampleActivity extends Activity {

  @Override
  protected void onCreate(Bundle savedInstanceState) {
    super.onCreate(savedInstanceState);
    setContentView(new CustomView(this));
  }

}
```

Adding the custom view using a layout file

To add our custom view using a layout file, we will have to first modify our previously created `example` layout file (found in **layouts** under **res**) and include our new custom View. To include a custom view in a layout file, you must include the full path to the view, unlike stock view components where you only have to include the view name. The following example layout file shows how to add the custom view to our layout file:

```
<?xml version="1.0" encoding="utf-8"?>
<com.example.CustomView
    xmlns:android="http://schemas.android.com/apk/res/android"
    android:layout_width="match_parent"
```

```
        android:layout_height="match_parent"/>
```

Once you have modified the layout file, you can then change the `SampleActivity` to use the layout file (as opposed to the programmatically created instance of the `CustomView`):

```
public class SampleActivity extends Activity {

  @Override
  protected void onCreate(Bundle savedInstanceState) {
    super.onCreate(savedInstanceState);
    setContentView(R.layout.example);
  }
}
```

Testing the CustomView

Following the same deployment procedures mentioned earlier in this chapter, build and deploy your example code to your device and you will get to see your custom view. If all goes well, fingers crossed, you will see something similar to the following screenshot. Although we could have achieved the same result using two views in a `LinearLayout` with a horizontal orientation, our custom view only requires one single view as opposed to three.

Here's the layout code for creating the same UI using three views:

```xml
<LinearLayout
    xmlns:android="http://schemas.android.com/apk/res/android"
    android:layout_width="match_parent"
    android:layout_height="match_parent">

    <View
        android:layout_weight="1"
        android:background="@android:color/black"
        android:layout_width="match_parent"
        android:layout_height="match_parent"/>

    <View
        android:layout_weight="1"
        android:layout_width="match_parent"
        android:layout_height="match_parent"/>

</LinearLayout>
```

The second custom view example

In the second custom view example, we will extend the TextView class and make it change the content to a random string every time the view is clicked. To do this, we will provide a list of strings and attach a click listener to the view to listen for user input.

Creating the CustomTextView class

As with our previous custom view example, we will create a new class in the com.example folder, where SampleActivity is currently located, and call the component CustomTextView. You can check the previous example for detailed instructions on how to do this using Android Studio.

As with our preview example, implement the first two constructors using the generate constructor functionality built into Android Studio.

Adding on-click behavior

After you have created the two constructors, add `OnClickListener` to the view. This will mean that whenever a user clicks on the custom view, the click listener will be fired and we will be able to react accordingly.

In the following code example, we will see how to add the click listener and how to update the contents of the `CustomTextView` when the click listener is fired. As there are two constructors, we move the view setup code into two methods: `setupLookAndFeel` and `setupClickListener`. In the first method, we programmatically set up how our custom `TextView` will look. As these methods will be called after the constructor has already called its super method, the properties we have set in the XML file for our custom `TextView` might be overwritten or completely ignored.

Setting `View` properties after the constructor has been called will override the properties specified by the XML. Be careful!

In the second method, we set up `OnClickListener`. When the click listener is called, we call `generateRandomWord`. This method generates a random number *n* between 0 and the size of the `WORDS` array and returns the word at the position *n*. Then, there is a call to `setText` to change the current text displayed in the `CustomTextView`. We must also call `generateRandomWord` and `setText` after setting up the `OnClickListener` to set the initial word displayed.

Other activities, fragments, or even views with a reference to our `CustomTextView` will also be able to set an `OnClickListener` on our `TextView`. This means that other Views could potentially break this functionality, and you should keep the scope of methods in mind when creating your own views.

Here's the full example:

```
public class CustomTextView extends TextView {

    private static final String[] WORDS = {
        "Hello",
        "World",
        "Testing!",
        "Boo",
        "Isn't this fun?"
    };
```

```
  public CustomTextView(Context context) {
    super(context);

    setupLookAndFeel();
    setupClickListener();
  }

  public CustomTextView(Context context, AttributeSet attrs) {
    super(context, attrs);

    setupLookAndFeel();
    setupClickListener();
  }

  private void setupLookAndFeel(){
    setTextSize(TypedValue.COMPLEX_UNIT_DIP, 22);
    setGravity(Gravity.CENTER);
    setTextColor(Color.BLACK);
  }

  private void setupClickListener() {
    setOnClickListener(new OnClickListener() {
      @Override
      public void onClick(View v) {
        setText(generateRandomWord());
      }
    });

    // Set the initial random word
    setText(generateRandomWord());
  }

  private String generateRandomWord() {
    // Grab the next random word
    int random = (int) (Math.random() * WORDS.length);
    return WORDS[random];
  }
}
```

Testing the CustomTextView

Following the same deployment procedures mentioned earlier in this chapter, build and deploy our example code to your device and you will get to see the CustomTextView. Again, if all goes well, you will see something similar to the following screenshot, changing the text dynamically as you click on **View**. Neat, right?

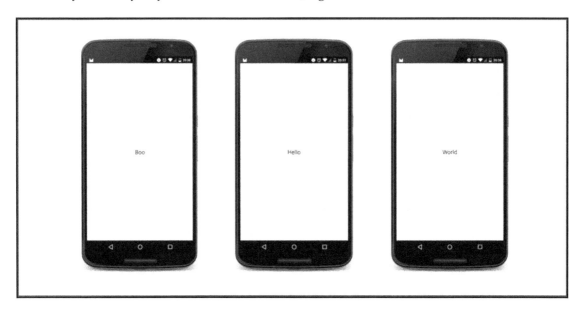

Overriding the onTouchEvent method

In our example, we added an onClick listener to the view. However, we could use the same logic without adding a listener, instead overriding the onTouchEvent method that all View classes have. In the following example, we show how to modify the class, removing the onClick listener and using the onTouchEvent method:

```
@Override
public boolean onTouchEvent(MotionEvent event) {

  if (event.getAction() == MotionEvent.ACTION_UP) {
    setRandomWord();
    return true;
  }

  return false;
}
```

With great power comes great responsibility! We have to be careful when overriding these methods; onTouchEvent has to return true if the event has been processed and false if it has not.

Additional user interface components

In this section, we will cover two additional user interface components that you will need to master to create an Android application. These components are very easy to understand, but we have included them here as you will use them over and over again during your time as an Android developer.

Toasts

First of all, despite the name, Toasts have nothing to do with bread and are in fact a super simple way to pop up text to your users. You have probably seen them 100 times but may not have paid too much attention to them. For example, when you connect to a Wi-Fi network, you might get a Toast popping up to let you know you are connected.

The great thing about Toasts is that they automatically hide after a few seconds and can be a great way to enhance your user experience without much additional effort. As a downside, something we have to be aware, users cannot interact with them.

 Although we can customize the look and feel of Toasts, be aware that your users will be used to seeing Toasts elsewhere on their device and might not understand a different design or UI. If in doubt, stick with the system design!

Creating a Toast is a piece of cake. All we need is Context reference (for example, your activity), some text to be displayed, and how long we should display the message. In the following sample, we create a Toast using our SampleActivity context to display **Hello there** using the short Toast duration. We finish by calling show() to display the Toast:

```
Toast.makeText(SampleActivity.this, "Hello there",
Toast.LENGTH_SHORT).show();
```

The following screenshot shows an example Toast notification:

Dialogs

A dialog is a small popup window that allows a user to input information; it also prompts a user to select an action. AlertDialog is one of the most commonly used dialog classes and presents a title, message, and up to three buttons to a user. AlertDialog can be easily created using AlertDialog.Builder. In the following example code, we show how to create a simple AlertDialog with a title and two buttons:

```
AlertDialog.Builder builder = new AlertDialog.Builder(SampleActivity.this);
builder.setTitle("Howdy!");
builder.setPositiveButton("OK", new DialogInterface.OnClickListener() {
  @Override
  public void onClick(DialogInterface dialog, int which) {
    // TODO
  }
});
builder.setNegativeButton("Cancel", new DialogInterface.OnClickListener() {
  @Override
  public void onClick(DialogInterface dialog, int which) {
    // TODO
  }
});
builder.show();
```

We could also pass `null` as the listener if we do not want to perform any action.

The following screenshot shows an example `AlertDialog`:

Summary

In this chapter, we introduced Android views and ViewGroups. We presented the most common views and ViewGroups, giving examples of each component and the common actions associated with them.

We also discussed two methods to create user interfaces: either by using layout files or doing it programmatically in Java.

Additionally, we walked through two examples of how to create custom views: the first example detailed a simple view with custom drawing code and the second example detailed how to add extra functionality to the `TextView` class.

Finally, we finished this chapter by reviewing additional UI components that are commonly used in Android development, including Toasts and dialogs.

In the next chapter, we will have a detailed look at how to add `ListViews` to our application, optimize them for performance, and replace them with `RecyclerViews`; we'll also look at how to use adapters to feed data to the list.

4
Lists and Adapters

Even in the simplest connected application, there is a list of things to be displayed. There is a list of items, users, locations, or for example, things to do. This is not the case always, but we can assume that a high percentage of applications show these items. Even in offline-only applications, there are many things to be shown as a list. In this chapter, we will focus on how to display lists using a `ListView` element. We'll see how to do this efficiently using a `RecyclerView` element and how to change and update the data shown on these lists by using adapters. We will end the chapter by introducing a more complex structure that will allow us to display a list in a more complex way, such as some well-known applications such as Pinterest or Etsy.

- `ListView` and `ListActivity`
- Adapters
- `RecyclerView`

ListView and ListActivity

As described in Google's documentation (http://developer.android.com/guide/topics/ui/layout/listview.html), a `ListView` element is a view group that displays a list of items and enables scrolling if the items do not fit the size of the `ListView` element. In this section, we will build a simple `ListView` element—introducing adapters briefly (we will cover them in more depth in the next section) but we will not spend much time on the `ListView` element, as we will favor the use of the newer `RecyclerView` element instead in later sections. Using `RecyclerView` over `ListView` is highly recommended as it is more flexible and does not leave performance improvements optional. `ListActivity` is like a normal activity, but with only one single element on it: `ListView`.

ListView

Let's begin, first of all, with the `ListView` element. Adding `ListView` is straightforward; just add it to an existing layout or view group and it will appear in the preview view, as shown in the following screenshot:

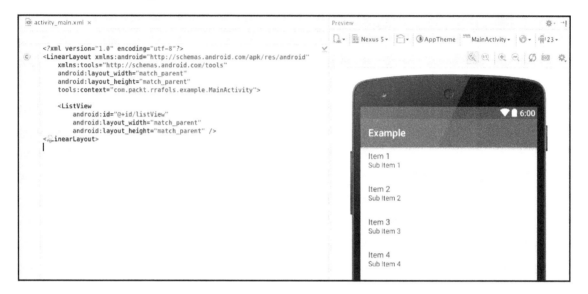

Once we have added the `ListView` element, we need to populate it. Let's use a simple array of fruits to do so:

```
"Orange", "Banana", "Pear", "Pineapple", "Mango", "Strawberry", "Apple",
"Peach", "Watermelon", "Kiwi", "Cherry", "Grape", "Fig", "Plum", "Quince",
"Avocado", "Pomegranate", "Lime", "Mandarin", "Grapefruit", "Raspberry",
"Melon", "Pomelo"
```

Then add the code shown in the following screenshot:

```
C MainActivity.java ×

    package com.packt.rrafols.example;

  import ...

    public class MainActivity extends AppCompatActivity {

        @Override
        protected void onCreate(Bundle savedInstanceState) {
            super.onCreate(savedInstanceState);
            setContentView(R.layout.activity_main);

            final String[] items = new String[] {"Orange", "Banana", "Pear", "Pineapple", "Mango", "Strawberry",
                    "Apple", "Peach", "Watermelon", "Kiwi", "Cherry", "Grape", "Fig", "Plum", "Quince",
                    "Avocado", "Pomegranate", "Lime", "Mandarin", "Grapefruit", "Raspberry", "Melon", "Pomelo"};

            ArrayAdapter<String> stringList = new ArrayAdapter<~>(this, android.R.layout.simple_list_item_1, items);

            ListView listView = (ListView) findViewById(R.id.listView);
            listView.setAdapter(stringList);
        }

    }
```

We need to provide items for the list using an adapter. An adapter, according to Google's documentation, provides access to data items and is also responsible for making a view for each item in the dataset. Visit http://developer.android.com/reference/android/widget/Adapter.html for more information.

As we do not want to over-complicate things here, we wrapped the String array into ArrayAdapter. An ArrayAdapter constructor is a very simple implementation of an Adapter object that is backed by an array. Visit http://developer.android.com/reference/android/widget/ArrayAdapter.html for more information.

To build the Adapter object, we need to specify the context, the resource ID of TextView (more on this later), and the list of items. Android provides many default layout items that can be freely used, for example, android.R.layout.simple_list_item_1.

> In the following page from the Android documentation, you'll find a comprehensive list:
> http://developer.android.com/reference/android/R.layout.html

Using the `android.R.layout.simple_list_item_1` layout will render the list as shown in the following screenshot:

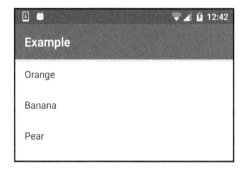

Showing a list without any kind of interaction is not very useful, although it is sometimes exactly what we want to do; however, if we want to trigger any action whenever an item on the list is clicked, we can easily achieve that by just adding the following code snippet to the previous code:

```
listView.setOnItemClickListener(new AdapterView.OnItemClickListener() {
    @Override
    public void onItemClick(AdapterView<?> parent, View view, int position, long id) {
        Toast.makeText(MainActivity.this, items[position], Toast.LENGTH_SHORT).show();
    }
});
```

Whenever an item is clicked, the `onItemClick` method of the `OnItemClickListener` instance set in `ListView` will be called; in that call, we will get the array position of the item that was clicked, among other things. In the code snippet, we are only showing a Toast with the text of the clicked item.

 Toasts are a very simple way of showing feedback to the user. Visit `http:/ /developer.android.com/guide/topics/ui/notifiers/toasts.html` for more information on the official Android developer.

ListActivity

Before showing how to change or improve the UI, let's do a quick visit to the
ListActivity class and explore why it can be useful. ListActivity is an activity that
contains a ListView and directly exposes the event handler when the user clicks on an item
on the list.

The next screenshot shows the same example as before, but this time it uses ListActivity
instead of having ListView inside our layout. Changes are minimal; instead of having to
find the ListView item and calling the setAdapter method on it, we can directly call
the setListAdapter method. The same applies to the onItemClick callback; instead of
having to create an instance of OnItemClickListener and set it to ListView, we can just
override the onListItemClick method on ListActivity.

```java
ListActivityExample.java ×

package com.packt.rrafols.example;

import ...

public class ListActivityExample extends ListActivity {

    private final String[] items = new String[] {"Orange", "Banana", "Pear", "Pineapple", "Mango", "Strawberry",
            "Apple", "Peach", "Watermelon", "Kiwi", "Cherry", "Grape", "Fig", "Plum", "Quince",
            "Avocado", "Pomegranate", "Lime", "Mandarin", "Grapefruit", "Raspberry", "Melon", "Pomelo"};

    @Override
    protected void onCreate(Bundle savedInstanceState) {
        super.onCreate(savedInstanceState);

        ArrayAdapter<String> stringList = new ArrayAdapter<>(this, android.R.layout.simple_list_item_1, items);
        setListAdapter(stringList);
    }

    @Override
    protected void onListItemClick(ListView l, View v, int position, long id) {
        Toast.makeText(this, items[position], Toast.LENGTH_SHORT).show();
    }
}
```

Even if ListActivity comes with a ListView item of its own, the layout can be
customized by providing a screen layout, as long as it contains a ListView object with the
ID @android:id/list. This custom layout can be set, using the regular setContentView
on the onCreate method.

This custom layout might optionally contain another view with the ID
@android:id/empty as well. This view will be shown when ListView is empty.

You can find detailed information on this at http://developer.android.com/reference/
android/app/ListActivity.html.

Customizing the item view

In the previous examples, we used `android.R.layout.simple_list_item_1` as the view resource for each item on the `ListView`. Android provides more default visualizations, for example `android.R.layout.two_line_list_item`, which cannot be used in a straightforward manner with an `ArrayAdapter` constructor. However, in the documentation page for `ListActivity`, there is an example on how to use a cursor to iterate through your phone contacts. Here, we will create our own item layout. Let's start with something very simple, just to mimic what Android already offers us. We will make it more complex later on.

Let's create a resource file named `item.xml` inside `res/layout` with the following content:

```xml
item.xml ×

<?xml version="1.0" encoding="utf-8"?>
<LinearLayout xmlns:android="http://schemas.android.com/apk/res/android"
    android:orientation="vertical"
    android:layout_width="match_parent"
    android:layout_height="match_parent"
    android:padding="16dp">

    <TextView
        android:id="@+id/item_text"
        android:layout_width="wrap_content"
        android:layout_height="wrap_content" />
</LinearLayout>
```

Let's update the `MainActivity` source code to use this layout rather than the default `simple_list_item_1` provided by Android. We can achieve this by only changing this line:

```java
ArrayAdapter<String> stringList = new ArrayAdapter<String>(this,
android.R.layout.simple_list_item_1, items);
```

Now refer to the following code:

```java
ArrayAdapter<String> stringList = new ArrayAdapter<String>(this,
R.layout.item, R.id.item_text, items);
```

For this one, what we have done is replace the default layout ID with the ID of the layout we have just created and, using an additional parameter, we have specified the ID of `TextView`.

We can make our layout more complex, otherwise there will be no point in creating our own layout; therefore, as an example, let's add some images. The layout file will be the same but with two additional `ImageView` views: one before `TextView` and one after.

The adapter will look for `TextView` using the ID inside the layout, so the code on the activity does not require any change, as we are already telling the adapter which item ID is `TextView`. As long as we do not remove the object, we will be fine.

We have used two default drawable bitmaps from Android in this example, only for the sake of simplicity and to show the example. In reality, we can make this layout as complex as we want; we'd need to be careful though as, if we make it unnecessarily complex, there will be performance issues. We have not really said anything about performance issues, but this is one of the major topics we will cover later on, as it gets very critical when talking about `ListView` objects.

```xml
item.xml ×

<?xml version="1.0" encoding="utf-8"?>
<LinearLayout xmlns:android="http://schemas.android.com/apk/res/android"
    android:orientation="horizontal"
    android:layout_width="match_parent"
    android:layout_height="match_parent"
    android:padding="16dp">

    <ImageView
        android:src="@android:drawable/star_big_on"
        android:layout_width="wrap_content"
        android:layout_height="match_parent"
        android:layout_gravity="center_vertical" />

    <TextView
        android:id="@+id/item_text"
        android:layout_width="wrap_content"
        android:layout_height="wrap_content"
        android:layout_gravity="center_vertical|center_horizontal"/>

    <ImageView
        android:src="@android:drawable/star_big_on"
        android:layout_width="wrap_content"
        android:layout_height="match_parent"
        android:layout_gravity="center_vertical"/>
</LinearLayout>
```

If we run the application with the preceding changes, we will have the following result:

Adapters

We have been using adapters already to populate our ListView, but we have only seen one kind of adapter and there are many. In this section, we will introduce the most common adapters and how they can be used. We will also cover performance optimization, as it is one of the critical topics when talking about lists.

ArrayAdapter

We have already introduced ArrayAdapter in all our previous examples and we know, quite clearly, how to use it. However, if we would like to use it with a more complex view than TextView, we can easily do so by overriding the getView(int, View, ViewGroup) method and returning the desired kind of view, as shown in the following screenshot:

```xml
two_lines_item.xml  ×

<?xml version="1.0" encoding="utf-8"?>
<LinearLayout xmlns:android="http://schemas.android.com/apk/res/android"
    android:orientation="horizontal"
    android:layout_width="match_parent"
    android:layout_height="match_parent"
    android:padding="16dp">

    <ImageView
        android:src="@android:drawable/star_big_on"
        android:layout_width="wrap_content"
        android:layout_height="match_parent"
        android:layout_gravity="center_vertical" />

    <LinearLayout xmlns:android="http://schemas.android.com/apk/res/android"
        android:orientation="vertical"
        android:layout_width="match_parent"
        android:layout_height="wrap_content"
        android:layout_gravity="center_vertical|center_horizontal"
        android:layout_marginLeft="10dp">

        <TextView
            android:id="@+id/item_text1"
            android:text="first line"
            android:textSize="22sp"
            android:layout_width="wrap_content"
            android:layout_height="wrap_content"
            />
        <TextView
            android:id="@+id/item_text2"
            android:text="second line"
            android:textSize="14sp"
            android:layout_width="wrap_content"
            android:layout_height="wrap_content" />
    </LinearLayout>
</LinearLayout>
```

First, we will start by creating the layout resource file that we would like to use for each list item. Once we have done that, we will have to modify the code to use this new layout and set the texts to the right views.

The code to do this is shown in the following screenshot:

```java
TwoItemsActivity.java ×

    package com.packt.rrafols.example;

    import ...

    public class TwoItemsActivity extends AppCompatActivity {

        final String[] fruits = new String[] {"Orange", "Banana", "Pear", "Pineapple", "Mango",
                "Strawberry", "Apple", "Peach", "Watermelon", "Kiwi", "Cherry", "Grape", "Fig",
                "Plum", "Quince", "Avocado", "Pomegranate", "Lime", "Mandarin", "Grapefruit",
                "Raspberry", "Melon", "Pomelo"};

        final String[] color = new String[] {"orange", "yellow", "green", "brown", "orangeish",
                "red", "red", "orange", "green", "brown", "red", "green", "burgundy", "burgundy",
                "yellow", "green", "red", "green", "orange", "orange", "red", "green", "green"};

        private static final int INVALID_LAYOUT = -1;

        @Override
        protected void onCreate(Bundle savedInstanceState) {
            super.onCreate(savedInstanceState);
            setContentView(R.layout.activity_main);

            ArrayAdapter<String> stringList = new ArrayAdapter<~>(this, INVALID_LAYOUT, fruits) {
                @Override
                public View getView(int position, View convertView, ViewGroup parent) {
                    LayoutInflater inflater = (LayoutInflater)
                            TwoItemsActivity.this.getSystemService (Context.LAYOUT_INFLATER_SERVICE);
                    View inflatedView = inflater.inflate(R.layout.two_lines_item, null);

                    ((TextView) inflatedView.findViewById(R.id.item_text1)).setText(fruits[position]);
                    ((TextView) inflatedView.findViewById(R.id.item_text2)).setText(color[position]);

                    return inflatedView;
                }
            };

            ListView listView = (ListView) findViewById(R.id.listView);
            listView.setAdapter(stringList);
        }

    }
```

We've changed many things in the code; let's go through them one by one. First, we have overridden the `getView` method and we are returning a view we are inflating from the layout resource. `LayoutInflater` builds the corresponding view objects from a layout XML resource. For more information, visit `http://developer.android.com/reference/android/view/LayoutInflater.html`.

Once we have our layout inflated, we can find the views we would like to set the text to, `item_text1` and `item_text2` in this specific case. Furthermore, you can see we used an `INVALID_LAYOUT` parameter, or its value -1, when calling the `ArrayAdapter` constructor. As we will not use the layout ID specified in the constructor, there is no need to put a valid layout ID.

Executing this code will provide us with the following results:

Performance considerations

If you look at the previous source code, you will see there is a lint warning. Android lint is a static code analysis tool that checks your source code for potential bugs and optimizations, as shown in the following screenshot. You will find more information on lint at `http://dev eloper.android.com/tools/help/lint.html`.

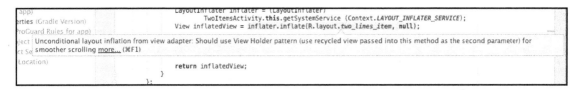

For unconditional layout inflation from a view adapter, use the View Holder pattern (use the recycled view passed into this method as the second parameter) for smoother scrolling.

This warning is telling us two things: we should use the recycled view passed into this method as `convertView` and we should use the View Holder pattern. Let's focus on the recycled view first. By evaluating the code carefully, you'll find it very easy to spot the fact that we are creating, or inflating, a whole new view hierarchy from the layout resource file every single time.

Let's make the assumption that all views on the list are the same; if this is the case, we will need as many unique views as views fit that the parent list size. As soon as a view is scrolled out of the viewing window, we will be able to reuse it and just change its contents. In the following image, we can see how the view used for **Item 0** is reused for **Item 9**.

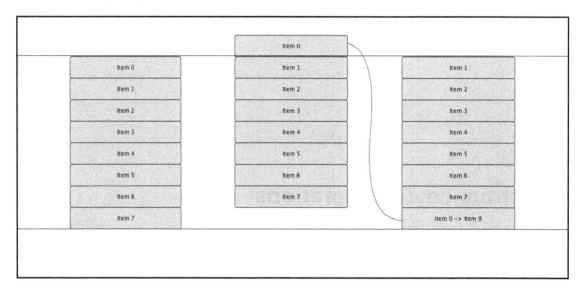

Android identifies whether a new view needs to be created or a previous one can be reused using the `convertView` parameter in the `getView` method. If `convertView` is `null`, we need to create or inflate one ourselves; if it contains a view, we can reuse it and will have to change the values we would like to show for the current item:

```
ArrayAdapter<String> stringList = new ArrayAdapter<~>(this, INVALID_LAYOUT, fruits) {
    @Override
    public View getView(int position, View convertView, ViewGroup parent) {
        if(convertView == null) {
            LayoutInflater inflater = (LayoutInflater)
                TwoItemsActivity.this.getSystemService(Context.LAYOUT_INFLATER_SERVICE);
            convertView = inflater.inflate(R.layout.two_lines_item, null);
        }

        ((TextView) convertView.findViewById(R.id.item_text1)).setText(fruits[position]);
        ((TextView) convertView.findViewById(R.id.item_text2)).setText(color[position]);

        return convertView;
    }
};

ListView listView = (ListView) findViewById(R.id.listView);
listView.setAdapter(stringList);
```

The only change we need to make in the code is to check whether `convertView` is `null` and just inflate a new view in that case. We assumed all items are shown with the same type of view. Later on, when covering `BaseAdapter`, we will explain how to manage different view types depending on the item or the item position.

The other performance issue mentioned in the lint warning was about using the View Holder pattern. Even if we are not creating more than the required views, we are still searching, multiple times, for the right views inside the view hierarchy using the `findViewById` method. This method has been declared particularly slow, and it gets worse if our view hierarchy becomes more complex. To avoid having to search for views, we need to get a view every single time we get a request from the list; we can create an object that will store the references of these views. This is the main idea behind the View Holder pattern.

First, we need to create a small class to contain the references:

```java
public class TwoItemsActivity extends AppCompatActivity {

    @Override
    protected void onCreate(Bundle savedInstanceState) {...}

    private static class ViewHolder {
        TextView text1;
        TextView text2;
    }
}
```

Then we need to modify the code to create a `ViewHolder` object for every view we create or inflate and store the references to the views we would like to use later on:

```java
ArrayAdapter<String> stringList = new ArrayAdapter<~>(this, INVALID_LAYOUT, fruits) {
    @Override
    public View getView(int position, View convertView, ViewGroup parent) {
        ViewHolder holder;

        if(convertView == null) {
            LayoutInflater inflater = (LayoutInflater)
                    TwoItemsActivity.this.getSystemService(Context.LAYOUT_INFLATER_SERVICE);

            convertView = inflater.inflate(R.layout.two_lines_item, null);

            holder = new ViewHolder();
            holder.text1 = ((TextView) convertView.findViewById(R.id.item_text1));
            holder.text2 = ((TextView) convertView.findViewById(R.id.item_text2));
            convertView.setTag(holder);
        } else {
            holder = (ViewHolder) convertView.getTag();
        }

        holder.text1.setText(fruits[position]);
        holder.text2.setText(color[position]);

        return convertView;
    }
};

ListView listView = (ListView) findViewById(R.id.listView);
listView.setAdapter(stringList);
}

private static class ViewHolder {
    TextView text1;
    TextView text2;
}
}
```

With this change, we will only create a `ViewHolder` object for every new view we will inflate, and we will only search for `TextView` views at that moment. At any other time, we will try to access a recycled view so that we can just reuse this stored information. Any view can store additional information using the `setTag` method, having regard to the fact that the object will have to be cast back to its original class when recovering it using the `getTag` method. For more information, refer to `http://developer.android.com/reference/andr oid/view/View.html#setTag(int,java.lang.Object)`.

In the previous code, we only set the text of two `TextViews`. However, if we have to change an image, or trigger its download for example, or something that might be really slow, it is a good idea to execute this on a background task. Android provides multiple options to execute code in background mode, but maybe the simplest solution here is to use `AsyncTask`. For more information, visit http://developer.android.com/refere nce/android/os/AsyncTask.html.

The next code is a small example of how can we achieve this. We will not go into the details of how to load an image or how the image is created; here we will only create a dummy image of 1 pixel width per 1 pixel height:

```java
private static class ImageLoader extends AsyncTask<ViewHolder, Void, Bitmap> {
    private ViewHolder holder;

    public ImageLoader(ViewHolder holder) {
        this.holder = holder;
    }

    @Override
    protected Bitmap doInBackground(ViewHolder... params) {
        // load real image here and return something more sensible
        return Bitmap.createBitmap(1, 1, Bitmap.Config.ARGB_8888);
    }

    @Override
    protected void onPostExecute(Bitmap bitmap) {
        holder.image.setImageBitmap(bitmap);
    }
}
```

We also need to modify the `ViewHolder` inner class to add the image:

```java
private static class ViewHolder {
    TextView text1;
    TextView text2;
    ImageView image;
}
```

We would also need to add an ID to `ImageView`, in the two-line item layout file `android:id="@+id/item_image"`, and set it together with `TextView`:

```
holder = new ViewHolder();
holder.text1 = (TextView) convertView.findViewById(R.id.item_text1);
holder.text2 = (TextView) convertView.findViewById(R.id.item_text2);
holder.image = (ImageView) convertView.findViewById(R.id.item_image);
```

Once we have performed all these steps, we just need to add one line to the `getView` method to trigger image loading:

```
new ImageLoader(position, holder).execute();
```

However, this code faces an important issue. As loading the image takes some time and this process is executed in the background, what would happen in the case where, after the image has finished loading, `ViewHolder` points to another item position because it has been recycled?

To solve this issue, we have to keep track of the position on `ViewHolder` as well and check it on `AsyncTask`. In addition, in a real application, we should avoid loading lots of background images if the user is scrolling very fast. This is because most of the images will not even be shown and will just waste time and data; additionally, this will make the user wait for the images he would really like to see, let's say, 200 rows, as shown in the following screenshot:

```
private static class ImageLoader extends AsyncTask<ViewHolder, Void, Bitmap> {
    private ViewHolder holder;
    private int position;

    public ImageLoader(int position, ViewHolder holder) {
        this.position = position;
        this.holder = holder;
    }

    @Override
    protected Bitmap doInBackground(ViewHolder... params) {
        // load real image here and return something more sensible
        return Bitmap.createBitmap(1, 1, Bitmap.Config.ARGB_8888);
    }

    @Override
    protected void onPostExecute(Bitmap bitmap) {
        if(position == holder.position) {
            holder.image.setImageBitmap(bitmap);
        }
    }
}
```

In the preceding code, we have added the item position to `ViewHolder`. While trying to set the image, if the position is different, we will ignore the image. The following screenshot shows the new `ViewHolder`, including the item position:

```
private static class ViewHolder {
    TextView text1;
    TextView text2;
    ImageView image;
    int position;
}
```

We also have to remember to update the `ViewHolder` position to the item position every time:

```
holder.text1.setText(fruits[position]);
holder.text2.setText(color[position]);
holder.position = position;
new ImageLoader(position, holder).execute();
```

for more information on how to make the scrolling of `ListView` smoother and faster and an example of how to use `AsyncTask` to change the image of `ImageView`, visit http://developer.android.com/training/improving-layouts/smooth-scrolling.html.

BaseAdapter

`BaseAdapter` is the basic implementation of an adapter. It is one of the simplest ways to implement our own adapter with its specific logic. To create our own custom adapter, we only have to create a class extending `BaseAdapter`:

```java
ExampleBaseAdapter.java ×

package com.packt.rrafols.example;

import android.view.View;
import android.view.ViewGroup;
import android.widget.BaseAdapter;

public class ExampleBaseAdapter extends BaseAdapter {
    @Override
    public int getCount() {
        return 0;
    }

    @Override
    public Object getItem(int position) {
        return null;
    }

    @Override
    public long getItemId(int position) {
        return 0;
    }

    @Override
    public View getView(int position, View convertView, ViewGroup parent) {
        return null;
    }
}
```

We will have to implement only four methods:

- The `getCount()` method returns the number of elements we have.
- The `getItem(int position)` method returns the actual object in the specified position.
- The `getItemId(int position)` method returns the ID of the object in the specified position. It can be used for our own purposes; alternatively, we can just return either 1 or 0, for instance, if we do not have any particular use for this method.
- The `getView(int position...)` method returns the view associated to this row. The same principles we saw before in the `getView` method of the `ArrayAdapter` class apply.

One of the main advantages of having our own implementation of an adapter is that we have control over the data in it. There is no need to destroy and create a new adapter whenever the dataset changes. For example, we can implement an adapter where we can add or remove rows dynamically.

Let's back the adapter by using `ArrayList` (to hold our elements):

```java
© ExampleBaseAdapter.java ×

    package com.packt.rrafols.example;

    import ...

    public class ExampleBaseAdapter extends BaseAdapter {
        private Context context;
        private ArrayList<String> list;

        public ExampleBaseAdapter(Context context) {
            this.context = context;
            list = new ArrayList<>();
        }

        @Override
        public int getCount() {
            return list.size();
        }

        @Override
        public Object getItem(int position) {
            return list.get(position);
        }

        @Override
        public long getItemId(int position) {
            return 0;
        }

        @Override
        public View getView(int position, View convertView, ViewGroup parent) {
            ViewHolder holder;

            if(convertView == null) {
                LayoutInflater inflater = (LayoutInflater) context.getSystemService(Context.LAYOUT_INFLATER_SERVICE);

                convertView = inflater.inflate(R.layout.two_lines_item, null);

                holder = new ViewHolder();
                holder.text1 = (TextView) convertView.findViewById(R.id.item_text1);
                holder.text2 = (TextView) convertView.findViewById(R.id.item_text2);

                convertView.setTag(holder);
            } else {
                holder = (ViewHolder) convertView.getTag();
            }

            holder.text1.setText(list.get(position));
            holder.text2.setText("pos: " +position);

            return convertView;
        }
```

So far it has been very easy; the `getView` implementation is almost the same as previous examples, except that we get the data from the list, and the only logic we have implemented comprises the `getCount()` method and the `getItem(int position)` method.

Let's add two new methods: one to add an element and another to remove one element from the list. This is shown in the following screenshot:

```
public void addItem(String str) {
    list.add(str);
    notifyDataSetChanged();
}

public void removeItem(String str) {
    list.remove(str);
    notifyDataSetChanged();
}
```

These new methods add and remove items from the list and they both call the `notifyDataSetChanged()` method. This method notifies all the observers of this data that it has changed and they should refresh themselves. As `notifyDataSetChanged` can only be called from the UI thread, we know `addItem` and `removeItem` will not be called at the same time and there is no need for synchronization blocks. To call `notifyDataSetChanged` from another thread, we can use, for example, `Activity.runOnUiThread` or a handler.

The following example is the modified activity with two buttons to add or remove an item from the list:

```java
© MainAdapterActivity.java ×

    package com.packt.rrafols.example;

  import ...

  public class MainAdapterActivity extends AppCompatActivity {

      private final String[] fruits = new String[] {"Orange", "Banana", "Pear", "Pineapple", "Mango", "Strawberry",
              "Apple", "Peach", "Watermelon", "Kiwi", "Cherry", "Grape", "Fig", "Plum", "Quince",
              "Avocado", "Pomegranate", "Lime", "Mandarin", "Grapefruit", "Raspberry", "Melon", "Pomelo"};

      private int index;
      private ExampleBaseAdapter adapter;

      @Override
      protected void onCreate(Bundle savedInstanceState) {
          super.onCreate(savedInstanceState);
          setContentView(R.layout.activity_main);

          adapter = new ExampleBaseAdapter(this);
          ListView listView = (ListView) findViewById(R.id.listView);
          listView.setAdapter(adapter);

          findViewById(R.id.addline).setOnClickListener((v) → {
                  if(index < fruits.length) {
                      adapter.addItem(fruits[index++]);
                  }
          });

          findViewById(R.id.delline).setOnClickListener(new View.OnClickListener() {
              @Override
              public void onClick(View v) {
                  if(adapter.getCount() > 0) {
                      int i = (int) (Math.random() * adapter.getCount());
                      adapter.removeItem((String) adapter.getItem(i));
                  }
              }
          });
      }
  }
```

RecyclerView

RecyclerView was introduced with Android 5.0 or Lollipop and was included directly in the support library, so it could be used in older versions of Android (we all know that firmware rollout is not always as fast as it should be because it might depend on operators and vendors). In this section, we will use the previous example to replace ListView with RecyclerView. We will see that it will take a bit more of code to set this up, but we will also be able to identify, quite clearly, its advantages: its flexibility and the uncoupling feature along with the ability to perform item layouts or item animation, helping us to keep a cleaner code architecture. In addition, `RecyclerView` was built with all the performance features we had to implement before in mind. This does not mean we do not have to do anything to implement them, but as we will see, the code is structured in a way that it will force us do to so naturally.

The official Android documentation defines it as a flexible view for providing a limited window into a large dataset. This definition could apply to any scrolling list, but the main keyword we have to take into consideration is "recycler." We have already explained how critical it is to recycle and reuse views in long scrolling lists, but with the introduction of `RecyclerView`, we can see that Google takes this concept very seriously as well. For more information, visit `http://developer.android.com/intl/es/reference/android/support/v7/widget/RecyclerView.html`.

Replacing ListView with RecyclerView

The first thing we need to do is add a dependency to the dependencies section of the `build.gradle` file of our application. As we have just mentioned, `RecyclerView` is included as part of the support library, so in order to use it, we will have to add the full package name from the support library, namely `android.support.v7.widget.RecyclerView`, as shown in the following screenshot:

```
dependencies {
    compile fileTree(dir: 'libs', include: ['*.jar'])
    testCompile 'junit:junit:4.12'
    compile 'com.android.support:appcompat-v7:23.1.1'
    compile 'com.android.support:recyclerview-v7:+'
}
```

After making this change, we will need to synchronize our Gradle file so Android Studio could fetch the new dependencies. Now, after performing this simple step, we could go to the layout file and replace the `ListView` item with `RecyclerView`, as shown in the following screenshot:

So, once we have the right layout item, we can proceed to perform the same change in our activity. We change the `ListView` class with `RecyclerView` and the appropriate cast:

```
RecyclerView recyclerView = (RecyclerView) findViewById(R.id.listView);
recyclerView.setAdapter(adapter);
```

This change will not just work out-of-the-box. `RecyclerView` has some additional requirements regarding the adapter. As we have mentioned before, `RecyclerView` will naturally force us to implement the performance improvements we had to do manually in the past. Instead of being able to use any adapter, we will have to extend from `RecyclerView.Adapter` and implement their abstract methods.

In the Android source code, this class is declared
`public static abstract class Adapter<VH extends ViewHolder> { ... }`
using generics to allow any class to extend `RecyclerView.ViewHolder`.

More information about generics can be found at the following links:

- `https://docs.oracle.com/javase/tutorial/java/generics/`
- `https://en.wikipedia.org/wiki/Generics_in_Java`

So, first of all, let's create a `ViewHolder` extending from `RecyclerView.ViewHolder`
instead of just creating our own independent class:

```
RecyclerViewHolder.java ×

package com.packt.rrafols.example;

import android.support.v7.widget.RecyclerView;
import android.view.View;
import android.widget.TextView;

public class RecyclerViewHolder extends RecyclerView.ViewHolder {
    private TextView text1;
    private TextView text2;

    public RecyclerViewHolder(View itemView) {
        super(itemView);

        text1 = (TextView) itemView.findViewById(R.id.item_text1);
        text2 = (TextView) itemView.findViewById(R.id.item_text2);
    }

    public TextView getText1() { return text1; }
    public TextView getText2() { return text2; }
}
```

This implementation is quite straightforward and very similar to our previous `ViewHolder`
implementation. The only thing we have to take into account is that we have to extend our
class from `RecyclerView.ViewHolder` and the constructor takes one parameter which is
the actual, already inflated, view. It is very common to have `ViewHolder` defined as an
internal class, as this would make it easier to access its elements. If you are a purist, there
will be no need to write the appropriate getters; however, in this specific case, it is on its
own public class so we can show it more clearly.

Now that we have our `ViewHolder` built, let's focus on the adapter. Let's create our class based on the previous definition, using the same name as in the previous section:

```
public class ExampleBaseAdapter extends
RecyclerView.Adapter<RecyclerViewHolder> { ... }
```

We will have to implement the abstract methods of `RecyclerView.Adapter`:

```
public RecyclerViewHolder onCreateViewHolder(ViewGroup parent, int
viewType)
public void onBindViewHolder(RecyclerViewHolder holder, int position)
public int getItemCount()
```

The `onCreateViewHolder` method will be called whenever a new `ViewHolder` (and a view) needs to be created. In our implementation, we will be responsible for returning a `ViewHolder` instance.

The implementation is also quite simple, assuming we would like to do the same as in our previous section; obviously, we could add all of the complexity we want depending on our needs and requirements. The following is a simple implementation of the `onCreateViewHolder` method:

```java
@Override
public RecyclerViewHolder onCreateViewHolder(ViewGroup parent, int viewType) {
    LayoutInflater inflater = (LayoutInflater) context.getSystemService(Context.LAYOUT_INFLATER_SERVICE);
    return new RecyclerViewHolder(inflater.inflate(R.layout.two_lines_item, parent, false));
}
```

Basically, we are inflating a new view and creating a new `ViewHolder` with it.

The `onBindViewHolder` method will be called whenever `RecyclerView` is binding a `ViewHolder` with a position in the list. Implementation in this case is also quite straightforward. The following is an example of how to reuse the view stored in the `ViewHolder`:

```java
@Override
public void onBindViewHolder(RecyclerViewHolder holder, int position) {
    holder.getText1().setText(list.get(position));
    holder.getText2().setText("pos: " + position);
}
```

As with our previous section, we are just setting the new text to the `TextViews` previously cached in `ViewHolder`.

Last but not least, the `getItemCount` method is simply the equivalent of the `getCount` method in a `BaseAdapter`. We have to return the total number of elements we want to show in `RecyclerView`.

To sum up this section, we have modified our previous `ExampleBaseAdapter` class to extend from `RecyclerView.Adapter` and adapted the implementation to follow the abstract methods we had to implement. We still back our elements with `ArrayList`, but we have slightly changed the `addItem` and `removeItem` methods. Instead of just calling `notifyDataSetChanged`, we will call the specific methods when an item has been inserted and when an item is removed from the list. Check the documentation for more specific methods as `RecyclerView` comes with many very helpful and more precise ways of notifying changes in the dataset. See the whole class with all the following changes:

```java
ExampleBaseAdapter.java ×
package com.packt.rrafols.example;

import ...

public class ExampleBaseAdapter extends RecyclerView.Adapter<RecyclerViewHolder> {
    private Context context;
    private ArrayList<String> list;

    public ExampleBaseAdapter(Context context) {
        this.context = context;
        list = new ArrayList<>();
    }

    @Override
    public RecyclerViewHolder onCreateViewHolder(ViewGroup parent, int viewType) {
        LayoutInflater inflater = (LayoutInflater) context.getSystemService(Context.LAYOUT_INFLATER_SERVICE);
        return new RecyclerViewHolder(inflater.inflate(R.layout.two_lines_item, parent, false));
    }

    @Override
    public void onBindViewHolder(RecyclerViewHolder holder, int position) {
        holder.getText1().setText(list.get(position));
        holder.getText2().setText("pos: " + position);
    }

    @Override
    public int getItemCount() { return list.size(); }

    public void addItem(String str) {
        list.add(str);
        notifyItemInserted(list.size());
    }

    public void removeItem(int position) {
        list.remove(position);
        notifyItemRemoved(position);
    }
}
```

In this case, we added the context to the constructor of the adapter, but because we only needed it on the `onCreateViewHolder` method, we could just retrieve it from `parent.getContext()`.

Are we ready to run our application again using `RecyclerView` instead of `ListView`? Almost, but not just yet. If we build and launch the application at this moment, it will crash with `NullPointerException` as soon as we add one item to the list. The reason is that `RecyclerView` does not know how to lay out the items so we have to provide `LayoutManager`. For more information, visit `http://developer.android.com/intl/es/reference/android/support/v7/widget/RecyclerView.LayoutManager.html`.

At the time of writing this book, `RecyclerView` provides three default implementations:

The straightforward `LinearLayoutManager`, `GridLayoutManager`, and `StaggeredGridLayoutManager`. We will talk about the last one in more detail later on, but for the time being we will just use `LinearLayoutManager` to run our application. To make the code work, just add a new `LinearLayoutManager` to `RecyclerView`:

```
recyclerView.setLayoutManager(new LinearLayoutManager(this))
```

For more information, visit the following links:

- `https://developer.android.com/training/material/lists-cards.html`
- `http://developer.android.com/intl/es/reference/android/support/v7/widget/LinearLayoutManager.html`

The resulting class is not really very different from our previous implementation. We have also modified how items are removed from the list; this time, we removed a random item from the list:

```java
© MainAdapterActivity.java ×

    package com.packt.rrafols.example;

    import ...

    public class MainAdapterActivity extends AppCompatActivity {

        private final String[] fruits = new String[] {"Orange", "Banana", "Pear", "Pineapple", "Mango", "Strawberry",
                "Apple", "Peach", "Watermelon", "Kiwi", "Cherry", "Grape", "Fig", "Plum", "Quince",
                "Avocado", "Pomegranate", "Lime", "Mandarin", "Grapefruit", "Raspberry", "Melon", "Pomelo"};

        private int index;
        private ExampleBaseAdapter adapter;

        @Override
        protected void onCreate(Bundle savedInstanceState) {
            super.onCreate(savedInstanceState);
            setContentView(R.layout.activity_main);

            adapter = new ExampleBaseAdapter(this);

            RecyclerView recyclerView = (RecyclerView) findViewById(R.id.listView);
            recyclerView.setAdapter(adapter);
            recyclerView.setLayoutManager(new LinearLayoutManager(this));

            findViewById(R.id.addline).setOnClickListener((v) -> {
                if(index < fruits.length) {
                    adapter.addItem(fruits[index++]);
                }
            });

            findViewById(R.id.delline).setOnClickListener((v) -> {
                if(adapter.getItemCount() > 0) {
                    int i = (int) (Math.random() * adapter.getItemCount());
                    adapter.removeItem(i);
                }
            });
        }
    }
```

CardView

The advantage of using `CardView` is that it comes with a default implementation for rounded corners and a shadow. This is precisely how it is defined in the official Android documentation (`https://developer.android.com/reference/android/support/v7/widget/CardView.html`).

In addition to this, many mobile applications use `CardView` widgets, and there are some interesting discussions about the future of cards as a UX pattern at the following links:

- `https://blog.intercom.io/why-cards-are-the-future-of-the-web/`
- `http://www.dtelepathy.com/blog/inspiration/ux-flows-how-to-champion-your-content-with-cards`

To use `CardViews` in our application, we will have to add the dependency to our application's `build.gradle` file:

```
dependencies {
    compile fileTree(dir: 'libs', include: ['*.jar'])
    testCompile 'junit:junit:4.12'
    compile 'com.android.support:appcompat-v7:23.1.1'
    compile 'com.android.support:recyclerview-v7:+'
    compile 'com.android.support:cardview-v7:+'
}
```

Let's create a new layout file, which includes a `CardView`. If we want to add a complex layout inside it, we need to add `RelativeLayout` or any other layout as a child. For this example, we do not really need that, as we will only add a background image and a single line of text.

```
cardview.xml ×

    <?xml version="1.0" encoding="utf-8"?>
    <LinearLayout xmlns:android="http://schemas.android.com/apk/res/android"
        android:orientation="horizontal"
        android:layout_width="match_parent"
        android:layout_height="match_parent"
        android:padding="16dp">

        <android.support.v7.widget.CardView
            xmlns:card_view="http://schemas.android.com/apk/res-auto"
            android:id="@+id/card_view"
            android:layout_gravity="center"
            android:layout_width="match_parent"
            android:layout_height="200dp"
            card_view:cardElevation="4dp"
            card_view:cardCornerRadius="10dp"
            card_view:cardUseCompatPadding="true">

            <ImageView
                android:id="@+id/item_background"
                android:layout_width="match_parent"
                android:layout_height="match_parent"
                android:scaleType="centerCrop" />

            <TextView
                android:id="@+id/item_text1"
                android:text="item name"
                android:textSize="22sp"
                android:textColor="@android:color/white"
                android:layout_width="wrap_content"
                android:layout_height="wrap_content"
                android:layout_marginLeft="20dp"
                android:layout_gravity="center_vertical"/>
        </android.support.v7.widget.CardView>

    </LinearLayout>
```

Double-check the `card_view` properties: `cardElevation`, `cardCornerRadius`, and `cardUseCompatPadding`.

- `cardElevation`: This property sets the card elevation in a backward-compatible mode. On Android L, we will use the elevation API, and on versions previous to Android L we will just change the shadow size.

- `cardCornerRadius`: This property sets the radius of the rounded corners.

- `cardUseCompatPadding`: This property adds a padding to Android L to have the same measurements as in the previous versions.

For detailed information and more parameters, check the official Android documentation.

Once we have created our new layout file, we will modify our `ViewHolder` class to only keep a reference to one single `TextField` and to the background image, as shown in the following screenshot:

```java
RecyclerViewHolder.java ×
    package com.packt.rrafols.example;

    import ...

    public class RecyclerViewHolder extends RecyclerView.ViewHolder {
        private TextView text1;
        private ImageView imageView;
        private CardView cardView;

        public RecyclerViewHolder(View itemView) {
            super(itemView);

            text1 = (TextView) itemView.findViewById(R.id.item_text1);
            imageView = (ImageView) itemView.findViewById(R.id.item_background);
            cardView = (CardView) itemView.findViewById(R.id.card_view);
        }

        public TextView getText1() { return text1; }
        public ImageView getImageView() { return imageView; }
    }
```

We just need a minor modification in our adapter to set the background and only one line. This example has not been optimized for performance or memory use; we just show the changes in the adapter to make the background of `CardView` appear.

```java
    @Override
    public void onBindViewHolder(RecyclerViewHolder holder, int position) {
        holder.getText1().setText(list.get(position));
        holder.getImageView().setImageResource(R.drawable.background);
    }
```

If we run our application now, we will see the rounded corners of `CardView` and a soft shadow due to the elevation of the item:

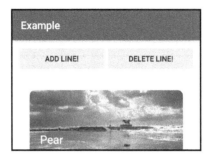

ItemAnimator

Let's do a quick modification of the `addItem` method in our adapter implementation so that the items will be inserted at the top of the list, not at the bottom:

```
public void addItem(String str) {
    list.add(0, str);
    notifyItemInserted(0);
}
```

If we now run our application, add a few items, and remove some of them, we see there are some animations. `RecyclerView` uses `DefaultItemAnimator` by default. Visit `http://developer.android.com/reference/android/support/v7/widget/DefaultItemAnimator.html` for more information.

Implementing our own `ItemAnimator` might be a bit complex, but we can extend `RecyclerView.ItemAnimator` and implement our own class. For more information, refer to `http://developer.android.com/reference/android/support/v7/widget/RecyclerView.ItemAnimator.html`.

This is not very easy, so our recommendation is to look at the Android source code (shown in the following link) and analyze the `DefaultItemAnimator` source code:

`https://android.googlesource.com/platform/frameworks/support/+/refs/heads/master/v7/recyclerview/src/android/support/v7/widget/DefaultItemAnimator.java`

ItemDecoration

In addition to animations, we can easily create our own decorations by just extending `RecyclerView.ItemDecoration`. It is quite common to use it to draw decorations or dividers between items in case we need them. `ItemDecoration` gives us the opportunity to draw something under item views or over them and change their positioning by overriding some of the methods of `RecyclerView.ItemDecoration`:

- The `onDraw` method allows us to draw before the `RecyclerView` child views are drawn. Anything drawn here will appear under them.
- The `onDrawOver` method is called after all child views are drawn, so anything drawn here will be drawn on top of the child views.
- The `getItemOffsets` method allows us to modify the outer bounds of the item. We can easily add an offset or additional margin here. If we need the item position, we have to use the `getChildAdapterPosition` method in `RecyclerView`.

For example, let's assume we would like to draw even rows slightly displaced to the right and fill that space with a solid color rectangle. First, we would have to create our own `ItemDecoration` class:

```java
RecyclerItemDecoration.java ×
package com.packt.rrafols.example;

import android.graphics.Canvas;
import android.graphics.Rect;
import android.support.v7.widget.RecyclerView;
import android.view.View;

public class RecyclerItemDecoration extends RecyclerView.ItemDecoration {
    @Override
    public void onDraw(Canvas c, RecyclerView parent, RecyclerView.State state) {
        super.onDraw(c, parent, state);
    }

    @Override
    public void onDrawOver(Canvas c, RecyclerView parent, RecyclerView.State state) {
        super.onDrawOver(c, parent, state);
    }

    @Override
    public void getItemOffsets(Rect outRect, View view, RecyclerView parent, RecyclerView.State state) {
        super.getItemOffsets(outRect, view, parent, state);
    }
}
```

That is quite straightforward, but now we would have to implement some of the methods in order to do something different.

Let's start by adding a configurable amount of displacement to the right for even rows. We will add the displacement as a parameter to the constructor:

```
RecyclerItemDecoration.java ×
package com.packt.rrafols.example;

import android.graphics.Rect;
import android.support.v7.widget.RecyclerView;
import android.view.View;

public class RecyclerItemDecoration extends RecyclerView.ItemDecoration {
    private int horDisplacement;

    public RecyclerItemDecoration(int horDisplacement) {
        this.horDisplacement = horDisplacement;
    }

    @Override
    public void getItemOffsets(Rect outRect, View view, RecyclerView parent, RecyclerView.State state) {
        super.getItemOffsets(outRect, view, parent, state);

        int position = parent.getChildAdapterPosition(view);
        if(position % 2 == 0) outRect.left = horDisplacement;
    }
}
```

As mentioned before, we are using the `getChildAdapterPosition` method in the parent `RecyclerView` to get the actual position of the view. Based on the position, we are modifying the left position of the item to be the displacement. By default, and according to the documentation, `getItemOffsets` sets all bounds to 0.

Let's take advantage of this empty space to draw something of our own. We will have to create a `Paint` object in our constructor. Let's not create it every single time we have to draw something, for performance reasons. This is to avoid unnecessary operations and memory allocations and to initialize it to fill the empty space with a solid color, which will be passed as a parameter as well.

Then, we have to iterate for all the even items in our parent `RecyclerView` and draw a rectangle, although we have chosen a round rectangle in our example, with appropriate coordinates. As we can get the child view using the `getChildAt` method in `RecyclerView`, we could use it to get the coordinates. In this specific example, we could use the top and bottom coordinates of the child view as they are, and we just need to calculate the left and right positions. Calculating the left side is quite easy; it will not depend on any other child or element, just the parent padding, so let's set it to the left padding of `RecyclerView`. For the right side, it is also quite straightforward. We know we have displaced the views to the right, so we can get the left coordinate of the child view and set it as the right coordinate of the rectangle we would like to draw. Please note that, in this example, we have hardcoded the radius of the oval used to make the round rectangle; we could have added it as another parameter if we customized it.

```
© RecyclerItemDecoration.java ×

    package com.packt.rrafols.example;

    import android.graphics.Canvas;
    import android.graphics.Paint;
    import android.graphics.Rect;
    import android.support.v7.widget.RecyclerView;
    import android.view.View;

    public class RecyclerItemDecoration extends RecyclerView.ItemDecoration {
        private int horDisplacement;
        private Paint paint;

        public RecyclerItemDecoration(int horDisplacement, int color) {
            this.horDisplacement = horDisplacement;

            this.paint = new Paint();
            this.paint.setStyle(Paint.Style.FILL);
            this.paint.setColor(color);
        }

        @Override
        public void onDraw(Canvas c, RecyclerView parent, RecyclerView.State state) {
            for(int i = 0; i < parent.getChildCount(); i += 2) {
                View child = parent.getChildAt(i);

                int top = child.getTop();
                int bottom = child.getBottom();
                int left = parent.getPaddingLeft();
                int right = child.getLeft();

                c.drawRoundRect(left, top, right, bottom, 10.f, 10.f, paint);
            }
        }

        @Override
        public void getItemOffsets(Rect outRect, View view, RecyclerView parent, RecyclerView.State state) {
            super.getItemOffsets(outRect, view, parent, state);

            int position = parent.getChildAdapterPosition(view);
            if(position % 2 == 0) outRect.left = horDisplacement;
        }
    }
```

Finally, we only have to set this `ItemDecoration` to `RecyclerView` in our activity and initialize it with some appropriate values. Ideally, both horizontal displacement and color should be defined as a XML resource and retrieved here, but for clarity reasons, we have put the immediate value here:

```
    adapter = new ExampleBaseAdapter(this);

    RecyclerView recyclerView = (RecyclerView) findViewById(R.id.listView);
    recyclerView.setAdapter(adapter);
    recyclerView.setLayoutManager(new LinearLayoutManager(this));
    recyclerView.addItemDecoration(new RecyclerItemDecoration(250, 0xff556688));
```

If we run our application now, and we add some lines, we will see them, as shown in the following screenshot. As we can see, even rows are displaced to the right and there is a bluish round rectangle on the left-hand side.

Let's do a quick update to our project to draw that bluish background on all the items and remove the displacement so we can reuse it in our next section:

```java
@Override
public void onDraw(Canvas c, RecyclerView parent, RecyclerView.State state) {
    for(int i = 0; i < parent.getChildCount(); i++) {
        View child = parent.getChildAt(i);

        int top = child.getTop();
        int bottom = child.getBottom();
        int left = child.getLeft();
        int right = child.getRight();

        c.drawRoundRect(left, top, right, bottom, 10.f, 10.f, paint);
    }
}

@Override
public void getItemOffsets(Rect outRect, View view, RecyclerView parent, RecyclerView.State state) {
    super.getItemOffsets(outRect, view, parent, state);
    outRect.bottom = 5;
}
```

Here we just drew the same round rectangle in all the child views, without adding the padding, and we also added a very small bottom offset to the items so there will be a small separation.

For more information about `ItemDecoration`, check the source code of one of the examples in the original Android source code, `DividerItemDecoration`. Visit `https://a ndroid.googlesource.com/platform/development/+/master/samples/Support7Demos/ src/com/example/android/supportv7/widget/decorator/DividerItemDecoration.jav a`.

StaggeredGridLayoutManager

There are many popular applications that show a special and more complex grid such as Etsy or Pinterest. Etsy was designed as an open source component, but it has been deprecated since September 2015 because Google added `StaggeredGridLayoutManager` to their default set of `LayoutManagers`.

Find the GitHub repository of the Etsy component at `https://github.com/etsy/AndroidS taggeredGrid`.

In this book, we will be using Google's `StaggeredGridLayoutManager` together with `RecyclerView`. What we want to achieve is basically a staggered grid layout. This is because items can have different sizes, and gaps between views have to be smartly managed.

The following is a screenshot of the Etsy application where we can see what we want to achieve:

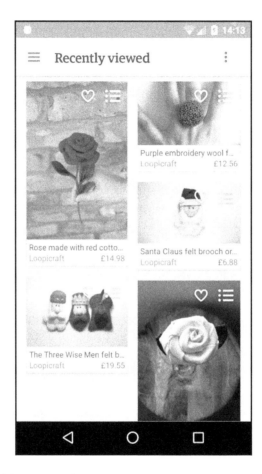

We can easily get started by just replacing our `LinearLayout` with `StaggeredGridLayoutManager` and see what happens:

```
//recyclerView.setLayoutManager(new LinearLayoutManager(this));
recyclerView.setLayoutManager(new StaggeredGridLayoutManager(2, StaggeredGridLayoutManager.VERTICAL));
```

We will not see that much difference as all the items have the same size. Let's randomize things a bit in our adapter. Every time we get a `ViewHolder` bind a call to a new position, we will randomly assign a new size to that view. Also, as we are inserting elements at the top, just calling `notifyItemInserted(0)` will not be enough as it does not propagate structural changes to the other views and assumes they have not been modified. There are two options here: either we insert elements at the end of the list or we call `notifyDataSetChanged()`. The following screenshot shows the changes to the adapter when you insert elements at the end of the list:

```java
    private HashMap<Integer, Integer> heightList;

    public ExampleBaseAdapter(Context context) {
        this.context = context;
        list = new ArrayList<>();
        heightList = new HashMap<>();
    }

    private static int dpToPixels(double dp) {
        return (int) (dp * Resources.getSystem().getDisplayMetrics().density);
    }

    @Override
    public void onBindViewHolder(RecyclerViewHolder holder, int position) {
        holder.getText1().setText(list.get(position));
        holder.getImageView().setImageResource(R.drawable.background);

        if(!heightList.containsKey(position)) {
            int height = dpToPixels(150 + Math.random() * 200);
            heightList.put(position, height);
        }

        holder.getCardView().getLayoutParams().height = heightList.get(position);
    }

    public void addItem(String str) {
        list.add(str);
        notifyItemInserted(list.size());
    }
```

We have chosen to insert elements at the end of the array and give each item a size between 150 and 350 density pixels (dp), which we would need to convert into pixels in order to use them.

`StaggeredGridLayoutManager`, by default, uses
`GAP_HANDLING_MOVE_ITEMS_BETWEEN_SPANS` as the gap-handling strategy. Whenever the
scroll state is changed to `SCROLL_STATE_IDLE`, it will check whether there are gaps
between the items and lay them out again. We could also disable this behavior by setting
the gap strategy to `GAP_HANDLING_NONE`.

For more detailed information on how `StaggeredGridLayoutManager` works, check the
Android source code and documentation:

- `https://android.googlesource.com/platform/frameworks/support/+/refs/heads/master/v7/recyclerview/src/android/support/v7/widget/StaggeredGridLayoutManager.java`
- `http://developer.android.com/reference/android/support/v7/widget/StaggeredGridLayoutManager.html`

The following screenshot shows the result after you randomize the `CardViews` height:

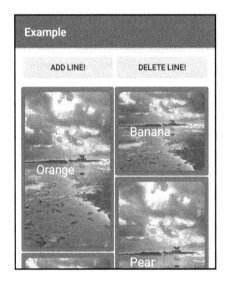

Summary

In this chapter, we learned how to add dynamic lists to our application. We also covered the performance issues that we might face if we do not do things in the right way, and we evolved our example from the good old `ListView` and `ListActivity` to the new and more efficient `RecyclerView`.

Additionally, we introduced a new `LayoutManager`, which is able to manage items with different sizes, and the ability to draw decorations before or after the `RecyclerView` child items are drawn.

For the time being, the source of data for the lists is quite static, but in upcoming chapters we will see how to make it more dynamic and have different data sources.

5
Remote Data

So far you have seen how to create dynamic lists with a static data source (a Java array in our previous examples). In this chapter, you will learn how to request and retrieve data from Internet origins. There is a huge market for hyperconnected and hypersocial applications, so we can imagine how critical it is to rely on a good implementation of the networking part of the application. If it is done wrong, it might cause serious performance issues, never-ending activity indicators, or even application crashes.

We will initially focus on how to request permissions and on background tasks and later move on to how networking works internally and how to add widely used third-party libraries to simplify all the connection needs our application might have.

Permissions

First of all, we need to understand the need for permissions. Permissions were introduced to let the user know what kind of operations the application will perform. These operations are potentially using services with a cost, for example, sending an SMS message or connecting to the Internet or getting potentially sensitive information from the phone or the user. As malicious applications might potentially abuse this, Android introduced a permission mechanism that will show all the required permissions to the user when he/she installs the application from Google Play. As this method did not show very clearly how these features that require special permission were used, Google introduced, in Android Marshmallow or API version 23, a new permission mechanism to check permissions at application runtime.

Android M permission mechanism

Permissions have to be declared in the `Manifest` file as with previous versions of Android, but there are some new methods to check and request permissions while the application is running, providing, this way, the right context to the user and giving him the flexibility to allow or deny these specific features of the application.

In previous versions of Android, when the user proceeded with the installation of the application, the user was, in fact, accepting all the permissions at the same time without the right context or knowledge of why the application was requesting those permissions.

This new permissions model is more convenient for the user since, if implemented correctly, it will give the right context before having to accept a specific permission, but adds some complex logic to handle when developing our applications. We do not have to assume that we always have permission to do everything in the application, for example, even if the user granted one permission, he/she can deny it later on from the application settings.

Let's see how we can do it; let's add Internet connectivity to our application. First of all, we have to add the Internet permission to our manifest file:

```xml
<?xml version="1.0" encoding="utf-8"?>
<manifest xmlns:android="http://schemas.android.com/apk/res/android"
    package="com.packt.rrafols.example">

    <uses-permission android:name="android.permission.INTERNET"/>

    <application
        android:allowBackup="true"
        android:icon="@mipmap/ic_launcher"
        android:label="Example"
        android:supportsRtl="true"
        android:theme="@style/AppTheme">
        <activity android:name=".MainAdapterActivity">
            <intent-filter>
                <action android:name="android.intent.action.MAIN" />
                <category android:name="android.intent.category.LAUNCHER" />
            </intent-filter>
        </activity>
    </application>

</manifest>
```

It is pretty straightforward. Just adding single line code
`<uses-permission android:name="android.permission.INTERNET"/>`, before the
application tag will do the job.

This covers all that we need for previous Android versions and if we still build our
application with a target API lower than 23. But if we target our application for Android M
(or API level 23), we will have to do some additional work. Let's check at runtime if the
Internet permission is granted:

```
@Override
protected void onResume() {
    super.onResume();

    if(checkSelfPermission(Manifest.permission.INTERNET) == PackageManager.PERMISSION_GRANTED) {
        Toast.makeText(this, "Internet permission granted", Toast.LENGTH_SHORT).show();
    } else {
        Toast.makeText(this, "Internet permission not granted", Toast.LENGTH_SHORT).show();
    }
}
```

If we execute the preceding code, we will see the permission has already been granted; we
do not have to request for it or do anything else. Also, this code will only run on Android M
and onward devices. To avoid performing constant checks for the API version, there are
some helper methods in the `app-compat` library that would make our lives a bit easier:

```
@Override
protected void onResume() {
    super.onResume();

    if(ContextCompat.checkSelfPermission(this, Manifest.permission.INTERNET)
            == PackageManager.PERMISSION_GRANTED) {
        Toast.makeText(this, "Internet permission granted", Toast.LENGTH_SHORT).show();
    } else {
        Toast.makeText(this, "Internet permission not granted", Toast.LENGTH_SHORT).show();
    }
}
```

Only changing the call `checkSelfPermission` to
`ContextCompat.checkSelfPermission` will do the work. This call will work and return
the appropriate value depending on the Android version of the device running the
application. From now on, we will be using all methods from the `app-compat` library and it
is actually a good recommendation to do so on all our applications.

As we saw earlier, the Internet permission was already granted. This is because the Internet permission belongs to a group of permissions categorized as normal.

Google classified some permissions as normal and others as dangerous. Normal permissions are granted by default, although they still need to be declared in the application `Manifest` file. For the list of normal permissions, refer to `http://developer.android.com/guide/topics/security/normal-permissions.html`.

 For more information on permissions, refer to `https://developer.android.com/reference/android/content/pm/PermissionInfo.html`.

Let's use the same approach with a dangerous permission: read contacts. As mentioned previously, we have to start by adding the `uses-permission` line in the application manifest:

```
<uses-permission android:name="android.permission.INTERNET"/>
<uses-permission android:name="android.permission.READ_CONTACTS"/>
```

And we change the `checkSelfPermission` with the right one:

```
@Override
protected void onResume() {
    super.onResume();

    if(ContextCompat.checkSelfPermission(this, Manifest.permission.READ_CONTACTS)
            == PackageManager.PERMISSION_GRANTED) {
        Toast.makeText(this, "Read contacts permission granted", Toast.LENGTH_SHORT).show();
    } else {
        Toast.makeText(this, "Read contacts permission not granted", Toast.LENGTH_SHORT).show();
    }
}
```

If we run the following code, we will see the permission is not granted. Let's request it:

```java
@Override
protected void onResume() {
    super.onResume();

    if(ContextCompat.checkSelfPermission(this, Manifest.permission.READ_CONTACTS)
            == PackageManager.PERMISSION_GRANTED) {
        Toast.makeText(this, "Read contacts permission granted", Toast.LENGTH_SHORT).show();
    } else {
        if(ActivityCompat.shouldShowRequestPermissionRationale(this,
                Manifest.permission.READ_CONTACTS)) {
            Toast.makeText(this, "Explain why we need this permission", Toast.LENGTH_LONG).show();
        } else {
            ActivityCompat.requestPermissions(this, new String[] {Manifest.permission.READ_CONTACTS},
                    PERMISSION_READ_CONTACTS);
        }
    }
}
```

We have introduced a call to the shouldShowRequestPermissionRationale method, which is an optional call and will return if we show an explanation to the user as to why we need this permission. It usually returns true whenever the user denies the permission request or disables it afterwards in the application settings. If the use of the permission is very obvious for the application, it is not really required, but if there are some doubts, it is always good to explain to the user why are we requesting this permission.

We should take into consideration that anything we do here to show the explanation to the user has to be done asynchronously and call an appropriate callback afterward. In this case, we are only showing a dummy Toast.

If we do not want to show any explanation or if shouldShowRequestPermissionRationale returns false, we can proceed and do the actual request of the permission with the requestPermissions method. This method is asynchronous and can be used to request multiple permissions at the same time, although in this example we are only requesting one.

As this method is asynchronous, we will have to override another method called onRequestPermissionsResult, which will be called with the results of what the user selected. The additional parameter to showShowRequestPermissionRationale is an int, which we can use to track the request.

In our implementation, we assume that we have requested only one permission. Code has to be refactored to be more generic and support multiple permissions at the same time.

If the user did not grant a permission, our application has to be smart enough to disable that functionality or implement a mechanism to keep asking, without being annoying, for that permission.

This implementation has been done in the `onResume` method, which might be the right location for a permission we would need to start the application, but in our case, the permission to read contacts should be placed in a more appropriate point in the code, which makes more sense to the end user:

```
@Override
public void onRequestPermissionsResult(int requestCode, @NonNull String[] permissions,
                                       @NonNull int[] grantResults) {
    switch(requestCode) {
        case PERMISSION_READ_CONTACTS:
            if(grantResults.length > 0 && grantResults[0] == PackageManager.PERMISSION_GRANTED) {
                Toast.makeText(this, "Permission granted!", Toast.LENGTH_SHORT).show();
            } else {
                Toast.makeText(this, "Permission denied!", Toast.LENGTH_SHORT).show();
            }
            break;

        default:
            Log.e(TAG, "Wrong permission request code: " + requestCode);
    }
}
```

As mentioned previously, even if the permission is granted, we should not assume that it will be always be that way. The user can deny the permission from the application settings. If that happens, Android will kill our application, and a lot of unexpected things might happen. Anyway, it is good practice to check if we have permission whenever we have to do a protected operation; this way we will have the most robust solution to permission changes.

Permission groups

Google grouped permissions into permissions groups. Whenever an application is requesting a permission and does not have any permission in the same group granted, it will ask the user to grant the permission to the group without going into detail of which specific permission. For example, if we ask permission to read contacts, it will show the following popup:

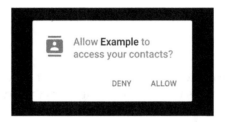

If the application asks for another permission from a group that has already a granted permission, it will immediately grant that permission.

For more information, refer to the following links:

- http://developer.android.com/reference/android/Manifest.permission_group.html
- http://developer.android.com/guide/topics/security/permissions.html

Background processing

Now that we have addressed how to request permission, we will slightly shift our focus on how to perform background operations. All network communications have to be done in the background. If we do it on the UI thread or main thread, we will block the UI layer and, most probably, throw an Application Not Responding (**ANR**) dialog. For more information, refer to http://developer.android.com/training/articles/perf-anr.html.

Anyway, any application targeted after Honeycomb will throw an exception `NetworkOnMainThreadException` if it detects any networking operations on the main thread. For more information, refer to `http://developer.android.com/reference/android/os/NetworkOnMainThreadException.html`.

We have several tools to address these points, but Android provides us with many useful mechanisms already.

Java threads

We can always use Java threads to do background work. It is good practice to use an Android provided mechanism, as using, or abusing, Java threads might lead to a complex and hard-to-maintain code.

For instance, if we want to load an image from the network (using the same example as that in the official documentation at `http://developer.android.com/guide/components/processes-and-threads.html`):

```
private void loadImage(final ImageView imageView, final String url) {
    new Thread(new Runnable() {
        public void run() {
            Bitmap b = loadImageFromNetwork(url);
            imageView.setImageBitmap(b);
        }
    }).start();
}
```

This would perform the downloading and creation of the bitmap in a background thread but will, actually, not work due to accessing the UI in a different thread than the UI thread. To solve this, we can use some additional mechanism provided by Android that makes sure that some code will be executed on the UI thread:

```
Activity.runOnUiThread(Runnable).
View.post(Runnable).
View.postDelayed(Runnable, long).
```

Modifying our code, now the `ImageView` class is only modified on the UI thread and we kept the downloading on the background thread, therefore not blocking any other thread:

```
private void loadImage(final ImageView imageView, final String url) {
    new Thread(new Runnable() {
        public void run() {
            final Bitmap b = loadImageFromNetwork(url);
            imageView.post(new Runnable() {
                @Override
                public void run() {
                    imageView.setImageBitmap(b);
                }
            });
        }
    }).start();
}
```

To solve this complexity when working on background processes and interacting with the UI, Android introduced the `AsyncTask` class.

AsyncTask

We saw the `AsyncTask` class in the previous chapter but we will go into more detail in this chapter.

As we have just mentioned, `AsyncTask` class is ideal when we have to do some background processing and interact with the UI layer with either the results or some intermediate process.

Implementation is very straightforward. We just have to subclass and implement the right methods and know when, and in which thread, they will be executed:

- `onPreExecute`: This is executed on the UI thread and is called before doing the background process
- `doInBackground`: This is invoked in a background thread
- `onProgressUpdate`: This is executed on the UI thread and is called after a call to `publishProgress` from `doInBackground`

- `onPostExecute`: This is executed on the UI thread and is called after the background process finishes

```
private static class ImageLoader extends AsyncTask<String, Void, Bitmap> {
    private ImageView imageView;

    private ImageLoader(ImageView imageView) {
        this.imageView = imageView;
    }

    @Override
    protected void onPreExecute() {
        imageView.setImageResource(R.drawable.placeholder);
    }

    @Override
    protected Bitmap doInBackground(String... params) {
        return loadImageFromNetwork(params[0]);
    }

    @Override
    protected void onPostExecute(Bitmap bitmap) {
        imageView.setImageBitmap(bitmap);
    }
}
```

Following are the parameters of the `AsyncTask` class:

- `Params`: Type of params sent to the `doInBackground` method
- `Progress`: Type of progress units, we will see it further down
- `Result`: Type of result done by `doInBackground`

It is also very easy to call, as shown in the following code:

```
private void loadImage(final ImageView imageView, final String url) {
    new ImageLoader(imageView).execute(url);
}
```

The execute call has to be done on the UI thread though.

Implementing `onProgressUpdate` method is a very useful way to update a progress bar or, basically, inform the UI about the progress of the background task.
The `progressUpdate` method has to be called from `doInBackground` method and update the progress value from there. For an example, check the official documentation at `http://developer.android.com/reference/android/os/AsyncTask.html`.

The `AsyncTasks` can be cancelled by just calling the `cancel` method. If the `AsyncTask` class has been cancelled, it will call `onCancelled` instead of `onPostExecute` when `doInBackground` finishes. What we have to take into consideration is periodically checking if the task has been cancelled in the `doInBackground` method, otherwise it might be doing lot of work for nothing and the background task will not be felt as though cancelled immediately.

Before HoneyComb, `AsyncTask` classes will be executed in parallel by default. In HoneyComb and later, all `AsyncTasks` will be executed serially unless called with the `executeOnExecutor(THREAD_POOL_EXECUTOR, ...)` method instead of just `execute(...)`:

```
private void loadImage(final ImageView imageView, final String url) {
    new ImageLoader(imageView).executeOnExecutor(AsyncTask.THREAD_POOL_EXECUTOR, url);
}
```

The `AsyncTask` class does not solve all our issues for free. If it is not implemented correctly, it can introduce lots of problems as well. For example, if the activity that spawned the `AsyncTask` class is destroyed, that does not destroy or stop the `AsyncTask`. We have to manually take care of all our `AsyncTask` classes and cancel them. As we saw previously, when we cancel an `AsyncTask`, it is not automatically stopped; it is our job to check whenever it is cancelled and stop the process.

This can be very easily reproduced if we have not taken care of it by just rotating the device for example. In addition, we have to be careful in the `onPostExecute` method of the `AsyncTask`; if the original activity that created the `AsyncTask` is no longer valid, the `ImageView` or any UI element we can reference might be potentially null. Also, as we are referencing these elements from inside the `AsyncTask`, they will not be garbage collected until the `AsyncTask` finishes, so, again, if we are not careful, we might introduce unnecessary memory use or even memory leaks.

IntentService

Another way to perform background operations is using an IntentService. As a difference from `AsyncTask`, an operation running on an IntentService could not interact directly with the UI and could not be interrupted, but it does not have the potential issues the `AsyncTask` had. For more information, refer to `http://developer.android.com/reference/android/app/IntentService.html`.

To create an IntentService, first of all, we will have to extend the `IntentService` class and implement `onHandleIntent` method. IntentService subclasses the `Service` class but provides the `onHandleIntent` method that is executed on a different thread than the main thread:

```java
public class DownloadService extends IntentService {

    public DownloadService() {
        super("DownloadService");
    }

    @Override
    protected void onHandleIntent(Intent intent) {

    }
}
```

Once this is done, we need to declare our service into our `Manifest` file:

```xml
AndroidManifest.xml ×

<?xml version="1.0" encoding="utf-8"?>
<manifest xmlns:android="http://schemas.android.com/apk/res/android"
    package="com.packt.rrafols.example">

    <uses-permission android:name="android.permission.INTERNET"/>
    <uses-permission android:name="android.permission.READ_CONTACTS"/>

    <application
        android:allowBackup="true"
        android:icon="@mipmap/ic_launcher"
        android:label="Example"
        android:supportsRtl="true"
        android:theme="@style/AppTheme">
        <activity android:name=".MainAdapterActivity">
            <intent-filter>
                <action android:name="android.intent.action.MAIN" />
                <category android:name="android.intent.category.LAUNCHER" />
            </intent-filter>
        </activity>

        <service
            android:name=".DownloadService"
            android:exported="false"/>

    </application>

</manifest>
```

Now that we have created an IntentService, which, in fact, will be used to connect to the Internet, we need to be able to pass parameters to it and get the output back.

IntentServices are invoked by calling the `startService` method with an Intent. Passing parameters is simple, for example, if we modify the `loadImage` method from our previous section to call the newly created IntentService rather than the `AsyncTask`, we could specify the URL in the `setData` method of the Intent:

```java
private void loadImage(final ImageView imageView, final String url) {
    Intent intent = new Intent(this, DownloadService.class);
    intent.setData(Uri.parse(url));
    startService(intent);
}
```

On the IntentService itself, we can retrieve the URL by reading the data string from the intent we get as parameter in the `onHandleIntent` method:

```java
@Override
protected void onHandleIntent(Intent intent) {
    String url = intent.getDataString();

    //...
}
```

More information on how to create a background service can be found at the official documentation page: `http://developer.android.com/training/run-background-servi ce/create-service.html`.

We can receive the output data from the IntentService through multiple ways. Maybe the simplest is to create our own `ResultReceiver` and pass it to the IntentService as a `Parcelable`. Another way is using a `BroadcastReceiver` and broadcasting an `Intent` with the result. We will not cover this in this book, but an example can be found at the official documentation page (`http://developer.android.com/training/run-background -service/report-status.html`).

```java
package com.packt.rrafols.example;

import ...

public class DownloadService extends IntentService {
    public static final String DOWNLOAD_PAYLOAD = "DownloadService.DOWNLOAD_PAYLOAD";
    public static final String DOWNLOAD_URL = "DownloadService.DOWNLOAD_URL";
    public static final String PARAM_RECEIVER = "DownloadService.RECEIVER";

    public static final int DOWNLOAD_SUCCESS = 0;
    public static final int DOWNLOAD_FAIL = 1;

    public DownloadService() { super("DownloadService"); }

    @Override
    protected void onHandleIntent(Intent intent) {
        String url = intent.getDataString();
        ResultReceiver receiver = intent.getParcelableExtra(PARAM_RECEIVER);

        byte[] data = loadDataFromUrl(url);

        Bundle bundle = new Bundle();
        bundle.putString(DOWNLOAD_URL, url);

        if(data != null) {
            bundle.putByteArray(DOWNLOAD_PAYLOAD, data);
            receiver.send(DOWNLOAD_SUCCESS, bundle);
        } else {
            receiver.send(DOWNLOAD_FAIL, bundle);
        }
    }
}
```

To avoid going into many details about HTTP connections right now, this implementation is rather simple. We receive an instance of a `DownloadReceiver`, our own implementation of `ResultReceiver`, in the intent extended data together with the URL. For more information on `ResultReceiver`, refer to `http://developer.android.com/reference/an droid/os/ResultReceiver.html`.

After downloading the data from the URL, we create a new `Bundle` class where we put the URL back to simplify tracking, which was the origin of the request, and if we get a positive response from the server, we put the payload as a byte array and deliver the result to the receiver asynchronously by calling the `send` function. As a `resultCode`, we used `DOWNLOAD_SUCCESS` to identify whether we were able to connect to the server. If we can not connect to the server, we do not put the payload but deliver a `DOWNLOAD_FAIL` message back to the receiver. In a real implementation, we would take care, for example, of the HTTP response code, and the `DownloadService` would have a specific logic depending on the response code value.

To create our own `ResultReceiver`, we have to create a class, extend from it, and implement the `onReceiveResult` method. In the following example, we created two empty methods that will be called accordingly to the `resultCode` we receive:

```
success(String url, byte[] data)
failure(String url)
```

As they are empty, we would have to subclass `DownloadReceiver` and implement these methods if we are interested in those callbacks:

```java
package com.packt.rrafols.example;

import android.annotation.SuppressLint;
import android.os.Bundle;
import android.os.Handler;
import android.support.v4.os.ResultReceiver;

@SuppressLint("ParcelCreator")
public class DownloadReceiver extends ResultReceiver {
    public DownloadReceiver(Handler handler) {
        super(handler);
    }

    @Override
    protected void onReceiveResult(int resultCode, Bundle resultData) {
        byte[] data = resultData.getByteArray(DownloadService.DOWNLOAD_PAYLOAD);
        String url = resultData.getString(DownloadService.DOWNLOAD_URL);
        if(resultCode == DownloadService.DOWNLOAD_SUCCESS) {
            success(url, data);
        } else {
            failure(url);
        }
    }

    public void success(String url, byte[] data) {}
    public void failure(String url) {}
}
```

Another way we could implement the `DownloadReceiver` is to declare an internal interface and a method to set an interface implementation:

```java
C DownloadReceiver.java ×

    package com.packt.rrafols.example;

    import android.annotation.SuppressLint;
    import android.os.Bundle;
    import android.os.Handler;
    import android.support.v4.os.ResultReceiver;

    @SuppressLint("ParcelCreator")
    public class DownloadReceiver extends ResultReceiver {
        private Receiver receiver;
        public DownloadReceiver(Handler handler) { super(handler); }

        public interface Receiver {
            void onReceivedResult(int resultCode, Bundle resultData);
        }

        public void setReceiver(Receiver receiver) {
            this.receiver = receiver;
        }

        @Override
        protected void onReceiveResult(int resultCode, Bundle resultData) {
            if(receiver != null) receiver.onReceivedResult(resultCode, resultData);
        }
    }
```

In case of having a valid instance of that implementation, we will just forward the `onReceivedResult` call to that receiver.

In our example, we will use the first implementation of `DownloadReceiver` and extend the success and failure methods to implement our own logic:

```java
        private void loadImage(final ImageView imageView, final String url) {
            Intent intent = new Intent(this, DownloadService.class);
            intent.setData(Uri.parse(url));
            intent.putExtra(DownloadService.PARAM_RECEIVER, imageReceiver);
            startService(intent);
        }


        private DownloadReceiver imageReceiver = new DownloadReceiver(new Handler()) {
            @Override
            public void success(String url, byte[] data) {

            }

            @Override
            public void failure(String url) {

            }
        };
```

We are currently not using the `imageView`, as, even if we could not do it, we do not want to pass the `ImageView` as a parameter to the `DownloadService`. A possible implementation would be the following; use a `HashMap` to map each URL to its associated `ImageView`:

```
private void loadImage(final ImageView imageView, final String url) {
    imageViewByUrl.put(url, imageView);
    Intent intent = new Intent(this, DownloadService.class);
    intent.setData(Uri.parse(url));
    intent.putExtra(DownloadService.PARAM_RECEIVER, imageReceiver);
    startService(intent);
}


private DownloadReceiver imageReceiver = new DownloadReceiver(new Handler()) {
    @Override
    public void success(String url, byte[] data) {
        ImageView iv = imageViewByUrl.get(url);
        if(iv != null) {
            Bitmap bm = BitmapFactory.decodeByteArray(data, 0, data.length);
            if(bm != null) iv.setImageBitmap(bm);
            imageViewByUrl.remove(url);
        }
    }

    @Override
    public void failure(String url) {
        imageViewByUrl.remove(url);

        Toast.makeText(MainAdapterActivity.this, "Error loading image: " + url,
                Toast.LENGTH_SHORT).show();
    }
};
```

We have to make sure to clean up our `HashMap` after we load, or fail to load, an image and also to clean it up whenever we do not need it anymore, for example, when our activity is destroyed:

```
@Override
protected void onDestroy() {
    imageViewByUrl.clear();

    super.onDestroy();
}
```

The preceding code works fine, but there is an issue: when we create the `DownloadReceiver`, we pass a new handler as a parameter. This new handler will be created in the looper of the current thread, so whenever we send a message, the `onReceiveResult` will be executed in the same thread as it was created, but as a posted message. Looper runs a message loop in a specific thread. For more information on looper, visit `https://developer.android.com/reference/android/os/Looper.html`.

As a consequence, if we do it this way, we are decoding the Bitmap on the main thread and potentially blocking any other process. To solve this, we pass a null handler to the `ResultReceiver`, which will execute the `onReceiveResult` on an arbitrary thread, and we make sure we modify the `ImageView` only on the UI thread:

```java
private DownloadReceiver imageReceiver = new DownloadReceiver(null) {
    @Override
    public void success(String url, byte[] data) {
        final ImageView iv = imageViewByUrl.get(url);
        if(iv != null) {
            final Bitmap bm = BitmapFactory.decodeByteArray(data, 0, data.length);
            if(bm != null) {
                iv.post(new Runnable() {
                    @Override
                    public void run() {
                        iv.setImageBitmap(bm);
                    }
                });
            }
            imageViewByUrl.remove(url);
        }
    }
}
```

Network code

Now that we have seen how to do some background processing and decode the data by ourselves, we will see how to implement the networking code. We will start by showing the standard classes and libraries Android provides us, and later we will cover widely used third-party networking libraries.

Android standard libraries

As we have just mentioned earlier, there are a lot of third party libraries that will make our lives easier, but it is important to know the basics. Android provides a set of standard classes and libraries which are not really used anymore by application developers unless there is something very specific of low-level access is required. Anyway, we will briefly show a possible implementation of an HTTP downloader and then will switch to higher level-party libraries.

In the previous example, we did not show the implementation of the `loadDataFromURL` method, as we will cover it here in this section:

```java
@Nullable
private byte[] loadDataFromUrl(@NonNull String urlString) {
    HttpURLConnection conn = null;
    BufferedInputStream is = null;
    try {
        URL url = new URL(urlString);
        conn = (HttpURLConnection) url.openConnection();

        is = new BufferedInputStream(conn.getInputStream());
        return readStream(is);
    } catch (IOException e) {
        Log.w(TAG, "Exception connecting to " + urlString, e);
    } finally {
        if(conn != null) conn.disconnect();
    }
    return null;
}

private byte[] readStream(InputStream is) throws IOException {
    ByteArrayOutputStream baos = new ByteArrayOutputStream();
    byte[] buffer = new byte[BUFFER_SIZE];
    int count;

    while((count = is.read(buffer)) != -1) {
        baos.write(buffer, 0, count);
    }

    return baos.toByteArray();
}
```

What we are doing in this implementation is to create an `HttpURLConnection` from the URL and read all the data from the `InputStream` of the connection as long as we have more information coming from it or as long as does not return -1. The `loadDataFromUrl` method is very similar to the method explained in the example in the official documentation at `http://developer.android.com/reference/java/net/HttpURLConnection.html`. However, here we are also provided with an implementation of the `readStream` method. A stream can be read in multiple ways, but we have chosen to read it by small blocks rather than byte per byte as this performs a lot better.

Volley

Volley is an HTTP library to make networking faster and easier for Android applications. It is included as a framework in the Android Open Source Project: `https://android.googlesource.com/platform/frameworks/volley`.

To include volley in your project, you can clone it from the original repository by using the following command:

```
git clone https://android.googlesource.com/platform/frameworks/volley
```

You can also add it as a subproject in Android Studio or by just adding a dependency to our `build.gradle` file:

```
compile 'com.android.volley:volley:1.0.0'
```

As documented at the official documentation page, `http://developer.android.com/training/volley/index.html`, what volley does better is to perform calls to web services that return structured data and comes with support for raw strings, images, and JSON.

Let's adapt our previous source code to request the images using Volley instead of our own implementations:

First of all, we have to initialize a `RequestQueue`. We could do this following the example in the documentation at `http://developer.android.com/training/volley/requestqueue.html`:

```
Cache cache = new DiskBasedCache(getCacheDir(), 1024 * 1024);
Network network = new BasicNetwork(new HurlStack());
requestQueue = new RequestQueue(cache, network);
requestQueue.start();
```

Or by simply using the following code:

```
requestQueue = Volley.newRequestQueue(this);
```

Initializing the queue this way, it will be already started and contain a default `DiskBasedCache` and `Network` object, like the ones we have created ourselves previously.

Once we have done this, we can replace the `loadImage` method by the following code, removing the background service, the intent, and `ResultReceiver`:

```java
private void loadImage(final ImageView imageView, final String url) {
    ImageRequest request = new ImageRequest(url,
        new Response.Listener<Bitmap>() {
            @Override
            public void onResponse(Bitmap response) {
                imageView.setImageBitmap(response);
            }
        }, 0, 0, ImageView.ScaleType.FIT_CENTER, null,
        new Response.ErrorListener() {
            @Override
            public void onErrorResponse(VolleyError error) {
                imageView.setImageResource(R.drawable.placeholder);
            }
        });

    requestQueue.add(request);
}
```

This new implementation is very simple and quite easy to understand. Volley has a specific type of request for images, and we can even specify the maximum width and height and the scaling type we want for the images. What we have to implement ourselves is two callbacks: firslty `Response.Listener<Bitmap>`, when we get a valid response from the server and we got the decoded Bitmap as a parameter; and secondly `Response.ErrorListener`, when we find any issue while connecting to the server.

In a case where we would like to have multiple connections from different parts of the app, Volley suggests creating a singleton and use that single instance to hold a single request queue. We could also take advantage of the `ImageLoader` and `NetworkImageView` to efficiently load and show images in a list for example. For more information and examples, refer to `http://developer.android.com/training/volley/request.html`.

If we want to connect to a REST service returning a JSON response, we could use a similar approach; for example, let's try to connect to Yahoo financial API and check for Yahoo, Google, and Apple symbols:

```
http://finance.yahoo.com/webservice/v1/symbols/YHOO,GOOG,AAPL/quote?format=json
```

```java
        String url = "http://finance.yahoo.com/webservice/v1/symbols/YHOO,GOOG,AAPL/quote?format=json";
        JsonObjectRequest request = new JsonObjectRequest(url, null,
                new Response.Listener<JSONObject>() {
                    @Override
                    public void onResponse(JSONObject response) {
                        Log.i(TAG, response.toString());
                    }
                },
                new Response.ErrorListener() {
                    @Override
                    public void onErrorResponse(VolleyError error) {
                        Toast.makeText(MainAdapterActivity.this, "Error processing json: " +
                                error.getMessage(), Toast.LENGTH_SHORT).show();
                    }
                });

        requestQueue.add(request);
```

As we can see, the code structure is very similar to the previous one. When creating the `JsonObjectRequest`, we can also send a `JSONObject` to the server. In case the `JSONObject` is present and not null, Volley will use the HTTP `POST` method instead of `GET`.

In a case where you would like to write more complex or custom requests, you could do so by following the guidelines in the documentation at `http://developer.android.com/training/volley/request-custom.html`.

There is also a nice presentation on YouTube about Volley done at the Google Developers conference Google I/O 2013; for more information, refer to `https://www.youtube.com/watch?v=yhv8l9F44qo`.

In the documentation, we can find a complete implementation of a `GsonRequest`. `Gson` is a Java serialization/deserialization library that we will cover in more detail in the next section, and basically it converts JSON to and from Java objects automatically. It uses reflection, so there will be a small performance impact but this will be insignificant compared to the time it takes to do any network operation. For more information on Gson, refer to `https://github.com/google/gson`.

In this implementation of a custom request, we can also see how to provide request headers, to manually set the HTTP request method, for example, and to put the response headers on the `Response` object:

```java
public class GsonRequest<T> extends Request<T> {
    private final Gson gson = new Gson();
    private final Class<T> clazz;
    private final Map<String, String> headers;
    private final Listener<T> listener;

    /**
     * Make a GET request and return a parsed object from JSON.
     *
     * @param url URL of the request to make
     * @param clazz Relevant class object, for Gson's reflection
     * @param headers Map of request headers
     */
    public GsonRequest(String url, Class<T> clazz, Map<String, String> headers,
            Listener<T> listener, ErrorListener errorListener) {
        super(Method.GET, url, errorListener);
        this.clazz = clazz;
        this.headers = headers;
        this.listener = listener;
    }

    @Override
    public Map<String, String> getHeaders() throws AuthFailureError {
        return headers != null ? headers : super.getHeaders();
    }

    @Override
    protected void deliverResponse(T response) {
        listener.onResponse(response);
    }

    @Override
    protected Response<T> parseNetworkResponse(NetworkResponse response) {
        try {
            String json = new String(
                    response.data,
                    HttpHeaderParser.parseCharset(response.headers));
            return Response.success(
                    gson.fromJson(json, clazz),
                    HttpHeaderParser.parseCacheHeaders(response));
        } catch (UnsupportedEncodingException e) {
            return Response.error(new ParseError(e));
        } catch (JsonSyntaxException e) {
            return Response.error(new ParseError(e));
        }
    }
}
```

Gson

Reusing the same API from Yahoo as previously and carefully checking its contents, we can recreate the same structure as Java objects:

```json
{
    "list":{
        "meta":{
            "type":"resource-list",
            "start":0,
            "count":3
        },
        "resources":[
            {
                "resource":{
                    "classname":"Quote",
                    "fields":{
                        "name":"Yahoo! Inc.",
                        "price":"36.320000",
                        "symbol":"YHOO",
                        "ts":"1459281600",
                        "type":"equity",
                        "utctime":"2016-03-29T20:00:00+0000",
                        "volume":"23598690"
                    }
                }
            },
            {
                "resource":{
                    "classname":"Quote",
                    "fields":{
                        "name":"Alphabet Inc.",
                        "price":"744.770020",
                        "symbol":"GOOG",
                        "ts":"1459281600",
                        "type":"equity",
                        "utctime":"2016-03-29T20:00:00+0000",
                        "volume":"1902687"
                    }
                }
            },
            {
                "resource":{
                    "classname":"Quote",
                    "fields":{
                        "name":"Apple Inc.",
                        "price":"107.680000",
                        "symbol":"AAPL",
```

```
          "ts":"1459281601",
          "type":"equity",
          "utctime":"2016-03-29T20:00:01+0000",
          "volume":"31165525"
        }
       }
      }
     ]
    }
   }
```

We have to create Java objects where the instance variable name matches the field name in the JSON data, and, in addition, we have to mimic, for example, the same kind of structures, subclasses, or arrays.

First of all, the whole model is wrapped into a list object, so we need to create a class representing this list object:

```
© Model.java ×
    package com.packt.rrafols.example.model;

    public class Model {
        public List list;

        public List getList() { return list; }
        public void setList(List list) { this.list = list; }
    }
```

The list object contains a meta object and a list of resource objects. The meta object is like the previous example, and we can easily represent the list of resource objects by creating an array:

```
© List.java ×
    package com.packt.rrafols.example.model;

    public class List {
        private Meta meta;
        private ResourceWrapper[] resources;

        public Meta getMeta() { return meta; }
        public void setMeta(Meta meta) { this.meta = meta; }
        public ResourceWrapper[] getResources() { return resources; }
        public void setResources(ResourceWrapper[] resources) { this.resources = resources; }
    }
```

The meta object will already have some primitives and not only objects. If we look carefully at the JSON file, we could appreciate that the start and count properties are just plain numbers instead of a string:

```java
© Meta.java ×
package com.packt.rrafols.example.model;

public class Meta {
    private String type;
    private int start;
    private int count;

    public String getType() { return type; }
    public void setType(String type) { this.type = type; }
    public int getStart() { return start; }
    public void setStart(int start) { this.start = start; }
    public int getCount() { return count; }
    public void setCount(int count) { this.count = count; }
}
```

One small detail that we have to pay attention to is that objects inside the list are wrapped in the JSON file with a resource object. To properly serialize those objects, we have to create a `ResourceWrapper` class and then the actual `Resource` object:

```java
© ResourceWrapper.java ×
package com.packt.rrafols.example.model;

public class ResourceWrapper {
    private Resource resource;

    public Resource getResource() { return resource; }
    public void setResource(Resource resource) { this.resource = resource; }
}
```

This `Resource` object will have a `classname` property, stored as a `String` data type, and a list of `Fields`:

```java
© Resource.java ×
package com.packt.rrafols.example.model;

public class Resource {
    private String classname;
    private Fields fields;

    public String getClassname() { return classname; }
    public void setClassname(String classname) { this.classname = classname; }
    public Fields getFields() { return fields; }
    public void setFields(Fields fields) { this.fields = fields; }
}
```

Fields will contain almost all the data, and as we can see in the following class implementation, there is a property mapping each JSON field:

```java
package com.packt.rrafols.example.model;

public class Fields {
    private String name;
    private String price;
    private String symbol;
    private String ts;
    private String type;
    private String utctime;
    private String volume;

    public String getName() { return name; }
    public void setName(String name) { this.name = name; }
    public String getPrice() { return price; }
    public void setPrice(String price) { this.price = price; }
    public String getSymbol() { return symbol; }
    public void setSymbol(String symbol) { this.symbol = symbol; }
    public String getTs() { return ts; }
    public void setTs(String ts) { this.ts = ts; }
    public String getType() { return type; }
    public void setType(String type) { this.type = type; }
    public String getUtctime() { return utctime; }
    public void setUtctime(String utctime) { this.utctime = utctime; }
    public String getVolume() { return volume; }
    public void setVolume(String volume) { this.volume = volume; }
}
```

Usually, in real-life applications or integration with complex data models, it is recommended to automate this step, as writing all the serialization classes and code can be tedious and quite error-prone.

Once we have created all the infrastructure or model classes, we can create the request with it:

```java
String url = "http://finance.yahoo.com/webservice/v1/symbols/YHOO,GOOG,AAPL/quote?format=json";
GsonRequest<Model> request = new GsonRequest<>(url, Model.class, null,
        new Response.Listener<Model>() {
            @Override
            public void onResponse(Model response) {
                Log.i(TAG, response.toString());
            }
        },
        new Response.ErrorListener() {
            @Override
            public void onErrorResponse(VolleyError error) {
                Toast.makeText(MainAdapterActivity.this, "Error processing json: " +
                        error.getMessage(), Toast.LENGTH_SHORT).show();
            }
        });

requestQueue.add(request);
```

After the call, the `Model` response object will be filled with all the JSON data and we will not have to worry about parsing the `data`. `Gson` takes care to serialize and unserialize Java objects to JSON and back. This is rather convenient, but depending on the API complexity, it is a laborious process and needs to be done very meticulously as any single mistake will leave us with some null fields that can be hard to debug where the bug or issue comes from.

Retrofit

Retrofit is an HTTP client for Java developed by Square. It is defined as a "Retrofit turns your HTTP API into a Java interface" at the official website (`http://square.github.io/retrofit/`).

Source code can be found in its Github repository (`https://github.com/square/retrofit`).

To include it in our Android application, we would only have to add a dependency line in our `build.gradle` file: `compile 'com.squareup.retrofit2:retrofit:2.0.0'` and

`compile 'com.squareup.retrofit2:converter-gson:2.0.0-beta3'` if we want to continue using Gson for serializing and deserializing JSON to and from Java objects. This library is still in beta at the time of writing this book.

Let's implement the same example of the Yahoo finances API but using Retrofit instead of Volley. We can use the same model classes as used previously as we will be using a Gson converter.

First of all, we will write a service interface with all the web service calls, and we will use the annotation extensions from Retrofit to map a specific interface call to a web service request.

At this point, we have to indicate only the relative path to the web service we want to map, as we will define the server URL in another part of our code when initializing the Retrofit classes. This will come in quite handy if we want to connect to our staging or testing server instead of production as we will not have to change anything in the web service interface:

```
 YahooFinanceService.java  ×
    package com.packt.rrafols.example;

    import com.packt.rrafols.example.model.Model;

    import retrofit2.Call;
    import retrofit2.http.GET;
    import retrofit2.http.Path;

    public interface YahooFinanceService {
        @GET("webservice/v1/symbols/{symbols}/quote?format=json")
        Call<Model> getQuote(@Path("symbols") String symbols);
    }
```

In the preceding code, we created a method, and with the `@Get` annotation, we specified the URL where it will perform the request. Also note that we can add dynamic parameters or dynamic parts of the URL by wrapping a variable with `{}` and then using the `@Path` annotation with our parameter to replace the variable with the content of the parameter. In this case, the symbols we want to request will be given by the parameter.

Now that we have the service interface created, we can write the code to initialize Retrofit and actually perform the request:

```
Retrofit retrofit = new Retrofit.Builder()
        .baseUrl("http://finance.yahoo.com/")
        .addConverterFactory(GsonConverterFactory.create())
        .build();

YahooFinanceService symbols = retrofit.create(YahooFinanceService.class);

Call<Model> symbolsCall = symbols.getQuote("YHOO,GOOG,AAPL");
symbolsCall.enqueue(new Callback<Model>() {
    @Override
    public void onResponse(Call<Model> call, retrofit2.Response<Model> response) {
        if(response.isSuccessful()) {

            Model model = response.body();
            //..

        } else {
            Toast.makeText(MainAdapterActivity.this, "Request not successful: " +
                    response.message(), Toast.LENGTH_SHORT).show();
        }
    }

    @Override
    public void onFailure(Call<Model> call, Throwable t) {
        Toast.makeText(MainAdapterActivity.this, "Error processing request: " +
                t.getMessage(), Toast.LENGTH_SHORT).show();
    }
});
```

From Retrofit 2.0.0 onwards, we would have to tell Retrofit to use a
`GsonConverterFactory` if we want to use Gson as it is not the default converter. In
previous versions, Gson was the default converter.

Retrofit allows us to create synchronous or asynchronous requests. We will not cover
synchronous requests, but information can be always found in the official documentation.
To create an asynchronous call, we have to queue a new callback to the `call` object wrapper
we got from the service interface. Callback is really simple and straightforward to
implement. Whenever we get a response from the server, the `onResponse` method will be
called, or if there has been any issue while connecting to the server, the `onFailure` method
is called. If we get an error due to the HTTP response code, we will get a response, but it
will not be a successful response. We will either check `response.isSuccessful` to see if
has been successful or the HTTP response code.

Retrofit also allows us, like other HTTP clients, to modify the HTTP headers statically or
send data as form encoded or even multipart. We mentioned that from Retrofit 2.0.0, it is by
default not using a GsonConverter, but we can very easily change that. If our server is using
another protocol, Retrofit comes with support for six different protocols, for example, XML,
wire, or protobuf.

Wire and protobuf are optimized binary protocols. For more information, check their
documentations at `https://github.com/square/wire`
and `https://developers.google.com/protocol-buffers/`, respectively.

In order to modify the headers dynamically, we would have to create an `OkHttp`
interceptor. `OkHttp` is an HTTP and HTTP/2 client for Android also built by Square, and
Retrofit uses it by default to perform HTTP connections. Interceptors are the way `OkHttp`
provides to observe requests and potentially modify them. Typically, they are used to
change headers on either the request or response.

`OkHttp` can be used as an independent library as well by just adding the following
dependency to our `build.gradle` file:

```
compile 'com.squareup.okhttp3:okhttp:3.2.0'
```

For more information on how to use it, check the official page and documentation at
`http://square.github.io/okhttp/`. Source code is available in its Github repository at
`https://github.com/square/okhttp`.

OkHttp

An HTTP & HTTP/2 client for Android and Java applications

Overview

HTTP is the way modern applications network. It's how we exchange data & media. Doing HTTP efficiently makes your stuff load faster and saves bandwidth.

OkHttp is an HTTP client that's efficient by default:

- HTTP/2 support allows all requests to the same host to share a socket.
- Connection pooling reduces request latency (if HTTP/2 isn't available).
- Transparent GZIP shrinks download sizes.
- Response caching avoids the network completely for repeat requests.

OkHttp perseveres when the network is troublesome: it will silently recover from common connection problems. If your service has multiple IP addresses OkHttp will attempt alternate addresses if the first connect fails. This is necessary for IPv4+IPv6 and for services hosted in redundant data centers. OkHttp initiates new connections with modern TLS features (SNI, ALPN), and falls back to TLS 1.0 if the handshake fails.

Using OkHttp is easy. Its request/response API is designed with fluent builders and immutability. It supports both synchronous blocking calls and async calls with callbacks.

OkHttp supports Android 2.3 and above. For Java, the minimum requirement is 1.7.

Real case scenario

One real case scenario of applying `OkHttp`, Retrofit, and Gson is the application we developed during the AngelHack Barcelona 2015 hackathon. After winning the local hackathon, we converted the idea into a product. To develop the prototype and the current version, we used all those libraries. In the very first version, though, connection to the server was handled by an IntentService, and all networking was done using the native Android classes, but as we can imagine, it is a lot better to switch to widely used and tested libraries.

In the following, you can see some parts of the code, how the API calls are mapped, how requests and responses are built, and some specificities, as some of the parameter names changed in our REST server and we had to use the annotations of Gson to use a different instance variable name than the property name returned in the JSON data.

The following source code is just for illustration purposes and does not contain the whole example.

The `InGroupService` class defines all the web service end points and which type of request we need and which type of response we will get back from the server. There will be some differences in comparison to our previous example, as we used Retrofit 1.9.0:

```java
InGroupService.java ×

package com.blinkingdash.ingroup.network;

import ...

public interface InGroupService {
    String API_VERSION = "v1";

    @POST("/" + API_VERSION + "/user/auth")
    void userAuth(@Body UserAuthRequest request,
                  Callback<UserAuthResponse> authResponse);

    @POST("/" + API_VERSION + "/question/list")
    void getQuestionList(@Body QuestionListRequest request,
                         Callback<QuestionListResponse> eventResponse);

    @POST("/" + API_VERSION + "/question/choose")
    void questionChoose(@Body QuestionChooseRequest request,
                        Callback<QuestionChooseResponse> eventResponse);

    @POST("/" + API_VERSION + "/question/skip")
    void questionSkip(@Body QuestionSkipRequest request,
                      Callback<QuestionSkipResponse> eventResponse);

    @POST("/" + API_VERSION + "/question/create")
    void questionCreate(@Body QuestionCreateRequest request,
                        Callback<QuestionCreateResponse> eventResponse);

    @POST("/" + API_VERSION + "/user/feedback")
    void userFeedback(@Body UserFeedbackRequest request,
                      Callback<UserFeedbackResponse> eventResponse);

    @POST("/" + API_VERSION + "/user/matches")
    void userMatches(@Body UserMatchesRequest request,
                     Callback<UserMatchesResponse> eventResponse);

    @POST("/" + API_VERSION + "/user/myprofile")
    void getUserProfile(@Body UserProfileGetRequest request,
                        Callback<UserProfileGetResponse> eventResponse);

    @POST("/" + API_VERSION + "/user/profile")
    void getMatchProfile(@Body MatchProfileGetRequest request,
                         Callback<MatchProfileGetResponse> eventResponse);

    @POST("/" + API_VERSION + "/user/questions")
    void getUserQuestions(@Body UserQuestionListRequest request,
                          Callback<UserQuestionListResponse> eventResponse);

    @PUT("/" + API_VERSION + "/user/myprofile")
    void getUserProfile(@Body UserProfileSetRequest request,
                        Callback<UserProfileSetResponse> eventResponse);

    @POST("/" + API_VERSION + "/question/log")
    void getQuestionLog(@Body QuestionLogRequest request,
                        Callback<QuestionLogResponse> eventResponse);
}
```

In the following, we can find how to build a request and wrap the response and how simple a response class object looks, thanks to Gson.

The way we created server requests was very simple – we need a request object with the data to be serialized and a response object wrapped into a callback. To keep things simple, we checked for the server response code, and we assumed that it was an error if the response status code was higher than or equal to 400:

```java
InGroupService.java ×

package com.blinkingdash.ingroup.network;

import ...

public interface InGroupService {
    String API_VERSION = "v1";

    @POST("/" + API_VERSION + "/user/auth")
    void userAuth(@Body UserAuthRequest request,
                  Callback<UserAuthResponse> authResponse);

    @POST("/" + API_VERSION + "/question/list")
    void getQuestionList(@Body QuestionListRequest request,
                         Callback<QuestionListResponse> eventResponse);

    @POST("/" + API_VERSION + "/question/choose")
    void questionChoose(@Body QuestionChooseRequest request,
                        Callback<QuestionChooseResponse> eventResponse);

    @POST("/" + API_VERSION + "/question/skip")
    void questionSkip(@Body QuestionSkipRequest request,
                      Callback<QuestionSkipResponse> eventResponse);

    @POST("/" + API_VERSION + "/question/create")
    void questionCreate(@Body QuestionCreateRequest request,
                        Callback<QuestionCreateResponse> eventResponse);

    @POST("/" + API_VERSION + "/user/feedback")
    void userFeedback(@Body UserFeedbackRequest request,
                      Callback<UserFeedbackResponse> eventResponse);

    @POST("/" + API_VERSION + "/user/matches")
    void userMatches(@Body UserMatchesRequest request,
                     Callback<UserMatchesResponse> eventResponse);

    @POST("/" + API_VERSION + "/user/myprofile")
    void getUserProfile(@Body UserProfileGetRequest request,
                        Callback<UserProfileGetResponse> eventResponse);

    @POST("/" + API_VERSION + "/user/profile")
    void getMatchProfile(@Body MatchProfileGetRequest request,
                         Callback<MatchProfileGetResponse> eventResponse);

    @POST("/" + API_VERSION + "/user/questions")
    void getUserQuestions(@Body UserQuestionListRequest request,
                          Callback<UserQuestionListResponse> eventResponse);

    @PUT("/" + API_VERSION + "/user/myprofile")
    void getUserProfile(@Body UserProfileSetRequest request,
                        Callback<UserProfileSetResponse> eventResponse);

    @POST("/" + API_VERSION + "/question/log")
    void getQuestionLog(@Body QuestionLogRequest request,
                        Callback<QuestionLogResponse> eventResponse);
}
```

We kept the response callback very simple by just having two methods, onSuccess and onError. In the case that the request was successful, the onSuccess method was called with the unserialized response as parameter:

```
InGroupAPIResponse.java ×

    package com.blinkingdash.ingroup.network;

    public interface InGroupAPIResponse<T> {
        void onSuccess(T t);
        void onError(int status, String reason);
    }
```

The response object is very simple; we had to change the name of the serialized field by using the SerializedName annotation, but without worrying about the complexity of the protocol and parsing the output we got ourselves a server response unserialized into a List of Question objects:

```
QuestionListResponse.java ×

    package com.blinkingdash.ingroup.responses;

    import ...

    public class QuestionListResponse extends GenericResponse {
        @SerializedName("question")
        private List<Question> questionList;

        public List<Question> getQuestions() { return questionList; }

        @Override
        public String toString() {
            return "result: " + result + " code: " + code + " message " + message +
                    " list size: " + ((questionList != null) ? questionList.size() : 0);
        }
    }
```

The following is example of a request that is pretty simple as well, but has a bit more logic than the response, as all the parameters are set by using a Builder pattern (Visit `https://en.wikipedia.org/wiki/Builder_pattern` for more information on Builder pattern) to simplify our code:

```java
QuestionListRequest.java ×

package com.blinkingdash.ingroup.requests;

public class QuestionListRequest extends GenericRequest {
    private String vstoken;
    private double lat;
    private double lon;
    private double alt;
    private int radius;
    private int limit;

    public static class Builder {
        private QuestionListRequest request;
        public Builder() { request = new QuestionListRequest(); }
        public Builder setVSToken(String vsToken) {...}
        public Builder setLat(double lat) {...}
        public Builder setLon(double lon) {...}
        public Builder setAlt(double alt) {...}
        public Builder setRadius(int radius) {...}
        public Builder setLimit(int limit) {...}
        public QuestionListRequest build() { return request; }
    }

    private QuestionListRequest() {}
    public String getVstoken() { return vstoken; }
    public double getLat() { return lat; }
    public double getLon() { return lon; }
    public double getAlt() { return alt; }
    public int getRadius() { return radius; }
    public int getLimit() { return limit; }
    public void setVstoken(String vstoken) { this.vstoken = vstoken; }
    public void setLat(double lat) { this.lat = lat; }
    public void setLon(double lon) { this.lon = lon; }
    public void setRadius(int radius) { this.radius = radius; }
    public void setLimit(int limit) { this.limit = limit; }
}
```

For more information, refer to `http://angelhack.com/215/1/22/meet-the-215-global-demo-day-finalists-the-22-startups/`.

Summary

In this chapter, you saw how to perform network connections. You started with permissions, both normal and dangerous, and covered how to do background processing and how to avoid doing heavy work on the main thread. We finished by explaining how to integrate widely used high-level networking libraries that will simplify our work and reduce the time to market of our application. We briefly looked at real case scenario of how these libraries can help us to quickly prototype and then build and improve on top of that.

6
Image Management

Nowadays, it is very hard to imagine an application without any kind of images. Images, and media in general, have become an essential part of our applications if we want to show appealing information. At the same time, images use a lot of resources, memory, and time to load, and so on. So, this is a relevant detail we have to take care when developing our application. Managing images in an inefficient way will prevent our application from running smoothly, and if we do not address memory constraints properly, our application will most probably crash. This is even more significant if we load user-generated images or images that come from sources out of our control. In addition, we always have to keep in mind that not everyone has the latest, most expensive Android smartphone on the market, and each smartphone will have different memory constraints.

To work these issues out, we will cover in this chapter how to cache images, both to local memory and to a local file; handle large images; and manage images efficiently, for example, when used in a large list or a **RecyclerView.** We will finish the chapter by introducing some widely used libraries for loading and managing images that will, definitely, help us when developing our application.

Caching remote data

We have seen previously how to load images and display them in our application. But what happens when we have to load a huge amount of images? Let's imagine a List or a RecyclerView and the end user scrolling back and forth. As RecyclerView is recycling the views and replacing the bitmap with another, we would have to download the same images from the Internet again and again. This is not only inefficient and slow, but it also drains the data plan and the user's battery. We can easily implement a cache to store the images so that we do not have to download them again and again. Let's see how we can do it.

Memory caches

The fastest way of accessing images is to store them in memory. We need to be careful as memory is a limited resource, and even more careful if we make assumptions, as every device has different amount of free memory. We will create a memory cache based on the amount of free memory and only use a small portion, leaving lots of memory for the app itself as well.

Since Honeycomb, and also part of the Android support library, there is a class that comes in really handy, the `LruCache` class. Visit `http://developer.android.com/reference/an droid/util/LruCache.html` for more information on the `LruCache` class.

 For more information on the Android support library, refer to `http://dev eloper.android.com/tools/support-library/index.html`.

The `LruCache` class is basically a cache that stores a limited number of entries. **LRU** stands for **Least Recently Used**. The maximum number of entries is specified at the time of creation, and the cache mechanism works by removing the elements at the end of a queue whenever the size of the cache will grow beyond its maximum size. Every time an element is accessed, it is moved to the top of the queue. With this mechanism, the elements that will be removed will be the least used elements. The `LruCache` class is currently backed by a `LinkedHashMap` class, flagged to iterate elements in the order they were accessed.

 For more details on the `LinkedHashMap` class, refer to `http://developer.android.com/reference/java/util/LinkedHashMap .html`.

In our case, we are more interested in the memory size of the images rather than number of images, but, as the documentation clearly shows, we can easily override the `sizeOf` method and return, for example, the amount of memory an image takes in memory:

```
int cacheSize = 4 * 1024 * 1024;
LruCache<String, Bitmap> bitmapCache = new LruCache<String, Bitmap>(cacheSize) {
    @Override
    protected int sizeOf(String key, Bitmap value) {
        return value.getByteCount();
    }
};
```

In the preceding example, which Google uses in the official documentation, we create a 4 MB cache where the size of each item is the byte count of the bitmap. We will be accessing the cache using a String as a key, so we can easily use an image name or the image URL, and we will get back a Bitmap.

If we want to get notified whenever an element gets removed from the cache, we can override the entryRemoved method. Also, if we want to be notified whenever there is a cache miss or have the chance to recreate the object at that point, we could do so by overriding the create method as follows:

```java
int cacheSize = 4 * 1024 * 1024;
LruCache<String, Bitmap> bitmapCache = new LruCache<String, Bitmap>(cacheSize) {
    @Override
    protected int sizeOf(String key, Bitmap value) {
        return value.getByteCount();
    }

    @Override
    protected void entryRemoved(boolean evicted, String key, Bitmap oldValue, Bitmap newValue) {
        if(evicted) {
            Log.d(TAG, "Key: " + key + " has been removed to make space");
        } else {
            Log.d(TAG, "Key: " + key + " has been replaced");
        }
    }

    @Override
    protected Bitmap create(String key) {
        Log.d(TAG, "cache miss for key: " + key);
        return null;
    }
};
```

To calculate the right amount of memory we need for the cache size, we should consider what kind of application we are building. For example, how many of these images are we going to show on-screen at the same time? Or what other parts of our application are using memory and how much memory are those parts using? Having considered these questions, we also have to check how much memory we have available for our application. We can do so by calling the getMemoryClass() method of our ActivityManager. In the following, there is a new implementation using this memory limit and checking on kilobytes instead of bytes, and this is the reason we are dividing both the byte count of a Bitmap and the maximum memory by 1,024. The size calculation, approximately 15% of the available memory per application, is taken directly from Picasso library, which will be introduced later in this chapter. Full details of Picasso's implementation can be found at https://githu b.com/square/picasso/blob/master/picasso/src/main/java/com/squareup/picasso/ Utils.java.

```java
static int calculateMemoryCacheSize(Context context) {
    ActivityManager am = getService(context, ACTIVITY_SERVICE);
    boolean largeHeap = (context.getApplicationInfo().flags &
            android.content.pm.ApplicationInfo.FLAG_LARGE_HEAP) != 0;

    int memoryClass = am.getMemoryClass();
    if (largeHeap &&
            android.os.Build.VERSION.SDK_INT >= android.os.Build.VERSION_CODES.HONEYCOMB) {
        memoryClass = ActivityManagerHoneycomb.getLargeMemoryClass(am);
    }

    // Target ~15% of the available heap.
    return (int) (1024L * 1024L * memoryClass / 7);
}


LruCache<String, Bitmap> bitmapCache =
        new LruCache<String, Bitmap>(calculateMemoryCacheSize(getApplicationContext())) {

    @Override
    protected int sizeOf(String key, Bitmap value) {
        return value.getByteCount() / 1024;
    }

};
```

To add and retrieve Bitmaps from this cache is relatively straightforward:

```
public void addBitmapToCache(String key, Bitmap bitmap) {
    bitmapCache.put(key, bitmap);
}

public Bitmap getBitmapFromCache(String key) {
    return bitmapCache.get(key);
}
```

In the event there is a Bitmap with the same key as another, the first bitmap will be replaced. Using the image URL as the hash key is usually a good practice as each image will have a different URL. Also, getBitmapFromCache might return null if the entry does not exist or it has been removed from the cache.

Whenever we want to load an image, we have to check the cache first; if the image is there, we can just work with it, otherwise we would have to load it remotely. Memory cache is really fast as it resides in memory, but loading images from the Internet or disk or any other potentially slow source needs to be done on a background thread:

```
public void loadBitmap(String url, ImageView imageView) {
    final Bitmap bitmap = getBitmapFromCache(url);
    if (bitmap != null) {
        imageView.setImageBitmap(bitmap);
    } else {
        loadRemoteBitmap(url, imageView);
    }
}
```

As shown in the following example, in the Android documentation, Google uses an `AsyncTask` class to load and decode a Bitmap, and, once decoded, it adds the Bitmap to the memory cache:

```
class BitmapWorkerTask extends AsyncTask<Integer, Void, Bitmap> {
    ...
    // Decode image in background.
    @Override
    protected Bitmap doInBackground(Integer... params) {
        final Bitmap bitmap = decodeSampledBitmapFromResource(
                getResources(), params[0], 100, 100));
        addBitmapToMemoryCache(String.valueOf(params[0]), bitmap);
        return bitmap;
    }
    ...
}
```

For more information on caching bitmaps, visit
`http://developer.android.com/training/displaying-bitmaps/cache-bitmap.html`.

Disk caches

We have seen how to load and cache images to a memory cache. A memory cache is very fast but not always reliable, as images might have been removed to make space for new images or, for example, the application might have been interrupted and killed while in the background and thus the memory cache is destroyed and all our hard work has been lost. If we are looking for a more reliable cache, although slower, we should go for a disk cache. A disk cache when used together with a memory cache will speed up things considerably. Images that no longer are in memory might still be persisting in the disk cache and avoid doing a network operation.

We can use an already existing implementation; there is one available in the Android source code, and also the version used in the Android documentation: `https://android.googles ource.com/platform/libcore/+/jb-mr2-release/luni/src/main/java/libcore/io/Di skLruCache.java`.

But, for example, we can also use the disk cache classes in Volley; visit `https://android.g ooglesource.com/platform/frameworks/volley/+/master/src/main/java/com/androi d/volley/toolbox/DiskBasedCache.java`.

Or, we can use the disk cache classes in OkHttp; visit `https://github.com/square/okhttp /blob/master/okhttp/src/main/java/okhttp3/internal/DiskLruCache.java`.

Later in this chapter, we will see how to take advantage of the disk cache embedded in these libraries when using them directly, but first we will focus on how we can use a plain disk cache to complement our memory cache.

Let's try to write our own `ImageCache` class using the `DiskBasedCache` class from Volley. Our own implementation will use both the memory cache and disk cache whenever there is a cache miss in the memory cache. Refer to the following android documentation to see more or less the same example, although more detailed, using the implementation found in the Android source code: `http://developer.android.com/training/displaying-bitmap s/cache-bitmap.html#disk-cache`.

First of all, the class constructor that initializes the memory cache and creates a disk cache is as follows:

```java
public ImageCache(Context context) {
    int maxMemory = (int) (Runtime.getRuntime().maxMemory() / 1024);
    int cacheSize = maxMemory / 8;

    bitmapCache = new LruCache<String, Bitmap>(cacheSize) {
        @Override
        protected int sizeOf(String key, Bitmap value) { return value.getByteCount() / 1024; }
    };

    File cacheDir = new File(context.getCacheDir(), DEFAULT_CACHE_DIR);
    diskCache = new DiskBasedCache(cacheDir);

    diskCacheInitialized = false;
    new InitializeDiskCache().execute();
}
```

Disk cache is initialized in a background thread as disk operations might take time and we do not want to block the UI thread. As it might take some time and we might receive, potentially, any requests before the disk cache is initialized, we need to implement a lock mechanism. All disk cache operations are synchronized using the diskCacheLock instance variable. Any request received to get an image from the disk cache before it has finished initializing will be blocked, thanks to the synchronization blocks and the wait and notifyAll methods; whenever that happens, all requests will be eventually executed:

```
class InitializeDiskCache extends AsyncTask<Void, Void, Void> {
    @Override
    protected Void doInBackground(Void... params) {
        synchronized (diskCacheLock) {
            diskCache.initialize();
            diskCacheInitialized = true;
            diskCacheLock.notifyAll();
        }
        return null;
    }
}
```

Let's also create an interface to get notified whenever there is a cache hit or a cache miss. We can use the cache miss to trigger a download of the image, for example:

```
public interface CacheNotifier {
    void cacheMiss(String key);
    void cacheHit(String key);
}
```

We have to use a background thread to store images on the disk cache, as it might take too much time. As usual, all input/output operations must not be done on the main thread, otherwise we will block it and cause our UI to become sluggish or stop responding:

```
class BitmapStorer extends AsyncTask<Void, Void, Void> {
    private String key;
    private Bitmap bitmap;

    BitmapStorer(String key, Bitmap bitmap) {
        this.key = key;
        this.bitmap = bitmap;
    }

    @Override
    protected Void doInBackground(Void... params) {
        synchronized (diskCacheLock) {
            diskCache.put(key, new BitmapCacheEntry(bitmap));
        }
        return null;
    }
}
```

In the preceding example, we are using a small helper class, `BitmapCacheEntry`, that we have created, as the `DiskBasedCache` implementation from Volley takes a `Cache.Entry` class. The `Cache.Entry` class only defines a bytearray to hold the data to cache. Our implementation is just a helper to use Bitmaps instead of bytearrays directly.

Implementation is very easy: we take a Bitmap in the constructor and we compress it using the WebP format to byte array. `BitmapCompressFormat` also has PNG and JPG support, but we will use WebP as, according to Google, it produces smaller files than PNG and JPG.

 For more information on WebP, refer to `https://en.wikipedia.org/wik i/WebP`.

```
class BitmapCacheEntry extends Cache.Entry {
    public BitmapCacheEntry(Bitmap bitmap) {
        ByteArrayOutputStream baos = new ByteArrayOutputStream();
        bitmap.compress(Bitmap.CompressFormat.WEBP, 100, baos);
        data = baos.toByteArray();
    }

    public Bitmap getBitmap() {
        return BitmapFactory.decodeByteArray(data, 0, data.length);
    }
}
```

To convert back from the byte array to a Bitmap, we just use the `decodeByteArray` method from the `BitmapFactory` class.

With this helper class, we can now implement the `getBitmapFromDisk` method, which will return a Bitmap if it is stored in the disk cache or `null` otherwise.

This method will check if the disk cache has been already initialized, otherwise it will block the current thread until then. The disk cache indexes the files and could take some time to initialize; doing a request for a file while it has not finished might lead to inaccurate responses:

```java
@Nullable
private Bitmap getBitmapFromDisk(String key) {
    synchronized (diskCacheLock) {
        while (!diskCacheInitialized) {
            try {
                diskCacheLock.wait();
            } catch (InterruptedException e) {}
        }

        BitmapCacheEntry cacheEntry = (BitmapCacheEntry) diskCache.get(key);
        if(cacheEntry != null) {
            return cacheEntry.getBitmap();
        }
        return null;
    }
}
```

If the file does not exist in the cache, this method will return `null`.

Now we can implement a Bitmap loader that tries to load a Bitmap from disk, calling the method we have just defined in a background thread, and notifies of a cache hit or cache miss.

`BitmapLoader` is also a very simple `AsyncTask` class that takes care of that. There should be some checks to see if the `ImageView` is still valid. Another good practice will be to hold a `WeakReference` of the `ImageView` and the `CacheNotifier`, and then add the proper checks in the `onPostExecute` method, but for clarity we have assumed that nothing wrong happens in our example:

```
class BitmapLoader extends AsyncTask<Void, Void, Bitmap> {
    private String key;
    private ImageView iv;
    private CacheNotifier notifier;

    BitmapLoader(String key, ImageView iv, CacheNotifier notifier) {
        this.key = key;
        this.iv = iv;
        this.notifier = notifier;
    }

    @Override
    protected Bitmap doInBackground(Void... params) { return getBitmapFromDisk(key); }

    @Override
    protected void onPostExecute(Bitmap bitmap) {
        if(bitmap != null) {
            notifier.cacheHit(key);
            iv.setImageBitmap(bitmap);
        } else {
            notifier.cacheMiss(key);
        }
    }
}
```

For more information on WeakReferences , refer to `http://developer.an droid.com/reference/java/lang/ref/WeakReference.html`.

Finally, we could implement the public interfaces to put and get an image from the cache. As we can see, it is using both the memory cache and the disk-based cache. When getting an image, if that image is already in the memory cache, it will notify us of a cache hit and return that image directly; otherwise it will launch the background task we created previously to load it if it exists on the disk cache:

```
public void putImage(String key, Bitmap bitmap) {
    bitmapCache.put(key, bitmap);
    new BitmapStorer(key, bitmap).execute();
}

public void getImage(String key, ImageView iv, CacheNotifier notifier) {
    final Bitmap bitmap = bitmapCache.get(key);
    if (bitmap != null) {
        notifier.cacheHit(key);
        iv.setImageBitmap(bitmap);
    } else {
        new BitmapLoader(key, iv, notifier).execute();
    }
}
```

Handling configuration changes

Memory caches can be destroyed very easily, for example, whenever the device screen is rotated. We should avoid this behavior since, when the device rotates, we would like to have the images rendered as soon as possible and skip the process of downloading them again.

Luckily, we can preserve a fragment if we set the `setRetainInstance` to `true`, and the same fragment will be reattached to the new activity. If we store the memory cache instance in the fragment, we still will have access to it after recreating the activity.

Look at the following example from the Android documentation:

```java
private LruCache<String, Bitmap> mMemoryCache;

@Override
protected void onCreate(Bundle savedInstanceState) {
    ...
    RetainFragment retainFragment =
            RetainFragment.findOrCreateRetainFragment(getFragmentManager());
    mMemoryCache = retainFragment.mRetainedCache;
    if (mMemoryCache == null) {
        mMemoryCache = new LruCache<String, Bitmap>(cacheSize) {
            ... // Initialize cache here as usual
        }
        retainFragment.mRetainedCache = mMemoryCache;
    }
    ...
}

class RetainFragment extends Fragment {
    private static final String TAG = "RetainFragment";
    public LruCache<String, Bitmap> mRetainedCache;

    public RetainFragment() {}

    public static RetainFragment findOrCreateRetainFragment(FragmentManager fm) {
        RetainFragment fragment = (RetainFragment) fm.findFragmentByTag(TAG);
        if (fragment == null) {
            fragment = new RetainFragment();
            fm.beginTransaction().add(fragment, TAG).commit();
        }
        return fragment;
    }

    @Override
    public void onCreate(Bundle savedInstanceState) {
        super.onCreate(savedInstanceState);
        setRetainInstance(true);
    }
}
```

The preceding example sets setRetainInstance to true in the RetainFragment and creates the cache only when mRetainedCache is null after the call to findOrCreateRetainFragment.

For more details, refer to `http://developer.android.com/training/dis playing-bitmaps/cache-bitmap.html#config-changes`.

An alternative would be to make the cache global to the whole application, simplifying this whole process.

Loading images

We have seen, so far, how to keep images in a local memory cache and in disk cache to avoid loading them from the network repeatedly in the quite common case when are used again. As mobile devices still have very limited resources, we will see how to deal with memory allocation and handling very large images.

Memory

As we have probably noticed, images take a big amount of space. For example, a 32 bit per pixel image 512 pixels wide and 512 pixels high will use around 1 megabyte of memory. So, having a lot of images can easily eat up all our memory. It is very important to take into consideration a few things when dealing with such amount of memory.

We don't really need to explain in detail how to manage bitmap memory on early releases of Android, as we will not probably have to support those versions, but just in case, it is good to know how it worked.

On Android 2.3.3 and lower versions, bitmap memory dedicated to store pixel data was stored in native memory and not in the Java heap, where the bitmap object and all the other Java objects resided. To ensure bitmap memory is cleaned as soon it was not needed anymore, we have to manually call the `recycle()` method. It is important to call it only when we are sure that the bitmap is no longer on the screen, otherwise Android will throw us a `Canvas: trying to use a recycled bitmap` error.

On the following page, there is a code snippet that shows how to maintain a reference count of the bitmap and recycle the bitmap at the right time whenever there is no cached or displayed reference and the bitmap has not been recycled before: `http://developer.andro id.com/training/displaying-bitmaps/manage-memory.html`.

Furthermore, the example included in the documentation uses a full class called
`RecyclingBitmapDrawable` that extends from `BitmapDrawable` and handles all the
reference count logic and calls recycle whenever it is needed. For the link to the source code
of `RecyclingBitmapDrawable`, refer to `http://developer.android.com/samples/Displ`
`ayingBitmaps/src/com.example.android.displayingbitmaps/util/RecyclingBitmapD`
`rawable.html`.

```
private int mCacheRefCount = 0;
private int mDisplayRefCount = 0;
...
// Notify the drawable that the displayed state has changed.
// Keep a count to determine when the drawable is no longer displayed.
public void setIsDisplayed(boolean isDisplayed) {
    synchronized (this) {
        if (isDisplayed) {
            mDisplayRefCount++;
            mHasBeenDisplayed = true;
        } else {
            mDisplayRefCount--;
        }
    }
    // Check to see if recycle() can be called.
    checkState();
}

// Notify the drawable that the cache state has changed.
// Keep a count to determine when the drawable is no longer being cached.
public void setIsCached(boolean isCached) {
    synchronized (this) {
        if (isCached) {
            mCacheRefCount++;
        } else {
            mCacheRefCount--;
        }
    }
    // Check to see if recycle() can be called.
    checkState();
}

private synchronized void checkState() {
    // If the drawable cache and display ref counts = 0, and this drawable
    // has been displayed, then recycle.
    if (mCacheRefCount <= 0 && mDisplayRefCount <= 0 && mHasBeenDisplayed
            && hasValidBitmap()) {
        getBitmap().recycle();
    }
}

private synchronized boolean hasValidBitmap() {
    Bitmap bitmap = getBitmap();
    return bitmap != null && !bitmap.isRecycled();
}
```

Starting from Android 3.0, the pixel data is stored in the Java heap together with the bitmap object. This does not mean we do not have to do anything related to memory. We could still improve the memory allocation process by only doing so when really needed.

Android 3.0 introduced a field `inBitmap` in `BitmapFactory.Options`. If this field is set with another bitmap, the bitmap decoder will try to reuse the memory of that already existing bitmap when loading the new one. This way, we remove the memory allocation and deallocation and we slightly improve performance. There are a few restrictions to this new field though, for example, before Android 4.4, it will only work for bitmaps with the same size.

For more information on the `inBitmap` field, refer to `http://developer.android.com/reference/android/graphics/BitmapFactory.Options.html#inBitmap`.

There was another field, called `inPurgeable`, that allowed Android 4.4 and below to allocate bitmap pixel data in such a way that it was easy to be purged to recycle memory. This field is deprecated since Android 5.0 and its not recommended, as it might have some performance implications due to decoding time and can lead to frames being skipped.

For more information on the `inPurgeable` field, including the reason why it has been deprecated, refer to `http://developer.android.com/reference/android/graphics/BitmapFactory.Options.html#inPurgeable`.

Looking at the Android documentation, there is a code snippet that shows how a bitmap that has been removed from an `LruCache` class can be reused by using the `inBitmap` field. Looking at the example, we notice that we have to set the field `inMutable` to `true` so that the bitmap decoder returns a mutable image required for the `inBitmap` to work:

```
private static void addInBitmapOptions(BitmapFactory.Options options,
        ImageCache cache) {
    // inBitmap only works with mutable bitmaps, so force the decoder to
    // return mutable bitmaps.
    options.inMutable = true;

    if (cache != null) {
        // Try to find a bitmap to use for inBitmap.
        Bitmap inBitmap = cache.getBitmapFromReusableSet(options);

        if (inBitmap != null) {
            // If a suitable bitmap has been found, set it as the value of
            // inBitmap.
            options.inBitmap = inBitmap;
        }
    }
}
```

For more information and examples for managing bitmap memory, visit `http://developer`
`.android.com/training/displaying-bitmaps/manage-memory.html`.

For a complete example of a disk cache, the use of fragment to retain the `ImageCache`
instance, and how to reuse memory by using the `inBitmap` property
of `BitmapFactory.Options`, check the example source code of the Android
documentation at `http://developer.android.com/samples/DisplayingBitmaps/src/co`
`m.example.android.displayingbitmaps/util/ImageCache.html`.

Handling large images

As with most of our applications, we will be loading images from the Internet or from user-generated content such as pictures from the gallery or those taken by the camera. An issue that we will face is how to handle big, or relatively big, images. When loading an Internet feed or getting images from a CMS, we do not know in advance the size of these images. There are basically two things we should take into consideration. First, the amount of data we will be transferring from the server to the mobile device. If the image is huge, it will take a considerable amount of time to download to our mobile device and might also consume a substantial amount of the data plan of the user.

Sometimes there is not much we can do if we do not have access to the server, but as recommended alternatives, we can try to rescale the image to an appropriate size and use a more optimized image format, for instance, WebP (`https://en.wikipedia.org/wiki/WebP`). Some image-loading libraries we will discuss later in this chapter have the ability to support progressive JPEG files. This will not resolve the amount of data downloaded from the network, but will improve the user experience of our application, as it partially disguises the loading by showing a reasonable preview. For more information on *Progressive JPEGs*, visit `http://frescolib.org/docs/progressive-jpegs.html`.

The second issue in handling large images is the amount of memory that we will consume on our mobile device. Imagine we have an image of 1,024 × 1,024 pixels that will be shown as a 64 × 64 pixels thumbnail. Do we really have to keep in memory the 4,194,304 bytes required to store it versus the 16,384 bytes that are required for the image that will be shown?

No, definitely it is not a good practice. Imagine many images like that in a scrolling list. Even using a RecyclerView and memory cache, we will be polluting the memory and taking all the space of the cache with very few images, making it almost useless. The scenario could be worse. Imagine the image is even bigger; we might get `java.lang.OutOfMemory` exceptions trying to load it. To prevent this from happening, we could use another field in `BitmapFactory.Options`, the `inJustDecodeBounds` property.

Setting `inJustDecodeBounds` to `true` will not decode the image data or allocate memory for it, but will set the image width and height. This will allow us to know beforehand the size of the image and load a scaled-down version that adjusts more efficiently to the size we really need. Let's see how we can do it.

First, let's see how we use the `inJustDecodeBounds` property:

```java
public static Bitmap decodeSampledBitmapFromStream(InputStream is, int width, int height) {
    // First decode with inJustDecodeBounds = true to check dimensions
    final BitmapFactory.Options options = new BitmapFactory.Options();
    options.inJustDecodeBounds = true;
    BitmapFactory.decodeStream(is, null, options);

    // Calculate inSampleSize
    options.inSampleSize = calculateInSampleSize(options, width, height);

    // Decode bitmap with inSampleSize set
    options.inJustDecodeBounds = false;
    return BitmapFactory.decodeStream(is, null , options);
}
```

Looking at the preceding source code snippet, we can see that the image loading is done in two steps: first with the `inJustDecodeBounds` property to true and later setting it to `false`. Between the two decode calls, we can calculate the value of the `inSampleSize` property of `BitmapFactory.Options`. `inSampleSize` is another property that allows us to load an image scaled down by values that are a power of 2. We can use the code from the Android documentation to calculate the right value for `inSampleSize`:

```
public static int calculateInSampleSize(
            BitmapFactory.Options options, int reqWidth, int reqHeight) {
    // Raw height and width of image
    final int height = options.outHeight;
    final int width = options.outWidth;
    int inSampleSize = 1;

    if (height > reqHeight || width > reqWidth) {

        final int halfHeight = height / 2;
        final int halfWidth = width / 2;

        // Calculate the largest inSampleSize value that is a power of 2 and keeps both
        // height and width larger than the requested height and width.
        while ((halfHeight / inSampleSize) > reqHeight
                && (halfWidth / inSampleSize) > reqWidth) {
            inSampleSize *= 2;
        }
    }

    return inSampleSize;
}
```

Looking at the preceding code, we can see that it will return the biggest `inSampleSize` that is a power of 2, with the resulting width and height bigger than the width and height requested, in order to maximize quality and not having to upscale the image afterwards. `inSampleSize` only works with power of 2 values, that is 1, 2, 4, 8, 16, and so on. If we set any other value, it will be rounded down to the nearest power of 2. Visit http://developer.android.com/reference/android/graphics/BitmapFactory.Options.html#inSampleSize for more information on `SampleSize` property.

Here we used an `InputStream` to decode a bitmap, but `BitmapFactory` supports decoding bitmaps from other sources. Check the Android documentation for the same example but, for decoding from a resource, visit http://developer.android.com/training/displaying-bitmaps/load-bitmap.html.

Different image types

As we have just seen, we might have to load images using different approaches. We will load them using an InputStream, a file, or from the application resources.

BitmapFactory comes with several mechanisms to load images to adjust to what we need; here are a few:

- BitmapFactory.decodeStream()
- BitmapFactory.decodeFile()
- BitmapFactory.decodeByteArray()
- BitmapFactory.decodeResource()

Let's see how we can also load images from the assets folder of the application using the method we created previously:

```java
public Bitmap decodeSampleBitmapFromAssets(String name, int width, int height) {
    InputStream is = null;
    try {
        is = getAssets().open(name);
        return decodeSampledBitmapFromStream(is, width, height);
    } catch(IOException e) {
        Log.w(TAG, "Error loading image " + name);
        return null;
    } finally {
        if (is != null) {
            try {
                is.close();
            } catch(Exception e) {
                //Nothing we can do about it
            }
        }
    }
}
```

Using the getAssets method we can open any asset by just using the file name, and once we have the InputStream from it, we can reuse our previous method.

Additionally, we can always use alternative methods to set images to ImageView. For instance, we can use imageView.setImageResource(r.drawable.<drawable_id>). Other methods are as follows:

- imageView.setImageBitmap(Bitmap bitmap)
- imageView.setImageResource (int resId)

- imageView.setImageDrawable (Drawable drawable)
- imageView.setImageURI(Uri uri)

We have to be very careful with the setImageURI method, as the image will be loaded and decoded on the UI thread.

> For more information on ImageView, refer to http://developer.androi d.com/reference/android/widget/ImageView.html.

Vector drawables

Starting with Android 5.0, there is support for vector drawables. We can easily add a new vector drawable to our application by using the Vector Asset Studio and use one of the standard material icons; or we can add our own SVG files, although not all features of SVG files are supported right now.

> See the documentation of the Vector Asset Studio for a comprehensive list at https://developer.android.com/studio/write/vector-asset-studio .html.

The main advantage of vector images is that they can be resized without any loss of image quality, and there is no need to have different sizes for all screen resolutions; so, in fact, this will help you reduce the size of the application. We have to be careful, though, as even if we do not see it on our project, if we target Android 4.4 or older versions, Android studio will generate PNG files in build time and store them in the generated folder. We can avoid this by using the support library and specifying the following command in our build.gradle:

```
android {
  defaultConfig {
    vectorDrawables.useSupportLibrary = true
  }
}

dependencies {
  compile 'com.android.support:appcompat-v7:23.2.0'
}
```

Otherwise, we can always explore, after triggering a build, the project view and see the `generated/pngs/<build configuration>`. As in this example, we can see the generated PNGs for different resolutions.

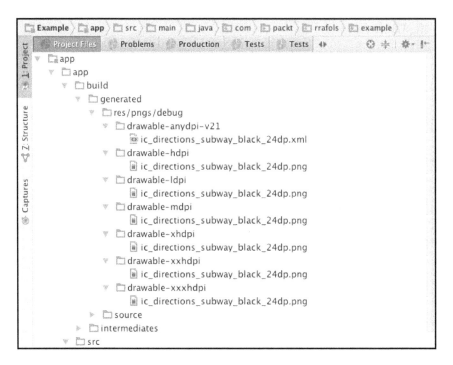

For more information on the support library v23.2, refer to `http://android-developers.blogspot.com.es/216/2/android-support-library-232.html`.

If we are not using the support library, we could do the following to reference a Vector Asset from code:

```
if (Build.VERSION.SDK_INT >= Build.VERSION_CODES.LOLLIPOP) {
    VectorDrawable vectorDrawable = (VectorDrawable) drawable;
} else {
    BitmapDrawable bitmapDrawable = (BitmapDrawable) drawable;
}
```

Not all the features are available; for instance, `autoMirrored` is only supported on Android 5.0 and higher.

Android Studio launches the Vector Asset Studio when we are try to add a new Vector Asset:

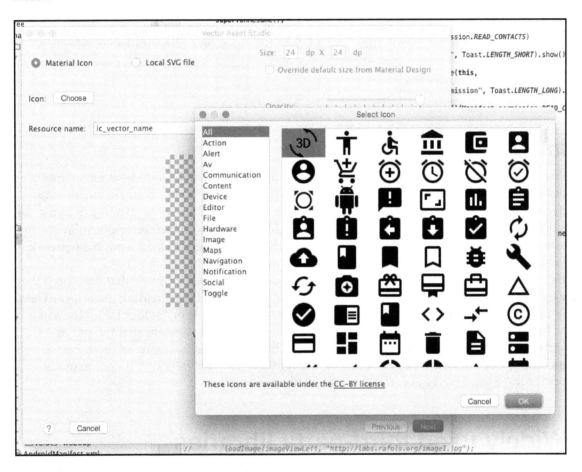

Depending on the application target, our recommendation is to either build one single APK, as it will be easier or because it is targeting Android 5.0 and higher, or build two separate APKs, one for Android 5.0 with vector drawables and another with raster images. This way we can reduce the application size for new devices. To see how to build multiple APKs, check the android development documentation at `https://developer.and roid.com/google/play/publishing/multiple-apks.html`.

 For more information and a DevBytes video on vector drawable, refer to `h ttps://youtube/w1FVIIstKmA` and `https://www.youtube.com/watch?v= 8e3I-PYJNHg`.

Images in a RecyclerView

We have to be aware that loading and decoding an image always has to be done in another thread rather than the main thread—not only loading from a file or network, but also the decoding and creating an image from an `InputStream`, a resource, or an array of bytes. As a direct consequence, we will have a lot of asynchronous calls, and if the application we are building contains a RecyclerView, where there are many images to load from the network for example, we will have to be careful to load and set the right image to the right `ImageView`. We have already seen in Chapter 4, *Lists and Adapters*, that we stored the view position in the ViewHolder as well as in the background task loading the image. Then, whenever the image is loaded, we check if the position of the ViewHolder is still the same as the position stored in the background task. If it is different, it means that the previous view has been recycled and is now used by another item. To solve many of these issues, including loading large images or setting them into a RecyclerView cell, there are many open source third-party libraries that can facilitate our job.

Widely used third-party libraries

We will see some of the most widely used libraries for handling images. These libraries have been developed and contributed by many developers and they will simplify our code, take care of all the underlying details, and reduce our application development time.

Glide

In order to use Glide, we have to add it to the dependencies section of our `build.gradle` file:

```
dependencies {
    compile 'com.github.bumptech.glide:glide:3.7.0'
    compile 'com.android.support:support-v4:23.2.1'
}
```

If our application is obfuscated, we need to add some lines to our proguard configuration, otherwise we will have some errors while the application is running:

```
-keep public class * implements com.bumptech.glide.module.GlideModule
-keep public enum
com.bumptech.glide.load.resource.bitmap.ImageHeaderParser$** {
    **[] $VALUES;
    public *;
}
```

We can simply use Glide to load images, either remote or local, to an `ImageView`. Glide will take care of the connection, the background thread, caching, and all the other details:

```
Glide.with(this).load("http://labs.rafols.org/image1.jpg").into(imageViewLeft);
Glide.with(this).load("http://labs.rafols.org/image2.jpg").into(imageViewRight);
```

We can add more complexity by just adding more calls. For example, if we want to use Glide to load images to an ImageView stored in a ViewHolder of a RecyclerView; center and crop the image; use a placeholder while loading and crossfade this placeholder to the downloaded image when the download and decoding are finished; we could use the following code:

```
@Override
public void onBindViewHolder(RecyclerViewHolder holder, int position) {
    ImageView imageView = holder.getImageView();
    Glide
            .with(context)
            .load("http://labs.rafols.org/image1.jpg")
            .centerCrop()
            .placeholder(R.drawable.placeholder)
            .crossFade()
            .into(imageView);
```

For more information on Glide, more complex examples as well as more transformations and animations, and how to change the underlying HTTP connection library, check the following official Github documentation and wiki at `https://github.com/bumptech/glide` and `https://github.com/bumptech/glide/wiki`.

UIL

As with Glide, we will also have to add a Gradle dependency to our `build.gradle` file to be able to use UIL. As an alternative, we can also download a JAR file and add it to our project, but using the Gradle or Maven dependency is recommended as it is very easy to update or change the version:

```
dependencies {
    compile 'com.nostra13.universalimageloader:universal-image-
loader:1.9.5'
}
```

This library seems to be unmaintained since November 2015, but anyway it is worth briefly covering it so that we can see how other libraries work and have a better general idea.

The Universal Image Library needs to be initialized; for example, in the following scenario, we initialize the library and we enable the memory and disk cache as, by default, they are disabled:

```
DisplayImageOptions options = new DisplayImageOptions.Builder()
        .cacheInMemory(true)
        .cacheOnDisk(true)
        .build();

ImageLoaderConfiguration config = new ImageLoaderConfiguration.Builder(getApplicationContext())
        .defaultDisplayImageOptions(options)
        .build();

ImageLoader.getInstance().init(config);
```

Also, to enable the disk cache, we need to request permission to write to external storage:

```
<uses-permission android:name="android.permission.WRITE_EXTERNAL_STORAGE"/>
```

To load images into an ImageView, we could simply do the following:

```
ImageLoader imageLoader = ImageLoader.getInstance();
imageLoader.displayImage("http://labs.rafols.org/image2.jpg", imageViewLeft);

imageLoader.loadImage("http://labs.rafols.org/image2.jpg", new SimpleImageLoadingListener() {
    @Override
    public void onLoadingComplete(String imageUri, View view, Bitmap loadedImage) {
        imageViewRight.setImageBitmap(loadedImage);
    }
});
```

The first method is the simplest. `ImageLoader.displayImage` just needs the URL and the ImageView. If we need some more control, we can create a `SimpleImageLoadingListener`, implement the `onLoadingComplete`, and use the `ImageLoader.loadImage` method with the listener we have just created.

Additionally, we could also implement `ImageLoadingListener` and have a lot more control, but if we do not require everything, it can be a bit cumbersome. Following is an example of calling `ImageLoader.displayImage` with an `ImageLoadingListener` and an `ImageLoadingProgressListener` with all the methods we can implement:

```
imageLoader.displayImage("http://labs.rafols.org/image3.jpg", imageViewRight, null,
        new ImageLoadingListener() {
    @Override
    public void onLoadingComplete(String imageUri, View view, Bitmap loadedImage) {
        Log.i(TAG, "Image loaded " + imageUri);
    }

    @Override
    public void onLoadingStarted(String imageUri, View view) {
        Log.i(TAG, "Image loading started " + imageUri);
    }

    @Override
    public void onLoadingFailed(String imageUri, View view, FailReason failReason) {
        Log.i(TAG, "Image loading failed " + imageUri);
    }

    @Override
    public void onLoadingCancelled(String imageUri, View view) {
        Log.i(TAG, "Image loading cancelled " + imageUri);
    }
}, new ImageLoadingProgressListener() {
    @Override
    public void onProgressUpdate(String imageUri, View view, int current, int total) {
        Log.i(TAG, "Progress " + imageUri + ", " + current + " / " + total);
    }
});
```

For more information, details, and complete examples, check the Github repository of the Universal Image Loader at `https://github.com/nostra` `13/Android-Universal-Image-Loader` and `https://github.com/nostra` `13/Android-Universal-Image-Loader/wiki/Useful-Info`.

Picasso

Picasso is an image downloading and caching library developed by square, although it is shared in Github and anyone can contribute as long as the Individual Contributor License Agreement is signed.

As with previous libraries, we will have to add the dependency into our `build.gradle` file:

```
dependencies {
    compile 'com.squareup.picasso:picasso:2.5.2'
}
```

As with previous libraries, to load an image into an ImageView is very simple. The following is an example of a very straightforward call, and another with many other parameters. For example, we could use an image as placeholder, another image when there is an error loading the image from the network, resize the image, or even apply a transformation:

```
Picasso.with(this).load("http://labs.rafols.org/image3.jpg").into(imageViewLeft);

Picasso.with(this)
        .load("http://labs.rafols.org/image1.jpg")
        .placeholder(R.drawable.placeholder)
        .error(R.drawable.error)
        .transform(new Transformation() {
            @Override
            public Bitmap transform(Bitmap source) {
                int size = Math.min(source.getWidth(), source.getHeight());
                int x = (source.getWidth() - size) / 2;
                int y = (source.getHeight() - size) / 2;
                Bitmap result = Bitmap.createBitmap(source, x, y, size, size);
                if (result != source) {
                    source.recycle();
                }
                return result;
            }

            @Override
            public String key() {
                return "crop_square_transformation";
            }
        })
        .resize(100, 100)
        .centerCrop()
        .into(imageViewRight);
```

The transformation is the same used in the Picasso library website, and it just crops the image into a square form based on the smallest dimension, either width or height.

While developing our application, we can see more details of how the image cache is working by enabling the cache indicators. Before doing any image request, we have to call the `setIndicatorsEnabled` method with the parameter `true` if we want to show color indicators on top of each image:

```
Picasso.with(context).setIndicatorsEnabled(true);
```

This will be very helpful, as we will not have to parse lines and lines of logs, and we will see on the device screen itself, which is the source of each image. For example, if the top-left corner is red, then it means the image has been downloaded from the network, if it is blue, it has been loaded from the disk cache, and if it is green, it has been loaded from the memory cache.

The following is how it looks in our small demo application:

Other very interesting features of Picasso are its handling of recycling in ImageViews and the automatic detection of adapter reuse and the cancellation of previous downloads. To get more information on all these and more complex examples, check the Picasso website at `http://square.github.io/picasso/`.

Fresco

The last library we would like to cover is Fresco. It has been developed by Facebook, although it is also shared in Github like other libraries.

Fresco needs to be initialized, but this can be done quite easily by just calling the initialize method during our activity's `onCreate` method:

```
Fresco.initialize(getApplicationContext());
```

Fresco uses a custom view called **Drawee** to render images; it adds many new features, for example, scaling the image to a specific focus point, showing rounded corners, or a custom overlay when the user presses the image.

It also gives the support to load remote images by just setting the URL as follows:

```
Uri uri = Uri.parse("http://labs.rafols.org/image1.jpg");
((SimpleDraweeView) findViewById(R.id.iv1)).setImageURI(uri);

uri = Uri.parse("http://labs.rafols.org/image2.jpg");
((SimpleDraweeView) findViewById(R.id.iv2)).setImageURI(uri);
```

But we need to change the normal ImageView for a `SimpleDraweeView`:

```xml
<LinearLayout
    android:orientation="horizontal"
    android:layout_width="match_parent"
    android:layout_height="wrap_content"
    android:padding="5dp"
    android:clipToPadding="false">

    <com.facebook.drawee.view.SimpleDraweeView
        android:id="@+id/iv1"
        fresco:placeholderImage="@drawable/placeholder"
        android:layout_width="0dp"
        android:layout_height="100dp"
        android:layout_weight="1"
        android:layout_margin="2dp"/>

    <com.facebook.drawee.view.SimpleDraweeView
        android:id="@+id/iv2"
        fresco:placeholderImage="@drawable/placeholder"
        android:layout_width="0dp"
        android:layout_height="100dp"
        android:layout_weight="1"
        android:layout_margin="2dp"/>
```

Fresco also has many additional features, but one of the main differentiators is memory optimization. On Android 4.x and earlier, Fresco put bitmap data in a separate memory area to avoid polluting the Java heap and triggering additional garbage collectors. Moreover, Fresco releases the memory from the image as soon as it is not shown on the screen, thus improving application performance. Furthermore, it adds support for WebP images, as well as animated GIF and progressive JPEG.

There is exhaustive documentation on the fresco website at `http://frescolib.org/`.

Summary

In this chapter, you saw how to cache images to avoid downloading them multiple times. This way we speed up our application, improve the user experience, and reduce the amount of data our application consumes. You also covered how to improve memory handling and how to solve some potential issues with large images. We finished the chapter by briefly covering multiple third-party libraries. These libraries are widely used by many applications, contributed by many developers, and are a way to reduce our development time and add many features without the complexity of having to develop them.

In the next chapter we will cover how to store information locally on the device. We have to make sure our application works properly whenever the device has no connection and avoid downloading information again and again. For performance reasons, responsiveness of our application and to save some data from the user's data plan.

7
Permanent Data

Even though Internet connection has improved quite noticeably in recent years and most mobile users have a data plan, there are always situations where we can't rely on mobile data. This is because either the user is in an area without network coverage or the user is not willing to pay for roaming costs, assuming that they are traveling to another country. In these situations, our application will benefit from having some data stored in the device itself to allow the user to work in, what we call, offline mode. With this, we will not only allow the user to do some work, but also greatly improve the user experience, as being able to store data on the device will reduce the time the application will take to display information.

In this chapter, we will explain different mechanisms to store data locally on the device: from how to store basic settings using **SharedPreferences** and writing internal and external files to how to use a SQLite database for a more complex way of storing data.

Storing preferences

One of the easiest ways to store information from our application is to store application preferences. Android provides us with a class named `SharedPreferences` to do this; however, it can be used to store anything that can be represented by a key-value. Refer to `ht tp://developer.android.com/reference/android/content/SharedPreferences.html` for more information.

Initialization

To use the `SharedPreferences` class, we have to get a reference to a preferences file. To do this, we can simply use the `getSharedPreferences(String name, int mode)` method in our context; refer to `http://developer.android.com/reference/android/content/Context.html#getShare dPreferences(java.lang.String,int)`. Alternatively, if we only need one single preference file, we can always use `getPreferences(int mode)` from our activity. `Context.getPreferences` will internally call `getSharedPreferences` and use the class name of the activity as the filename.

There are three different modes to get the preferences file:

- `MODE_PRIVATE` or : Here, only the application that created the file will be able to access it.
- `MODE_WORLD_READABLE`: Here, all other applications will be able to read the file. The use of this flag is discouraged, and it is deprecated since API level 17. To give access to other applications to the application data, a service, `ContentProvider,` or `BroadcastReceiver` should be used to expose the data in the most appropriate way. It is not guaranteed that it will remain in this state after a backup and restore operation.
- `MODE_WORLD_WRITABLE`: In this, all other applications will be able to read and write data. As with the previous flag, the use of this flag is discouraged and deprecated, and it is not guaranteed that it will remain in this state after a backup and restore operation.

More information about file-opening modes is available at `http://developer.android.com/reference/android/content/Context .html`.

Basic use

Let's write a simple application to see how can we write and read some values. We can start by creating a simple layout file with two checkboxes:

```
activity_main.xml ×

<?xml version="1.0" encoding="utf-8"?>
<RelativeLayout xmlns:android="http://schemas.android.com/apk/res/android"
    xmlns:tools="http://schemas.android.com/tools"
    android:layout_width="match_parent"
    android:layout_height="match_parent"
    android:paddingBottom="@dimen/activity_vertical_margin"
    android:paddingLeft="@dimen/activity_horizontal_margin"
    android:paddingRight="@dimen/activity_horizontal_margin"
    android:paddingTop="@dimen/activity_vertical_margin"
    tools:context="com.packt.rrafols.example.MainActivity">

    <CheckBox
        android:layout_width="wrap_content"
        android:layout_height="wrap_content"
        android:text="@string/checkbox1"
        android:id="@+id/checkBox1"
        android:layout_alignParentTop="true"
        android:layout_alignParentStart="true" />

    <CheckBox
        android:layout_width="wrap_content"
        android:layout_height="wrap_content"
        android:text="@string/checkbox2"
        android:id="@+id/checkBox2"
        android:layout_below="@+id/checkBox1"
        android:layout_alignParentStart="true" />

</RelativeLayout>
```

Not too fancy, but this will get the job done. Going back to our activity, we will save the status of the checkboxes in the `onDestroy` method. So every time the application is closed and opened again, it will preserve the status of the checkboxes.

In order to do so, we need to get a `SharedPreferences.Editor` object. Using the `Editor` object, we can save some primitive values:

- `boolean`
- `String`
- `int`
- `float`
- `long`
- Set of strings

For more information on the `SharedPreferences.Editor` class, refer
to http://developer.android.com/reference/android/content/SharedP
references.Editor.html.

We will only store the status of the two checkboxes by calling their `isChecked` method:

```java
@Override
protected void onDestroy() {

    SharedPreferences sharedPreferences = getPreferences(Context.MODE_PRIVATE);
    SharedPreferences.Editor prefEditor = sharedPreferences.edit();

    prefEditor.putBoolean(getString(R.string.checkbox1_property), checkbox1.isChecked());
    prefEditor.putBoolean(getString(R.string.checkbox2_property), checkbox2.isChecked());
    boolean saved = prefEditor.commit();
    if(!saved) Log.e(TAG, "Error saving to SharedPreferences");

    super.onDestroy();

}
}
```

To save the changes, we can either use `commit()` or `apply()`. The latter will apply the
changes to the memory and trigger an asynchronous task to write the new values to a disk.
If we read from a `SharedPreference` object immediately after calling `apply()`, we will
get the right values because `SharedPreference` objects are singletons and `apply()` stores
all the changes to the memory in a flash. If we call `commit()`, it will block the current
thread until it finishes writing the file.

Now that we are persisting the status of the checkboxes when the application finishes, we
need to read those values when the application starts and do something useful with them.
In our `onCreate` method, we check whether the properties exist in
the `SharedPreferences` file, and if they do, we toggle the status of the checkbox to either
check or uncheck.

The property key is stored in the `Strings` file, so we can access it from any part of the code without having to type it again.

```java
@Override
protected void onCreate(Bundle savedInstanceState) {
    super.onCreate(savedInstanceState);
    setContentView(R.layout.activity_main);

    SharedPreferences sharedPreferences = getPreferences(Context.MODE_PRIVATE);

    checkbox1 = (CheckBox) findViewById(R.id.checkBox1);
    String checkbox1Property = getString(R.string.checkbox1_property);
    if (sharedPreferences.contains(checkbox1Property)) {
        checkbox1.setChecked(sharedPreferences.getBoolean(checkbox1Property, false));
    }

    checkbox2 = (CheckBox) findViewById(R.id.checkBox2);
    String checkbox2Property = getString(R.string.checkbox2_property);
    if (sharedPreferences.contains(checkbox2Property)) {
        checkbox2.setChecked(sharedPreferences.getBoolean(checkbox2Property, false));
    }
}
```

We also specify a default value and if the key is not found, the `getBoolean` method will return `false` and leave the checkbox unchecked.

We could actually slightly reduce the code to the following:

```java
@Override
protected void onCreate(Bundle savedInstanceState) {
    super.onCreate(savedInstanceState);
    setContentView(R.layout.activity_main);

    SharedPreferences sharedPreferences = getPreferences(Context.MODE_PRIVATE);

    checkbox1 = (CheckBox) findViewById(R.id.checkBox1);
    String checkbox1Property = getString(R.string.checkbox1_property);
    checkbox1.setChecked(sharedPreferences.getBoolean(checkbox1Property, false));

    checkbox2 = (CheckBox) findViewById(R.id.checkBox2);
    String checkbox2Property = getString(R.string.checkbox2_property);
    checkbox2.setChecked(sharedPreferences.getBoolean(checkbox2Property, false));
}
```

As with the default behavior of `getBoolean` and the other getters, there is no need to check whether the key exists beforehand.

Additional features

In addition to the standard read/write operations, `SharedPreferences` allows us to directly remove the keys using the remove method and register an `onSharedPreferenceChangeListener` listener to get notified whenever a key/value is changed in our `SharedPreferences` file.

According to the documentation, `SharedPreferences` does not store a strong reference of the listener, so it is the responsibility of the code calling `registerOnSharedPreferenceChangeListener` to keep a strong reference of it. For example, as per the following code, we log in whenever a preference is changed:

```
private SharedPreferences.OnSharedPreferenceChangeListener preferenceChangeListener = new
    SharedPreferences.OnSharedPreferenceChangeListener() {
        @Override
        public void onSharedPreferenceChanged(SharedPreferences sharedPreferences, String key) {
            Log.i(TAG, key + " has been changed on SharedPreferences");
        }
    };
```

We need to change the `onCreate` method as well to register the listener, `sharedPreferences.registerOnSharedPreferenceChangeListener(preferenceChangeListener);`.

 More information on `SharedPreferences` is available at `http://developer.android.com/training/basics/data-storage/shared-preferences.html`.

Files

Shared preferences are the perfect solution if we want to store key-value sets of data, but if we want to store some complex data, it is not enough. In addition to shared preferences, Android allows us to read and write files in its file system. Depending on our needs, we can use internal or external storage. For information on file storage, check out `http://developer.android.com/training/basics/data-storage/files.html`.

Let's look at the differences between internal and external storage.

Internal storage

It is highly recommended that you save files in internal storage when these files need to be kept private from other applications. Moreover, Android guarantees that all the files saved in internal storage will be removed when the user uninstalls the application.

To create a file in internal storage, we need to get the base directory first. We can easily get it from the current context by calling the getFilesDir method. If we have to write a temporary file or, for example, an on-disk cache, we should call the getCacheDir method. We should not store anything critical in the cache directory as Android might delete it at any time and without any warning if the system is running low on space.

As an example, to facilitate comparison, let's store and retrieve the same information as with did before with SharedPreferences.

To simplify our data, we will just store two bytes: the first one will indicate the status of the first checkbox and the second will do the same for the second checkbox. If the value of a byte is 1, the respective Checkbox will be checked. If the value is 0, the checkbox is not checked:

```
private void saveState() {
    FileOutputStream fos = null;
    try {
        File settingsFile = new File(getFilesDir(), "settings.properties");
        fos = new FileOutputStream(settingsFile);
        fos.write(checkbox1.isChecked() ? 1 : 0);
        fos.write(checkbox2.isChecked() ? 1 : 0);
        fos.flush();
        fos.close();
    } catch(IOException e) {
        Log.w(TAG, "Exception writing settings file", e);
    } finally {
        if(fos != null) {
            try {
                fos.close();
            } catch(IOException e) {}
        }
    }
}
```

Once we create a file using `getFilesDir` and an appropriate filename, we need to open `FileOutputStream` so we can start writing data to it. To read data, we need to follow a similar approach once we have the file reference; we check whether the file exists and then open `FileInputStream` and read two bytes from it. If the file does not exist, it means it is the first time we have run the application or the internal file has been deleted.

```java
private void readState() {
    FileInputStream fis = null;
    try {
        File settingsFile = new File(getFilesDir(), "settings.properties");
        if(settingsFile.exists()) {
            fis = new FileInputStream(settingsFile);
            checkbox1.setChecked(fis.read() == 1);
            checkbox2.setChecked(fis.read() == 1);
        } else {
            Log.i(TAG, "Settings file does not exist yet. Setting default properties");
        }
    } catch(IOException e) {
        Log.w(TAG, "Exception reading settings file", e);
    } finally {
        if(fis != null) {
            try {
                fis.close();
            } catch(IOException e) {}
        }
    }
}
```

Alternatively, instead of having to get a file and the path with `getFilesDir`, we could use `openFileOutput` and `openFileInput`, which returns `FileOutputStream` or `FileInputStream` directly:

```java
private void saveState() {
    FileOutputStream fos = null;
    try {
        fos = openFileOutput("settings.properties", Context.MODE_PRIVATE);
        fos.write(checkbox1.isChecked() ? 1 : 0);
        fos.write(checkbox2.isChecked() ? 1 : 0);
        fos.flush();
        fos.close();
    } catch(IOException e) {
        Log.w(TAG, "Exception writing settings file", e);
    } finally {
        if(fos != null) {
            try {
                fos.close();
            } catch(IOException e) {}
        }
    }
}
```

One small thing we have to pay attention to is that we can't check whether the file exists, as we do not have the `File` reference; however, `openFileInput` will throw `FileNotFoundException` if the file we're trying to open does not exist.

```
private void readState() {
    FileInputStream fis = null;
    try {
        fis = openFileInput("settings.properties");
        checkbox1.setChecked(fis.read() == 1);
        checkbox2.setChecked(fis.read() == 1);
    } catch(FileNotFoundException fnfe) {
        Log.i(TAG, "Settings file does not exist yet. Setting default properties");
    } catch(IOException e) {
        Log.w(TAG, "Exception reading settings file", e);
    } finally {
        if(fis != null) {
            try {
                fis.close();
            } catch(IOException e) {}
        }
    }
}
```

External storage

From the point of view of writing and reading files, using external storage is the same thing as using internal, but there are some details we have to pay attention to.

External storage might become unavailable at any time. Most of the time, external storage refers to a removable storage medium; however, some devices might mount the external storage area as a partition of the total storage of the device. It goes without saying that, if the external storage is a removable medium, it might be removed or ejected at any time. Also, external storage can be mounted as USB storage and then be logically, not physically, ejected from the device.

To check whether the external storage is mounted and we can write or at least read from it, we can use the code example shown in the official documentation; refer to http://developer.android.com/guide/topics/data/data-storage.html#filesExternal:

```java
/* Checks if external storage is available for read and write */
public boolean isExternalStorageWritable() {
    String state = Environment.getExternalStorageState();
    if (Environment.MEDIA_MOUNTED.equals(state)) {
        return true;
    }
    return false;
}

/* Checks if external storage is available to at least read */
public boolean isExternalStorageReadable() {
    String state = Environment.getExternalStorageState();
    if (Environment.MEDIA_MOUNTED.equals(state) ||
        Environment.MEDIA_MOUNTED_READ_ONLY.equals(state)) {
        return true;
    }
    return false;
}
```

In addition to this, files stored in external storage can be read by anyone. For example, if we write the same `settings.properties` file as before in the external storage, we could retrieve it by doing the following:

```
adb pull
/storage/emulated/0/Android/data/com.packt.rrafols.example/files/settings.p
roperties
```

If we try to do the same with the internal file, we will get the following error:

```
adb pull /data/user/0/com.packt.rrafols.example/files/settings.properties
adb: error: remote object
'/data/user/0/com.packt.rrafols.example/files/settings.properties' does not
exist
```

Another thing we have to check is permissions. If we are targeting devices, such as an Android version lower than KitKat (4.4 or API level 19), we would need to request permission to read and write the external storage. Write permission includes read access, but read permission does not include write access. We can add this permission when needed by adding the `maxSdk` keyword and limiting it to `API level 18`:

```
<manifest ...>
    <uses-permission android:name="android.permission.WRITE_EXTERNAL_STORAGE"
                     android:maxSdkVersion="18" />
    ...
</manifest>
```

Starting with Android 4.4, permissions are only required if the application wants to access or write files to the device's public folders. To get a public folder, we could use the `Environment.getExternalStoragePublicDirectory(String type)` method and specify the type of file we want to access or write. For example, to save a picture, we can get the path of the pictures folder:

```
File path =
Environment.getExternalStoragePublicDirectory(Environment.DIRECTORY_PICTURE
S);
```

As the folder may not have been created, it is always a good practice to call `path.mkdirs()`. If the directory already exists, it will not do anything.

 To get more information about the public folders available, check the `Environment` class documentation at http://developer.android.com/reference/android/os/Environment.html.

Additional methods

Android also provides us with some more methods to manage the file system:

- `delete`: This is to delete a file (http://developer.android.com/reference/android/content/Context.html#deleteFile(java.lang.String))
- `fileList`: This returns a list of private files (http://developer.android.com/reference/android/content/Context.html#fileList())

SQLite

We have seen how to store key-value data in the `SharedPreferences` class and more complex data in the form of files in either internal or external storage. But, if we want to store structured data, we should go for a database-like storage option. Android provides us with an implementation of SQLite we can use to store and query data.

 More information about SQLite is available at `https://www.sqlite.org/`. For more information on the SQLite applied to Android, refer to `http://developer.android.com/training/basics/data-storage/databases.html`.

Schema and contract definition

As a good practice, it is recommended that you define your database structure in a contract class. Doing it this way will make things very easy, for example, changing a column name and propagating all the changes to everywhere the database is used.

In addition to this, if we implement the `BaseColumns` interface, it will automatically add an `_ID` field, which we can use as the primary `autoincrement` key.

Returning to the example we used in Chapter 5, *Remote Data*, in order to get finance information using the Yahoo finance API with retrofit, we could store the data in a local database. Just after we receive the response on the retrofit callback, we will store it in the database.

```java
public static abstract class ModelContractElement implements BaseColumns {
    public static final String TABLE_NAME = "element";

    public static final String COLUMN_NAME_NAME = "name";
    public static final String COLUMN_NAME_PRICE = "price";
    public static final String COLUMN_NAME_SYMBOL = "symbol";
    public static final String COLUMN_NAME_TS = "ts";
    public static final String COLUMN_NAME_TYPE = "type";
    public static final String COLUMN_NAME_UTCTIME = "time";
    public static final String COLUMN_NAME_VOLUME = "volume";
}
```

In this contract class, we could also define other constants required by the database implementation. For example, we could define the filename to be used; the version of the database; and (to keep it together), the SQL queries we need to, for example, create or destroy tables.

In the full class illustrated in the following screenshot, we can see we defined the SQL query to create the table. We can also see that it refers to `ModelContractElement._ID`, the inherited field from `BaseColumn`, as the primary key.

```java
ModelContract.java ×
    package com.packt.rrafols.example.storage;

    import android.provider.BaseColumns;

    public final class ModelContract {
        public static final String DB_NAME = "model.db";
        public static final int DB_VERSION = 1;

        private ModelContract() {}

        public static abstract class ModelContractElement implements BaseColumns {
            public static final String TABLE_NAME = "element";

            public static final String COLUMN_NAME_NAME = "name";
            public static final String COLUMN_NAME_PRICE = "price";
            public static final String COLUMN_NAME_SYMBOL = "symbol";
            public static final String COLUMN_NAME_TS = "ts";
            public static final String COLUMN_NAME_TYPE = "type";
            public static final String COLUMN_NAME_UTCTIME = "time";
            public static final String COLUMN_NAME_VOLUME = "volume";
        }

        public static final String TEXT_TYPE = " TEXT";
        public static final String COMMA_SEP = ",";
        public static final String SQL_CREATE_ENTRIES =
                "CREATE TABLE " + ModelContractElement.TABLE_NAME + " (" +
                    ModelContractElement._ID + " INTEGER PRIMARY KEY," +
                    ModelContractElement.COLUMN_NAME_NAME + TEXT_TYPE + COMMA_SEP +
                    ModelContractElement.COLUMN_NAME_PRICE + TEXT_TYPE + COMMA_SEP +
                    ModelContractElement.COLUMN_NAME_SYMBOL + TEXT_TYPE + COMMA_SEP +
                    ModelContractElement.COLUMN_NAME_TS + TEXT_TYPE + COMMA_SEP +
                    ModelContractElement.COLUMN_NAME_TYPE + TEXT_TYPE + COMMA_SEP +
                    ModelContractElement.COLUMN_NAME_UTCTIME + TEXT_TYPE + COMMA_SEP +
                    ModelContractElement.COLUMN_NAME_VOLUME + TEXT_TYPE +
                    " )";
    }
```

Note that, in order to avoid anyone using this contract to make an instance of this class, the constructor has been declared private. In addition to this, the class is final, thereby preventing anybody from extending it as well.

 To read more about contract classes, take a look at the content provider documentation at http://developer.android.com/guide/topics/providers/content-provider-basics.html.

Helper implementation

Android provides us with a helper class called `SQLiteOpenHelper` to manage everything related to database creation and its upgrade and downgrade. We just have to extend it and, at least, implement the `onCreate(SQLiteDatabase)` and `onUpgrade(SQLiteDatabase, int, int)` methods with the logic of our database. There are other methods we can implement if we need them, but they are not mandatory, such as `onDowngrade(SQLiteDatabase, int, int)` and `onOpen(SQLiteDatabase)`. Visit http://developer.android.com/reference/android/database/sqlite/SQLiteOpenHelper.html for more information on Android documentation.

Let's just build a basic implementation using the SQL query we defined before in the contract to create the database:

```java
ModelStorageHelper.java ×

    package com.packt.rrafols.example.storage;

    import android.content.Context;
    import android.database.sqlite.SQLiteDatabase;
    import android.database.sqlite.SQLiteOpenHelper;


    public class ModelStorageHelper extends SQLiteOpenHelper {

        public ModelStorageHelper(Context context) {
            super(context, ModelContract.DB_NAME, null, ModelContract.DB_VERSION);
        }

        @Override
        public void onCreate(SQLiteDatabase db) { db.execSQL(ModelContract.SQL_CREATE_ENTRIES); }

        @Override
        public void onDowngrade(SQLiteDatabase db, int oldVersion, int newVersion) {}

        @Override
        public void onUpgrade(SQLiteDatabase db, int oldVersion, int newVersion) {}
    }
```

Once we have the basics, we could write the specific implementation to store Model objects, although we will only store the field values instead of the whole model. In order to do so, first we need to get writeable access to the database. **SQLiteOpenHelper** provides us with two simple methods to access the database: `getWritableDatabase` and `getReadableDatabase`. The latter will return the same database object as the first method unless there is an issue or something crops up that prevents the database from being written.

Using the access to the database, we could call an insert operation with the values of all the fields in the model; refer to the following example:

```
public void storeModel(Model model) {
    SQLiteDatabase db = getWritableDatabase();

    for(ResourceWrapper resourceWrapper : model.getList().getResources()) {
        Resource res = resourceWrapper.getResource();
        Fields fields = res.getFields();

        ContentValues values = new ContentValues();
        values.put(ModelContract.ModelContractElement.COLUMN_NAME_NAME, fields.getName());
        values.put(ModelContract.ModelContractElement.COLUMN_NAME_PRICE, fields.getPrice());
        values.put(ModelContract.ModelContractElement.COLUMN_NAME_SYMBOL, fields.getSymbol());
        values.put(ModelContract.ModelContractElement.COLUMN_NAME_TS, fields.getTs());
        values.put(ModelContract.ModelContractElement.COLUMN_NAME_TYPE, fields.getType());
        values.put(ModelContract.ModelContractElement.COLUMN_NAME_UTCTIME, fields.getUtctime());
        values.put(ModelContract.ModelContractElement.COLUMN_NAME_VOLUME, fields.getVolume());

        long newRowId = db.insert(ModelContract.ModelContractElement.TABLE_NAME, null, values);
        Log.d(TAG, "storing rowid: " + newRowId);
    }
}
```

Now that we have some data stored locally in a database, let's see how we can retrieve the data stored. First, we need to create a projection of the columns we will be using after executing our query. Just creating an array with the constants we defined in our contract will do:

```
String[] projection = {
        ModelContract.ModelContractElement._ID,
        ModelContract.ModelContractElement.COLUMN_NAME_NAME,
        ModelContract.ModelContractElement.COLUMN_NAME_PRICE,
        ModelContract.ModelContractElement.COLUMN_NAME_SYMBOL,
        ModelContract.ModelContractElement.COLUMN_NAME_TS,
        ModelContract.ModelContractElement.COLUMN_NAME_TYPE,
        ModelContract.ModelContractElement.COLUMN_NAME_UTCTIME,
        ModelContract.ModelContractElement.COLUMN_NAME_VOLUME
};
```

Then, when we execute the query with that projection, we will have a `Cursor` object with all of the data. We could also use `null` as the projection, but then we will get all of the data. Retrieving more data than we will use is not good practice:

```
String sortOrder = ModelContract.ModelContractElement._ID + " DESC";

SQLiteDatabase db = getReadableDatabase();
Cursor cursor = db.query(ModelContract.ModelContractElement.TABLE_NAME,
                         projection,
                         null,
                         null,
                         null,
                         null,
                         sortOrder);
```

So, in order to get the data from `Cursor`, we will have to iterate. Therefore, as long as the cursor is not positioned after the last elements, we will retrieve the object from the database and store it in a local list so that it can be easily manipulated by Java classes in the memory:

```
LinkedList<Fields> fieldList = new LinkedList<>();

cursor.moveToFirst();
while (!cursor.isAfterLast()) {
    Fields field = new Fields();
    field.setName(cursor.getString(
            cursor.getColumnIndex(ModelContract.ModelContractElement.COLUMN_NAME_NAME)));
    field.setPrice(cursor.getString(
            cursor.getColumnIndex(ModelContract.ModelContractElement.COLUMN_NAME_PRICE)));
    field.setSymbol(cursor.getString(
            cursor.getColumnIndex(ModelContract.ModelContractElement.COLUMN_NAME_SYMBOL)));
    field.setTs(cursor.getString(
            cursor.getColumnIndex(ModelContract.ModelContractElement.COLUMN_NAME_TS)));
    field.setType(cursor.getString(
            cursor.getColumnIndex(ModelContract.ModelContractElement.COLUMN_NAME_TYPE)));
    field.setUtctime(cursor.getString(
            cursor.getColumnIndex(ModelContract.ModelContractElement.COLUMN_NAME_UTCTIME)));
    field.setVolume(cursor.getString(
            cursor.getColumnIndex(ModelContract.ModelContractElement.COLUMN_NAME_VOLUME)));

    fieldList.add(field);
    cursor.moveToNext();
}
cursor.close();

String sortOrder = ModelContract.ModelContractElement._ID + " DESC";

SQLiteDatabase db = getReadableDatabase();
Cursor cursor = db.query(ModelContract.ModelContractElement.TABLE_NAME,
                         projection,
                         null,
                         null,
                         null,
                         null,
                         sortOrder);
```

Third-party libraries

We have seen how to store data in multiple ways but, as with previous chapters, there are many libraries out there that simplify this job. As usual, depending on what your project requires and common sense, we recommend that you either use a third-party library or build your own implementation. If you wish to use a third-party library, let's briefly talk about Realm, `http://www.realm.io`.

Realm

Realm is a mobile database that aims to replace SQLite. For more information, full examples, and documentation go to the official website.

For details about the latest Java and Android release, refer to `https://realm.io/docs/java/latest/`.

To start with Realm, we need to add the dependencies to our gradle file. In our top folder root, add the following:

```
buildscript {
  repositories {
    jcenter()
  }
  dependencies {
    classpath "io.realm:realm-gradle-plugin:1.1.0"
  }
}
```

If we already have jcenter as the repository, we just need to add the line with the classpath pointing to Realm. In the `app` folder, we need to add the following to apply the plugin:

```
apply plugin: 'realm-android'
```

Furthermore, if we want to reuse the code as much as possible from the previous case, we will implement a `ModelStorage` interface and change all the `ModelStorageHelper` references to `ModelStorage`:

```java
// ModelStorage.java

package com.packt.rrafols.example.storage;

import com.packt.rrafols.example.model.Fields;
import com.packt.rrafols.example.model.Model;

import java.util.List;

public interface ModelStorage {
    void storeModel(Model model);
    List<Fields> retrieveFieldList();
}
```

Both the SQLite implementation and the new Realm implementation of the persistence layer will implement this simple interface. The real implementation is quite simple and straightforward:

```java
// ModelStorageRealm.java

package com.packt.rrafols.example.storage;

import ...

public class ModelStorageRealm implements ModelStorage {
    private static final String TAG = ModelStorageRealm.class.getSimpleName();

    private RealmConfiguration realmConfig;
    private Realm realm;
    private Context context;

    public ModelStorageRealm(Context context) { this.context = context; }

    @Override
    public List<Fields> retrieveFieldList() {
        checkAndCreate();

        return realm.where(Fields.class).findAll();
    }

    @Override
    public void storeModel(Model model) {
        for(ResourceWrapper resourceWrapper : model.getList().getResources()) {
            Resource res = resourceWrapper.getResource();
            Fields fields = res.getFields();

            checkAndCreate();

            realm.beginTransaction();
            realm.copyToRealm(fields);
            realm.commitTransaction();
        }
    }

    private void checkAndCreate() {
        if(realm == null) {
            realmConfig = new RealmConfiguration.Builder(context).build();
            realm = Realm.getInstance(realmConfig);
        }
    }
}
```

To persist an object, we use the `copyToRealm` method; to return the elements in a list, we can use the `findAll` method on the where clause of the filter. In addition, to be able to persist instances of the `Fields` class, we have to modify the `Fields` class to extend from `RealmObject`:

```
Fields.java ×

    package com.packt.rrafols.example.model;

    import io.realm.RealmObject;

    public class Fields extends RealmObject {

        // ...

    }
```

Summary

In this chapter, we learned how to persist some data to the local storage of the device. We learned how to write and read from a key-value preferences file and a standard file and how to use SQLite or a third-party database library. Finally, we briefly saw how to integrate Realm and how to convert the example from a previous chapter to use Realm.

8

Testing Your Application

OK! You have built your mobile application and you are ready to publish it to the store, but how do you know the application will work the way it was designed and will not crash? In addition to this, how do you know you did not break any functionality when you added that last-minute change to one of the screens? Even if you manually tested the change, there might be something related to your change you may have missed or forgotten to test.

In this chapter, we will see how to write automatic tests for your application, covering topics that range from testing your application logic to application UI and navigation. This does not mean everything will be automatically tested and there will be no need for any further manual and exploratory tests, but adding automatic tests as early as possible when developing software will help us identify and discover issues in the very early stages of our development. As documented multiple times, the cost of fixing software development defects is much smaller if done in the early stages, by factors of 50 to 200, rather than in the later stages, for instance when our application is already published and distributed.

This was originally published in the *Understanding and Controlling Software Costs* paper back in 1988.

Barry W. Boehm and Philip N. Pappacio, *Understanding and Controlling Software Costs*, IEEE Transactions on Software Engineering, Vol. 14, issue: 10, p. 1466, Oct. 1988, http://ieeexplore.ieee.org/xpl/articleDetails.jsp?arnumber=6191.

This is also crucial when working in teams. Developing automatic tests is an easier way to verify, if tests have been done properly, that nothing critical is broken when merging code from multiple developers. This principle applies perfectly to situations where you have to build one functionality on top of another, which is already built. By running automatic tests, you can quickly check whether the old functionality and features still work as intended.

Testing logic

Usually, the most straightforward tests you can write for your applications are unit tests. As the name indicates, each unit test should test a single unit or individual piece of the software and should be relatively simple. These types of tests are useful, for example, to check whether the logic or the business logic of your application is working as intended. If done right, logic should be isolated or abstracted from other components and even from Android SDK classes and methods. It could be run directly on the IDE, Android Studio, or even from the command line.

To show how to create some simple unit tests in your application, we will write a small and simple calculator application and write some tests for it. Later, we will add some more functionality so we will see other kinds of test in action.

Simple calculator application

The aim of this calculator application is to provide an example of how to create and run tests, so the functionality aspect will be very limited and we will not focus on how to build the UI and interactions. It will only contain two EditText fields, where we can put the numbers, and a TextView field to show the result and two buttons, one to perform an addition operation and another to perform a multiplication operation.

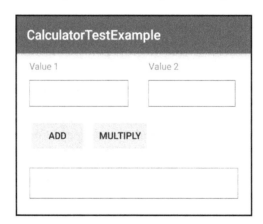

All of the calculation logic will be placed in a specific class, isolated from any other functionality of the application. Let's call this class `CalculatorLogic`. We will implement only two straightforward methods to add and multiply long numbers:

```
@    static long add(long x, long y) {
         return x + y;
     }

@    static long multiply(long x, long y) {
         return x * y;
     }
```

Also, we'll add two additional methods to support addition and multiplication from numbers provided as strings with the obvious checks:

```
final static String NOT_A_NUMBER = "NaN";

static String add(String xs, String ys) {
    if(xs == null || ys == null || xs.length() == 0 || ys.length() == 0)
        return NOT_A_NUMBER;

    try {
        long x = Long.parseLong(xs);
        long y = Long.parseLong(ys);

        long result = add(x, y);
        return String.valueOf(result);
    } catch(NumberFormatException e) {
        return NOT_A_NUMBER;
    }
}

static String multiply(String xs, String ys) {
    if(xs == null || ys == null || xs.length() == 0 || ys.length() == 0)
        return NOT_A_NUMBER;

    try {
        long x = Long.parseLong(xs);
        long y = Long.parseLong(ys);

        long result = multiply(x, y);
        return String.valueOf(result);
    } catch(NumberFormatException e) {
        return NOT_A_NUMBER;
    }
}
```

As you can see, we will return the constant NOT_A_NUMBER if any string does not contain a number or is empty or null.

Unit tests

After we create the project, we will be able to see two classes in green in the Android project structure: one is `ExampleInstrumentationTest` and the other is `ExampleUnitTest`. As we will see later, instrumentation tests are those tests that require the components of the Android framework or, for instance, an application context. On the other hand, plain unit tests only require the class logic and plain Java dependencies.

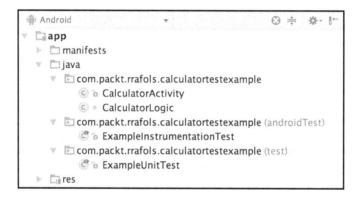

Let's focus on the `ExampleUnitTest` class file first; the code is shown in the following screenshot:

```
ExampleUnitTest.java ×
    import org.junit.Test;

    import static org.hamcrest.CoreMatchers.is;
    import static org.junit.Assert.*;

    public class ExampleUnitTest {

        @Test
        public void addition_isCorrect() throws Exception {
            assertEquals(4L, StaticCalculatorLogic.add(2L, 2L));
            assertEquals(2L, StaticCalculatorLogic.add(0L, 2L));
            assertEquals(0L, StaticCalculatorLogic.add(0L, 0));
        }

        @Test
        public void multiplication_isCorrect() throws Exception {
            assertEquals(8L, StaticCalculatorLogic.multiply(2L, 4L));
            assertEquals(0L, StaticCalculatorLogic.multiply(0L, 250L));
            assertEquals(125L, StaticCalculatorLogic.multiply(25L, 5L));
        }
    }
```

We have implemented two tests. Any method preceded by the `@Test` annotation will be executed as a unit test. These two tests are responsible for making sure that the `add` and `multiply` methods work as they are supposed to work. Here, we added some random but simple tests; however, if we leave aside that nothing critical core functionality, edge cases will be the next main things to test.

We have been using a static class, very easy to use in a test; however, if we need an instance of a class or have some initialization to do before every test, we could easily do so in any method as long as it has the `@Before` annotation. To prevent side-effects, JUnit executes every test, so each method is annotated with `@Test` in a new instance of the class. Before the execution, JUnit will always call the methods annotated with `@BeforeTest`; after the execution, it will call test methods annotated with `@AfterTest`. So it is easy to allocate and set up anything that is needed for every test and then shut it down in a clean way.

If we need to initialize something that has to be shared between all the tests, we can do so by creating a static method and adding the `@BeforeClass` annotation. For example, this will be the right approach if we want to initialize a huge data array or read and process a big file during our tests.

Changing our class from a static reference to creating an instance of the logic, and changing the methods in `CalculatorLogic` to be instance methods rather than static methods, will look like the following class:

```
CalculatorUnitTests.java ×

    public class CalculatorUnitTests {
        private CalculatorLogic logic;

        @BeforeClass
        public static void initClass() {
            // Nothing for the moment being
        }

        @Before
        public void initTest() {
            logic = new CalculatorLogic();
        }

        @Test
        public void addition_isCorrect() throws Exception {
            assertEquals(4L, logic.add(2L, 2L));
            assertEquals(2L, logic.add(0L, 2L));
            assertEquals(0L, logic.add(0L, 0));
        }

        @Test
        public void multiplication_isCorrect() throws Exception {
            assertEquals(8L, logic.multiply(2L, 4L));
            assertEquals(0L, logic.multiply(0L, 250L));
            assertEquals(125L, logic.multiply(25L, 5L));
        }
    }
```

We also added methods to `CalculatorLogic` to calculate these operations from strings; let's add some more tests for those methods:

```
@Test
public void stringAddition_isCorrectForPositiveNumbers() throws Exception {
    assertThat("30", is(logic.add("25", "5")));
    assertThat("5", is(logic.add("0", "5")));
}

@Test
public void stringAddition_isCorrectForNegativeNumbers() throws Exception {
    assertThat("20", is(logic.add("25", "-5")));
    assertThat("-5", is(logic.add("20", "-25")));
}

@Test
public void stringAddition_isCorrectForInvalidNumbers() throws Exception {
    assertThat(CalculatorLogic.NOT_A_NUMBER, is(logic.add(null, null)));
    assertThat(CalculatorLogic.NOT_A_NUMBER, is(logic.add("25", null)));
    assertThat(CalculatorLogic.NOT_A_NUMBER, is(logic.add("", "")));
    assertThat(CalculatorLogic.NOT_A_NUMBER, is(logic.add("Invalid Number", "dummy")));
}
```

We start seeing some tests, but how do we execute them? The easy way is to right-click on top of the class in the Android project structure and select **Run**:

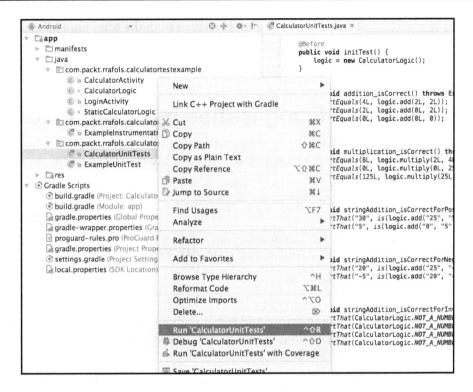

We will also check out a direct shortcut to run it. Once we press **Run**, Android Studio will execute the test without an emulator or real device. We will get the results in the bottom part of Android Studio, where we can check whether everything went fine, something similar to the following screen:

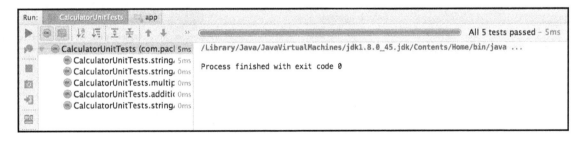

Android Studio will show us the number of tests that passed, the total time taken, and the details of every test executed (whether passed or not and the time taken by that specific test).

Discovering and fixing issues by creating tests

As mentioned earlier, in addition to the core functionality, we should test for edge cases and special values. Let's see what happens if we add a test to check the addition of 1 to `Long.MAX_VALUE`:

```
@Test
public void addition_isCorrectEdgeCases() throws Exception {
    assertEquals(0L, logic.add(Long.MAX_VALUE, 1L));
}
```

If we run the test, we can do it like before and run it with all the other tests. Alternatively, we can just execute the test by pressing the small red, or green if the test has passed before time, bullet placed on the left-hand side of the method.

The test does not work, as when we add 1 to `Long.MAX_VALUE`, it does not return 0. It actually returns `Long.MIN_VALUE`. We could add a test for this, but it does not seem to be the right solution. We'd need to modify the code in such cases to throw an arithmetical exception:

```java
public long add(long x, long y) throws ArithmeticException {
    long result = x + y;

    if(x > 0 && y > 0 && result < 0) throw
            new ArithmeticException("Numbers out of bounds: " + x + ", " + y);

    if(x < 0 && y < 0 && result > 0) throw
            new ArithmeticException("Numbers out of bounds: " + x + ", " + y);

    return result;
}
```

Then, we'd need to modify the test accordingly:

```java
@Test(expected = ArithmeticException.class)
public void addition_isCorrectEdgeCases() throws Exception {
    logic.add(Long.MAX_VALUE,  1L);
}
```

In this case, instead of writing an assert method call, we added an attribute to the `@Test` annotation specifying that we will receive an `ArithmeticException` error.

If we execute the test now, we can see the test will pass:

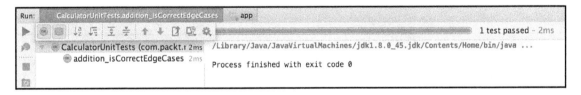

These tests can be easily run on the command line as well by running the following code:

```
./gradlew test
```

Results in XML format can be found at
`<application path>/app/build/test-reports` and in HTML format
at `<application path>/app/build/reports/test`.

 For general information on unit tests in Android, refer to `https://develo`
`per.android.com/training/testing/unit-testing/local-unit-tests`
`.html`. And more information on JUnit is available
at `http://junit.org/junit4/`.

Instrumentation tests

So far, the execution of tests has been quite easy as all of the code was independent of
Android SDK classes and their methods. But, what about those cases where we need a
context or something that Android runtime provides, such as **SharedPreferences** or
a Parcelable interface? This is called an instrumentation test, and it will be executed either
on our emulator or a real device.

In our previous example, we returned a constant string when the operation was invalid.
Let's change this constant and read it from our application resources, more specifically,
from the `Strings.xml` file.

```
public String NOT_A_NUMBER;

public CalculatorLogic(Context context) {
    NOT_A_NUMBER = context.getResources().getString(R.string.not_a_number);
}
```

Let's build an instrumentation test to check whether this is working as well. If we look at the Android project structure, we can see, next to the unit tests, there is a class with instrumentation tests. In the instrumentation test class, we have to specify the class that will act as the runner of the test, instead of the default runner: JUnit. As we want to run Android instrumentation tests, we will specify the `AndroidJUnit4` class:

```
@RunWith(AndroidJUnit4.class)
```

There is also a size classification of the test; for instance, in our case, we could use the `@SmallTest` annotation to specify that it will be a relatively small test that will not access resources such as files, networks, or databases. Generally, we can assume small tests almost as unit tests, medium tests as integration tests, and large tests as end-to-end tests. We could use the following table, which is taken from a code-testing blogging site from Google, as a reference point (refer to `http://googletesting.blogspot.com.es/21/12/test-sizes.html`):

Feature	Small	Medium	Large
Network access	No	localhost only	Yes
Database	No	Yes	Yes
File system access	No	Yes	Yes
Use external systems	No	Discouraged	Yes
Multiple threads	No	Yes	Yes
Sleep statements	No	Yes	Yes
System properties	No	Yes	Yes
Time limit (seconds)	60	300	900+

Leaving aside these details, we can use the previous annotations and mechanisms to implement the tests:

```
ExampleInstrumentationTest.java ×

    package com.packt.rrafols.calculatortestexample;

    import ...

    @SmallTest
    @RunWith(AndroidJUnit4.class)
    public class ExampleInstrumentationTest {

        private CalculatorLogic logic;
        private Context appContext;

        @Before
        public void initTest() {
            appContext = InstrumentationRegistry.getTargetContext();
            logic = new CalculatorLogic(appContext);
        }

        @Test
        public void useAppContext() throws Exception {
            String nan = appContext.getResources().getString(R.string.not_a_number);
            assertThat(nan, is(logic.add(null, null)));
        }
    }
```

We used the `InstrumentationRegistry` class to get the current `appContext` variable so that we could access the resources and get the not a number string.

For more methods and information about `InstrumentationRegistry`, refer to `https://d eveloper.android.com/reference/android/support/test/InstrumentationRegistry. html`.

If we run this test, it might take some time, as it has to build the APK and deploy it to either a real device or an emulator and run it from there.

More information about instrumented tests is available at `https://developer.android.com/training/testing/unit-testing/instrumented-unit-t ests.html`.

To see how to run instrumented tests on Google Cloud Test Lab, check out `https://develo per.android.com/training/testing/start/index.html#run-instrumented-tests`.

Testing integrations

Instrumentation tests also allow us to test the Android components we have in our application, such as services and content providers. For example, in order to test a service, not IntentService as it is not supported, we need to use `ServiceTestRule`. `ServiceTestRule` will start and shut down our service for the duration of the tests. Once `ServiceTestRule` is created, we can start or bind to our service, call methods directly, and test its correctness.

For more information, refer to the Android documentation site at `https://developer.andr oid.com/training/testing/integration-testing/index.html`.

Mocking Android dependencies

As we have seen, instrumented tests take much more time than unit tests. If we do not want to depend specifically on the Android SDK classes and methods, we could mock them. We could use Mockito as a mock framework, although we have to be aware that, by design, we will not be able to mock any static method with Mockito.

To use it, we have to just add a reference to our app's `build.gradle` file:

```
testCompile 'org.mockito:mockito-core:1.10.19'
```

And, as we did before, to run it with `AndroidJUnit4`, set the `@RunWith` annotation in our test to `@RunWith(MockitoJUnitRunner.class)`.

To mock any Android dependency, we have to add a `@Mock` annotation before the field declaration.

We need to define the behavior; for example, if we are mocking the application context, we can tell Mockito to return a specific constant string when the code requests for a string from the resources:

```
when(appContext.getString(R.string.not_a_number)).thenReturn(NaN);
```

Let's create a test with Mockito mocking the application context:

```java
MockedCalculatorUnitTests.java ×

package com.packt.rrafols.calculatortestexample;

import ...

@RunWith(MockitoJUnitRunner.class)
public class MockedCalculatorUnitTests {
    private static final String NaN = "NaN";

    private CalculatorLogic logic;

    @Mock
    private Context appContext;

    @Before
    public void initTest() {
        when(appContext.getString(R.string.not_a_number)).thenReturn(NaN);

        logic = new CalculatorLogic(appContext);
    }

    @Test
    public void useAppContext() throws Exception {
        String nan = appContext.getString(R.string.not_a_number);
        assertThat(nan, is(logic.add(null, null)));
    }
}
```

If we run this test, it should run as fast as standard unit tests and there is no need to deploy the APK file to the device or the emulator.

More information about mocking Android dependencies is available at
`https://developer.android.com/training/testing/unit-testing/local-unit-tests.html#mocking-dependencies`.

The source code along with more information about Mockito is available at `https://github.com/mockito/mockito`.

Testing the UI

Now that we have the mechanisms to test our application logic, and at the same time we're sure nothing was broken when we added new functionality or modified the already existing features, we could add some more tests to check whether the UI behaves as it should.

Writing UI tests with the Espresso framework is quite similar to writing plain instrumentation tests; the difference is in navigating and performing checks and actions on UI views and the elements on the screen. When a UI test is executed, the emulator or real Android device will show the changes and actions in real time as if somebody was triggering those actions.

Setup

To set up the Espresso framework, we will not require additional work if we have configured our project for instrumentation tests already. We have to be sure that our `build.gradle` file contains the Espresso dependencies:

```
androidTestCompile 'com.android.support.test.espresso:espresso-core:2.2.2'
androidTestCompile 'com.android.support.test:runner:0.5'
```

Be aware that Espresso is added to the `androidTestCompile` configuration and not the standard compile, as we do not want to include espresso in our final application when deployed to Google Play. For the same reason, JUnit and Mockito are added to the `testCompile` configuration, but not to either of the standard compile or `androidTestCompile` configurations.

For more information about build configurations in Gradle, check their documentation at `https://docs.gradle.org/current/userguide/artifact_dependencies_tutorial.html`.

In addition to this, to prevent errors from occurring once the process is automated—elements appearing after a long animation, for instance—we should disable animations on our device by toggling off the following options inside **Settings | Developer Options**:

- Window animation scale
- Transition animation scale
- Animator animation scale

Once we have performed these simple steps, we can start using Espresso.

Creating UI tests

To create a new UI test, we should create a new instrumentation test. Once this has been created, in a way that is quite similar to standard instrumentation tests, we set the JUnit runner to AndroidJUnit4; however, this time we use the @LargeTest annotation to determine the size of the test. As the documentation states, as a rule of thumb, all UI tests are large tests.

Let's create a test, which verifies that once we press the add button, the correct result appears on the right-hand side of the field. In order to do this, we need to introduce some values to both the EditText fields, simulate a button click, and then check TextView to see whether the result is shown.

To achieve this, we will have to launch the activity first; we can use the ActivityTestRule class, annotated by @Rule, to launch the activity we need before running the test. Even if the activity is not the main activity, it will be launched:

```java
CalculatorUITest.java ×

    package com.packt.rrafols.calculatortestexample;

  + import ...

    @RunWith(AndroidJUnit4.class)
    @LargeTest
▷ public class CalculatorUITest {

        private String value1 = "10";
        private String value2 = "20";
        private String result = "30";

        @Rule
        public ActivityTestRule<CalculatorActivity> calculatorActivityTestRule =
                new ActivityTestRule<CalculatorActivity>(CalculatorActivity.class);

        @Test
▷   public void checkResultShown_calculatorActivity() {
            onView(withId(R.id.value1)).perform(typeText(value1), closeSoftKeyboard());
            onView(withId(R.id.value2)).perform(typeText(value2), closeSoftKeyboard());
            onView(withId(R.id.add_button)).perform(click());
            onView(withId(R.id.result_viewer)).check(matches(withText(result)));
        }
    }
```

Once we have it, we can start performing our actions in all the screen elements by using the EspressoAPI. For instance, check the imports of our previous example:

```
import android.support.test.filters.LargeTest;
import android.support.test.rule.ActivityTestRule;
import android.support.test.runner.AndroidJUnit4;

import org.junit.Rule;
import org.junit.Test;
import org.junit.runner.RunWith;

import static android.support.test.espresso.Espresso.onView;
import static android.support.test.espresso.action.ViewActions.click;
import static android.support.test.espresso.action.ViewActions.closeSoftKeyboard;
import static android.support.test.espresso.action.ViewActions.typeText;
import static android.support.test.espresso.assertion.ViewAssertions.matches;
import static android.support.test.espresso.matcher.ViewMatchers.withId;
import static android.support.test.espresso.matcher.ViewMatchers.withText;
```

We can appreciate the use of the import static of Espresso classes. If we statically import a static field or method, we could use it as if it was declared on our class directly. This avoids a lot of boilerplate code and typing. More information about static imports is provided by Oracle; refer to `http://docs.oracle.com/javase/1.5.0/docs/guide/language/static-import.html`.

To trigger actions on views, we need to find them first. Using `onView` and `ViewMatcher` on it, we could pinpoint the exact view where we would like to perform an action. For instance, if we use the `withId` matcher, it will find a view that matches that exact ID. We have to be careful, as there might be more than one view with that ID, and if that is the case, Espresso will throw an `AmbiguousViewMatcherException` error. To avoid this, we can use more matchers, and even combine them, to finally have one single view matching our criteria. However, if we are too strict and not even a single view matches our criteria, Espresso will throw `NoMatchingViewException`, so we always have to be careful.

Espresso uses Hamcrest matchers and provides many alternatives. Check out the full documentation at `https://developer.android.com/reference/android/support/test/espresso/matcher/ViewMatchers.html`.

More information about Hamcrest matchers is available at `http://hamcrest.org/JavaHamcrest/`.

If you want to have a spinner or an adapter that shows lots of data, we can also filter by data instead of using view properties. For example, we could use the following:

```
onView(withId(R.id.spinner_simple)).perform(click());
onData(allOf(is(instanceOf(String.class)),
is("Americano"))).perform(click());
```

To perform a click on the spinner with ID `spinner_simple` and then, find all the views that are strings and the content is "Americano". Once the view is found, perform a click on it.

On the Espresso page, there are detailed examples; refer to `https://google.github.io/android-testing-support-library/docs/espresso/basics/`.

In addition, there is an Espresso online cheat sheet for all the View Matchers, Intent Matchers, View Actions, and so on: (`https://google.github.io/android-testing-support-library/docs/espresso/cheatsheet/index.html`).

Simplifying UI test creation

In Android Studio 2.2, Google introduced the Espresso test recorder. It is still not available on the current preview at the time of writing this book, but this feature will be able to record our clicks and actions on a running application and recreate them directly on Espresso code, while being able to introduce assertions.

Check out `https://www.youtube.com/watch?v=csaXml4xtN8`. This is the link to the Google I/O 2016 presentation on *What's new in Android development tools?* The part about the Espresso test recorder starts around 22:50. The following screenshot shows the cheat sheet for espresso 2.1, including view matchers, intent matchers and object matchers:

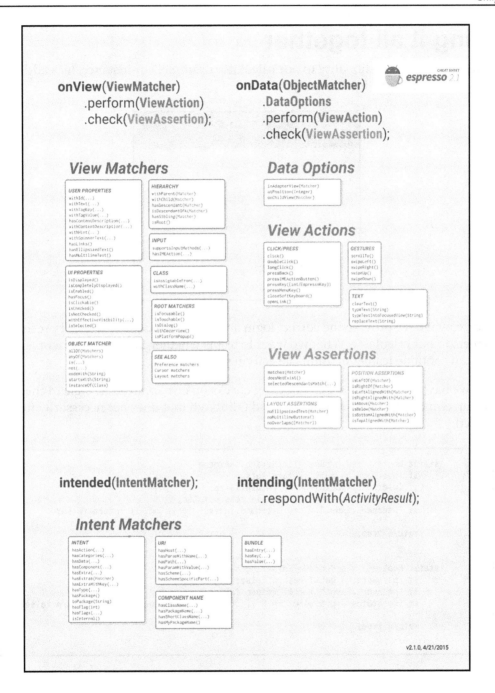

Putting it all together

Let's add some more functionality to our calculator example. For instance, let's add a login screen and test the whole functionality:

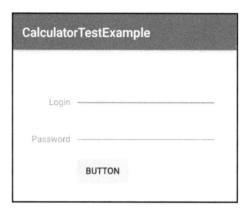

In this case, when we provide the correct login and password details, we will proceed to the next screen, to our calculator. What we want to test is whether the transition works and how we can continue testing on multiple activities.

Imagine we have implemented the following checks on our application logic to check whether an e-mail ID and password are valid (although that does not necessarily mean they are correct):

```
@      static boolean isUsernameValid(String username) {
            if (username == null) return false;
            if (username.length() < 6) return false;
            if (username.indexOf('@') == -1) return false;
            if (username.indexOf('.', username.indexOf('@')) == -1) return false;

            return true;
        }

@      static boolean isPasswordValid(String password) {
            if (password == null) return false;
            if (password.length() < 6) return false;
            if (countDigits(password) == 0 || countLetters(password) == 0) return false;

            return true;
        }
```

We can add many unit tests to these methods, but let's just add few of them and focus on UI tests:

```java
LoginUnitTests.java ×
package com.packt.rrafols.calculatortestexample;

import org.junit.Test;
import static junit.framework.Assert.assertEquals;

public class LoginUnitTests {
    @Test
    public void checkUsernameValidity_isCorrect() {
        assertEquals(true, LoginActivity.isUsernameValid("john@doe.net"));
        assertEquals(false, LoginActivity.isUsernameValid("john@doenet"));
        assertEquals(false, LoginActivity.isUsernameValid("johndoe.net"));
        assertEquals(false, LoginActivity.isUsernameValid("j@d.t"));
    }

    @Test
    public void checkPasswordValidity_isCorrect() {
        assertEquals(true, LoginActivity.isPasswordValid("letters110"));
        assertEquals(false, LoginActivity.isUsernameValid("onlytext"));
        assertEquals(false, LoginActivity.isUsernameValid("123456789"));
        assertEquals(false, LoginActivity.isUsernameValid("ab12"));
    }
}
```

With regard to UI tests, first of all let's add some simple tests that will validate that an error is shown if either the username or password is invalid.

```java
        findViewById(R.id.login_button).setOnClickListener((v) -> {
            String username = usernameEditText.getText().toString();
            String password = passwordEditText.getText().toString();

            if(!isUsernameValid(username)) {
                showError("Invalid username");
            } else if(!isPasswordValid(password)) {
                showError("Invalid password");
            } else if(!areCredentialsCorrect(username, password)) {
                showError("Incorrect username/password");
            } else {
                startActivity(new Intent(LoginActivity.this, CalculatorActivity.class));
                finish();
            }
        });
```

When we press the login button, we check for the validity and then for the correctness of the username and password; if something goes wrong, we show an error.

To show the error, we change the visibility of a `TextView` field (initially set to invisible) to visible, and we set the text of the error in such a way that it shows up.

```java
private void showError(int stringResource) {
    errorTextView.setText(getString(stringResource));
    errorTextView.setVisibility(View.VISIBLE);
}
```

We can easily test the functionality by using different checks/matches, `withEffectiveVisibility`, to see whether the `TextView` field is visible after we introduce wrong data.

```java
 LoginUITest.java  ×

    package com.packt.rrafols.calculatortestexample;

    import ...

    @RunWith(AndroidJUnit4.class)
    @LargeTest
    public class LoginUITest {

        private String username = "john@doe.net";
        private String password = "admin1234";
        private String incorrectPassword = "invalid1234";
        private String invalidUsername = "invalid1234";

        @Rule
        public ActivityTestRule<LoginActivity> calculatorActivityTestRule =
                new ActivityTestRule<LoginActivity>(LoginActivity.class);

        @Test
        public void checkLogin_incorrectCredentials() {
            onView(withId(R.id.login_username)).perform(typeText(username), closeSoftKeyboard());
            onView(withId(R.id.login_password)).perform(typeText(incorrectPassword), closeSoftKeyboard());
            onView(withId(R.id.login_button)).perform(click());

            onView(withId(R.id.login_error_text)).check(matches(
                    withEffectiveVisibility(ViewMatchers.Visibility.VISIBLE)));

            onView(withId(R.id.login_error_text)).check(matches(withText(
                    "Incorrect username/password")));

        }

        @Test
        public void checkLogin_invalidUsername() {
            onView(withId(R.id.login_username)).perform(typeText(invalidUsername), closeSoftKeyboard());
            onView(withId(R.id.login_password)).perform(typeText(password), closeSoftKeyboard());
            onView(withId(R.id.login_button)).perform(click());

            onView(withId(R.id.login_error_text)).check(matches(
                    withEffectiveVisibility(ViewMatchers.Visibility.VISIBLE)));

            onView(withId(R.id.login_error_text)).check(matches(withText(
                    "Invalid username")));

        }
```

Let's test what happens when we use the right credentials:

```
@Test
public void checkLogin_correctCredentials() {
    onView(withId(R.id.login_username)).perform(typeText(username), closeSoftKeyboard());
    onView(withId(R.id.login_password)).perform(typeText(password), closeSoftKeyboard());
    onView(withId(R.id.login_button)).perform(click());

    onView(withId(R.id.login_error_text)).check(matches(
            withEffectiveVisibility(ViewMatchers.Visibility.INVISIBLE)));

    onView(withId(R.id.add_button)).check(matches(isDisplayed()));
}
```

In this case, to check that we have changed to another activity, we could simply check whether one of the views of the second activity is displayed. Espresso will continue to run tests even if activities are changed, and ViewMatcher will match the views on the current activity.

Even if this allows us to build huge tests that can go from the login screen of our application to all the screens and functionality, it is recommended (and a good practice) to write many small tests rather than a few large tests. The smaller the test, the more concrete it is; if the test fails, it will provide more details to the developer so they can discover what is going on and fix it.

Summary

In this chapter, we learned how to add automatic tests to our application. We started with testing basic logic, which should be isolated from Android SDK classes and methods, using unit tests to instrumentation tests for those tests that had dependencies with Android. Eventually, we progressed to performing UI tests to check whether the UI layer behaves in the way it was designed to.

Automating tests is very important. Not only does it help the programmer develop the code while proactively thinking about quality, but it also solves a lot of issues when merging code from other colleagues and prevents regression issues when adding new features on top of an already existing functionality. Tests have to be smart and test the right thing; we could add almost infinite tests that would test useless functionalities, which would definitely be a waste of time and money as well. As a recommendation, test the critical functionality, edge cases, and, if you are working in a team, get an agreement as to what should constitute the minimum set of test cases. Later on, if you find an issue, extend the tests to check and correct it.

We have not mentioned test coverage in this chapter as it is often misunderstood as a quality metric. Test or code coverage is only useful to see which parts of the code are being tested. For more information, read Martin Fowler's page at `http://martinfowler.com/bli` `ki/TestCoverage.html`.

9
Publishing Your Application

After adding some tests to your application and polishing any last-minute defects, now you are ready to publish it to Google Play. Publishing an application is the way to make your work available to a larger public.

In this chapter, we will see what we need to do before publishing, how to create an account in Google Play, and finally, how to upload our application binary.

Preparation steps

There are a few minor details that we have to pay attention to before we publish the application.

Application signing

Android Studio has been signing all our debug builds with a debug dummy certificate. You will not be able to publish an application to Google Play signed with a debug certificate. You will need to generate a signed production build with your release certificate. Signing an application with your own certificate will help you identify yourself as the author of the application in Google Play.

In order to generate a signed build, go to the Build menu and select **Generate Signed APK**:

If you have not created a keystore before or you would like to use a new one, Android Studio will allow you to create a keystore or select a previously created one. Once an application is signed with a key and published to the store, it will have to be always signed with that key; otherwise, users with the previous version of the app will not be able to update it. So, once you create a keystore, store the keystore file safely.

The steps to create the keystore are very easy. You just have to enter your personal or business details, set the password of the keystore and the key, and introduce the path where the keystore will be saved.

If you already have a keystore and would like to use it, or if you have just created it, press the **Choose existing...** button and select the keystore file.

Once we have selected the keystore and key combination, Android Studio will ask us where to save the final APK and which build type and flavor to use. Android Studio will take some time to build, and when it finishes, we will have a small notification on the top-right border telling us whether the build was successful.

For more information about the signing process, keystore, and key generation, check the Android documentation about signing at `https://developer.android.com/studio/publi sh/app-signing.html?hl=cs`.

Account creation

To create an account on Google Play, go to the *Google Play Developer Console* (`https://play. google.com/apps/publish/`).

It only requires an e-mail address registered with Google or a Gmail e-mail address, our personal or business details, and $25 in order to activate the account.

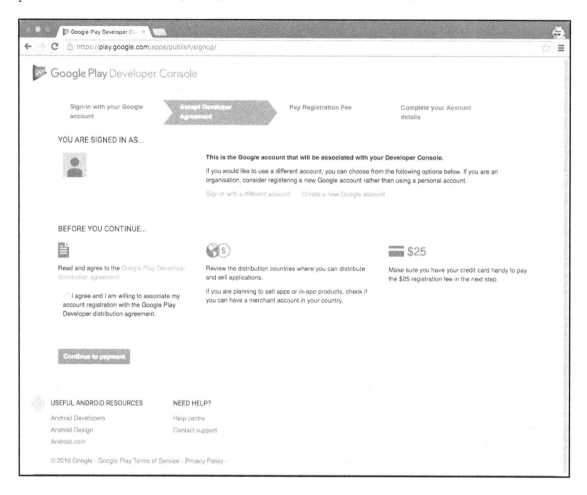

Publishing your application on Google Play

Once we have created an account and have paid the $25, we are able to add and publish Android applications. We are only required to do some previous steps before actually publishing an Android application: prepare the store listing with all the screenshots, marketing material, and texts and promotional images, and upload the application binaries.

Adding a new application

Our first step will be to add a new application to our account. We have to select the default language of the application, which will be the default language in which we will be editing our texts in Google Play and our application title.

If we have our APK ready, we can start by uploading it; otherwise, we can start by preparing the store listing.

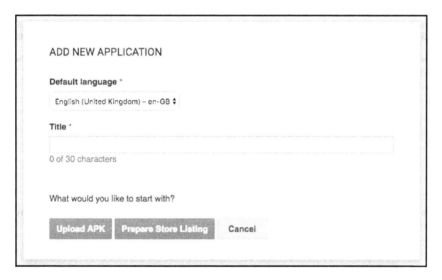

Preparing the Store Listing

As mentioned before, an application is not only a binary. When we upload it to the store, we have to add a lot of marketing material. With the huge number of applications in the market, unless the application's marketing material is exceptional, well-targeted, and well maintained, it might be very difficult to discover and reach all the potential customers or users.

Texts are also very important. Google Play provides us with different types of texts, from the title to the short description and full description. We can also have these texts in many languages. It is also recommended that you have texts in the native languages of the countries targeted in the application. It might depend on the type of application and content but you'll have to keep the target audience in mind; for instance, Spanish users do not only prefer Spanish texts to English, but many of them will not even understand English at all.

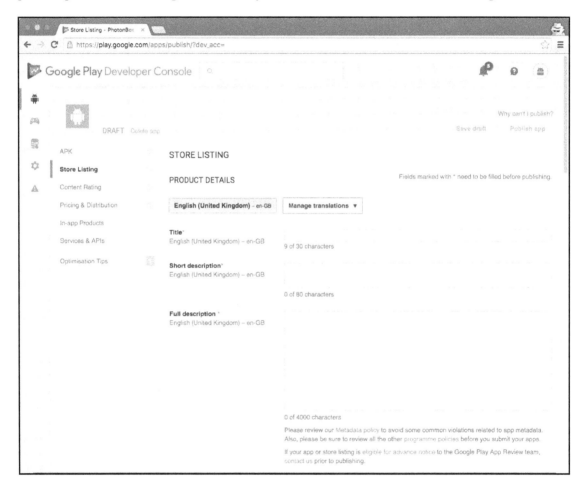

As the popular idiom says, a picture is worth a thousand words. The first thing the potential users of the application will see on the store is the application's graphical assets: either the app icon or the feature graphic, or even the screenshots of the application. If the first impression does not convince them, they will move along and will not even read the texts we have carefully created in our previous step.

If you need to capture some screenshots from your application, you can take them from an emulator or a real device by using Android Device Monitor, accessible from the **Tools** menu under the **Android** submenu. On the Android Device Monitor, there will be an active camera icon on the **Devices** tab that will take a screenshot of the connected device or the emulator. Another option is to take a screenshot from the device itself, for instance, by pressing the volume and power buttons down at the same time on some devices.

Please be aware that each graphic asset has a specific resolution and format and Google Play is very restrictive with that. For example, the high resolution icon is, at this moment, a 512 x 512 32 bpp PNG file, while the featured graphic is a 1024 x 500 JPEG or 24 bpp PNG.

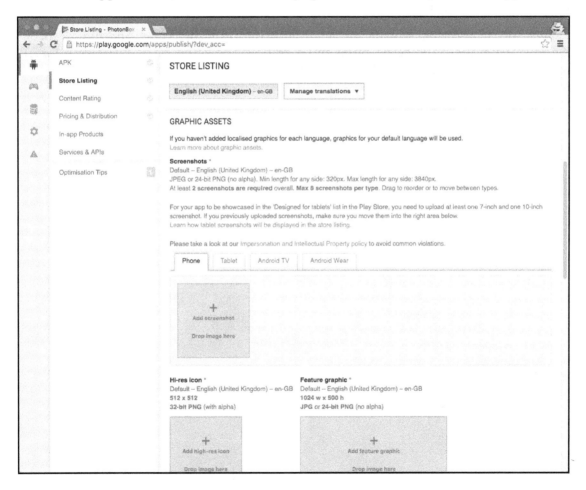

After adding our graphical assets, we still have to fill out our contact details, privacy policy, application category, and content rating. However, note that Google Play will not allow us to fill out the content rating until we have uploaded an APK.

We also have to fill out our pricing and distribution model. Here, we can choose whether our application is free or paid and, in the latter case, select what will be the price in every country that is available. In order to create a paid application, Google Play will ask us to create a merchant account first so that Google can process the application payments with the right TAX information. As part of the pricing and distribution section, we will also have to mention whether our application contains advertisements and we can access Google's advertising policy from there.

Finally, we can also select whether our application is for **Android Wear**, **Android TV**, or **Android Auto**. There are specific terms and conditions and additional requirements; for example, we need to upload an **Android Wear** screenshot if we want to distribute our application for Android Wear devices.

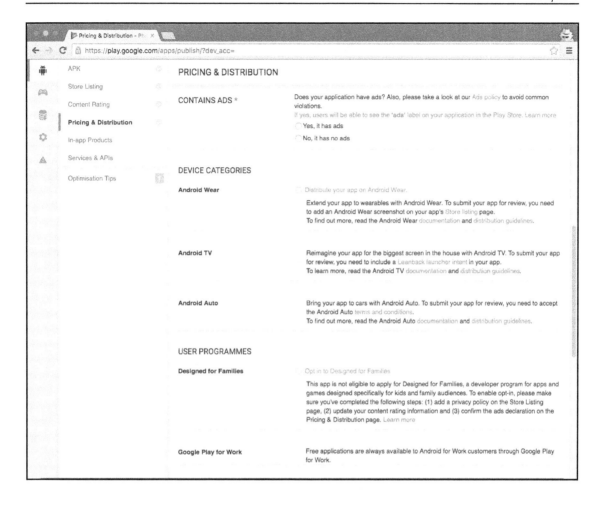

Uploading the application APK

We have seen how to add and modify the store listing information of our application; now we can upload our first application APK to the store. Our application needs to be versioned; there are two properties in the application manifest related to the application version:

- `android:versionCode`: This is the numeric property that represents the application version. It is a plain number up to 2,147,483,647 that allows us to easily check whether there has been an update programmatically. Google Play will not allow you to publish another APK with the same `versionCode` property as the previous one.
- `android:versionName`: This is a string literal that is basically shown to the user.

Users will not understand or pay attention to the application version 32,848 for instance, but 4.0.0 will be more user-friendly for them.

For more information on versioning, refer to `https://developer.androi d.com/studio/publish/versioning.html`.

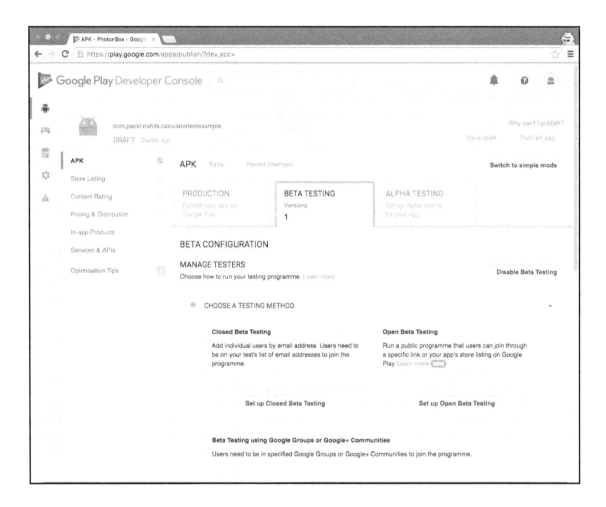

Google Play will not allow us to upload an APK to production. We could set beta testing or alpha testing with a set of users before switching the application to production. How to run the alpha or beta testing is up to us. We can do a public beta, only to a closed Google+ group or an e-mail list. It all depends on what we want to achieve with our beta program. It is very useful to distribute a new version of the application to a few selected or a small percentage of the users, so that if something goes wrong, it will only affect a few and not everyone. There is always time to make a beta release with the fix and when everything is working fine, make the switch to production.

 For more information about alpha/beta testing, refer to `https://support.google.com/googleplay/android-developer/answer/3131213`.

If our application is rather huge and we would like our users to have a smaller download and updates, Google Play allows us to upload and keep multiple active APKs as long as they have a different `versionCode` number, they are signed with the same certificate, and do not overlap the specific devices supported. To filter the list of devices for each individual APK, we have to use Google Play's splitting configurations:

- OpenGL texture compression format
- Screen size
- Device feature sets
- API level
- CPU architecture (ABI)

Although it is recommended that we have one single APK, as it simplifies the build and distribution process significantly, sometimes we can have smaller APKs, for example, if we have a lot of images supporting multiple screen densities or relatively big native, JNI, libraries. There are many people in the world with access to slow connections or metered data connections that will be glad to have a smaller download. Also, people running with low-end devices have very limited space on their device. If the user wants to install a new application and does not have enough space on the device, Android will show a list of all the currently installed applications sorted by decreasing size.

Our application should avoid being on top of that list; otherwise, it might be very quickly uninstalled.

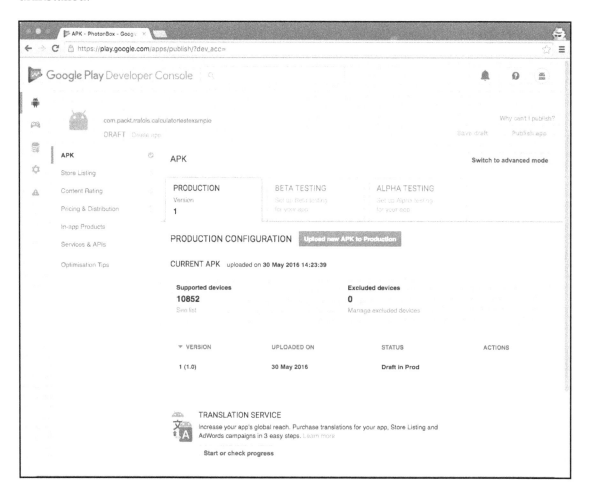

For more information on multiple APKs, go to the Android documentation at `https://developer.android.com/google/play/publi shing/multiple-apks.html`.

In addition to this, in the previous URL, there is a recommendation from Google about application versioning when developers have multiple APKs. It can be a bit complicated to comply with all the rules defined. Google's suggestion is to use a seven-digit number, where the first two digits will indicate the API level, the following two numbers will indicate the minimum and maximum screen size, and the last three will be the last three digits of the application version. For example, 0412310 will be for API level 04, where the minimum screen size supported is 1 (small), maximum screen size supported is 2 (medium), and the application version is 3.1.0.

Summary

In this chapter, we learned how to generate, version, and sign a Google Play build and how to create a Google Play Developer Console account and fill all the data that enables our application to be distributed on Google Play. It is now time to upload our beloved creation and start monetizing it! A mobile application is not something we can treat as fire-and-forget. We need to analyze how it is performing, get maximal feedback from the users, learn from all of the data, and iterate on our design and development again to fine-tune and optimize it.

For more information on the Google Play Developer Console, refer to `http s://developer.android.com/distribute/googleplay/developer-cons ole.html`.

10
Monetization – Make Money with Your App

Now that we have launched our application on the market and it is beginning to get downloaded by people, it is time to start earning some money from it. Whether it is our main business or a spare-time hobby, it took us a considerable amount of time to design, develop, and test the application. So, it would be good to monetize it somehow.

In this chapter, we will see different monetization strategies. Simply putting a price on our application is the most straightforward approach and might actually work out quite well, but we will also see how to enable in-app purchase elements in our application and how to add advertisements. It will depend on the type of application we are working with to decide the use of one mechanism or another, or even a combination of them; for example, we can have a free application with advertisements and an in-app purchase to disable advertisements. Or, for instance, we can have two versions of the same application: one could be free with advertisements and the other could be the exact same application but paid, with advertisements.

At the end of the day, market status and past experience combined with good analytics are the best way we can learn what works and what does not.

Paid apps

Paid apps are the most straightforward approach. At the moment of uploading the application to Google Play, we set the download price. As mentioned just now, some applications have a freemium version that includes advertisements or, for example, have limited functionality. And then, we have a paid version that can be considered the full, professional version or the one without advertisements.

Creating a paid app

When we created an application in Google Play, under the pricing and distribution section, we can choose whether we would like to publish it as free or paid. A paid application can always be converted to free, but a free application, once it has been published as free, cannot be changed to paid:

The only option would be to change the package name and upload it as a brand new application. For more information, refer to `https://support.google.com/googleplay/android-developer/answer/6334373?rd=1#paid_free`.

We have to set the price of our application. There is a default price that will be applied to all countries where the application is distributed and do not have a specific price (the price will be converted into local currency in such cases). This default price is without tax; Google Play will automatically add the right tax amount for each country (as shown in the following screenshot). We can manage the countries where our application is distributed and actually set the price for that country. In some countries, we can even choose to distribute only to users from one or many specific carriers if we want to do so. One advantage of using the automatic currency converter with local prices is that Google Play will automatically update the price based on the current day exchange rate and country-specific pricing pattern.

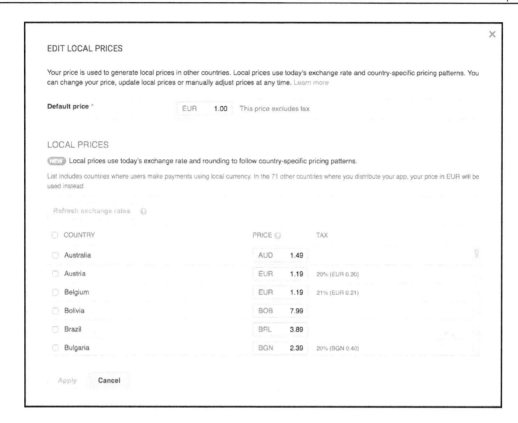

EDIT LOCAL PRICES

Your price is used to generate local prices in other countries. Local prices use today's exchange rate and country-specific pricing patterns. You can change your price, update local prices or manually adjust prices at any time. Learn more

Default price *   EUR   1.00   This price excludes tax

LOCAL PRICES

NEW Local prices use today's exchange rate and rounding to follow country-specific pricing patterns.

List includes countries where users make payments using local currency. In the 71 other countries where you distribute your app, your price in EUR will be used instead.

Refresh exchange rates

COUNTRY	PRICE		TAX
Australia	AUD	1.49	
Austria	EUR	1.19	20% (EUR 0.20)
Belgium	EUR	1.19	21% (EUR 0.21)
Bolivia	BOB	7.99	
Brazil	BRL	3.89	
Bulgaria	BGN	2.39	20% (BGN 0.40)

Apply   Cancel

For more information, refer to .

Finance tracking

Google Play allows us to see the overall status of our application sales from the **Finances** tab. There is also information about **Average Revenue Per Paying User** (**ARPPU**) and the average value per transaction. This information makes more sense and carries a lot more value when you have in-app purchases with different prices. For more detailed information about transactions, visit the Google Payments Merchant Console at `https://payments.goo gle.com/merchant`.

In-app purchases

Another mechanism to monetize our application is to add in-app purchases. In-app purchases are, usually, microtransactions that can be used to enable specific functionality in our application. It is also very common to use in-app purchases to let the user purchase consumables or local in-game currency if, for instance, we develop a game.

Initial setup

One of the first things we have to do if we want to add support for in-app purchases in our application is to install **Google Play Billing Library** from the Android SDK Manager:

| | SDK Platforms | SDK Tools | SDK Update Sites |

Below are the available SDK developer tools. Once installed, Android Studio will automatically check for updates. Check "show package details" to display available versions of an SDK Tool.

Name	Version	Status
Android SDK Build Tools		Update Available: 24.0.0 rc4
Android Auto API Simulators	1	Not installed
Android Auto Desktop Head Unit emulator	1.1	Not installed
Android SDK Platform-Tools 24-rc3	24.0.0 rc3	Installed
Android SDK Tools 25.1.7	25.1.7	Installed
Android Support Library	23.2.1	Installed
Android Support Repository	32.0.0	Installed
CMake	3.4.1	Not installed
Documentation for Android SDK	1	Installed
GPU Debugging tools	1.0.3	Not installed
Google Play APK Expansion library	1	Not installed
Google Play Billing Library	5	Installed
Google Play Licensing Library	1	Not installed
Google Play services	30	Not installed
Google Repository	28	Installed
Google Web Driver	2	Not installed
Intel x86 Emulator Accelerator (HAXM installer), rev 6.0.1	6.0.1	Installed
LLDB 2.0	2.0.2558144	Not installed
LLDB 2.1	2.1.2852477	Not installed
LLDB 2.2	2.2.2904772	Not installed
NDK	12.0.2867246 rc2	Not installed
com.android.support.constraint:constraint-layout-solver:1.0.0-alpha2	1	Not installed
com.android.support.constraint:constraint-layout:1.0.0-alpha2	1	Not installed

Google Play Billing Library provides us with an **Android Interface Definition Language** (**AIDL**) file; refer to `https://developer.android.com/guide/components/aidl.html`. Once we install this, we need to copy the In-app Billing Version 3 service interface definition called `IInAppBillingService.aidl` to our project. The build system will automatically generate a Java class we can directly use from our code. By using this class, we will not have to manage any network connections to Google Play and it will simplify our work.

The `IInAppBillingService.aidl` file will be located in `<sdk>/extras/google/play_billing/` and we will have to copy it into our project in `app/src/main/aidl/` with the `com.android.vending.billing` package:

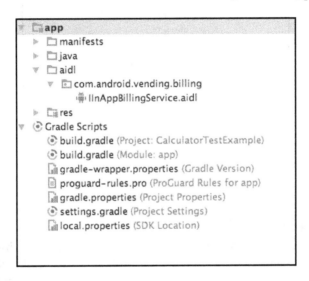

Once we build our project, we will see it generates a Java file inside the `app/build/generated/source/aidl` directory, as we can see in the project structure view.

Our next step will be to declare the billing permission in our manifest. This permission is a bit different from the other permissions we are requesting in our app, as it is declared in the Google Play Store application in the `com.android.vending` package.

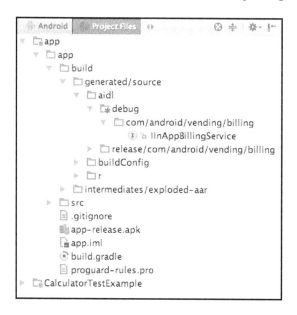

Adding in-app products

From Google Play Developer Console, we can create and manage our in-app products, but before Google Play allows us to do so, we need to upload an APK file with the billing permission declared. There is no need to publish it, so we do not have to worry about the application not being finished; alternatively, we can just upload it to the Beta or Alpha channel, even before we set up any beta testing program or add any users at all.

We can either add in-app products one by one or if we have multiple products, import a CSV file:

When adding a product, we can add it as a managed product or a subscription. Managed products can be bought only once until they are consumed from the application. Depending on the type of application or game, we might be interested in consuming the products or leaving them as a one-time purchase only. For example, if we have one application with an in-app purchase to remove all the advertisements, it would not be consumed; once the user has purchased it, it will stay that way. Also, we will not have to worry about storing the purchase in the app, as Google Play will save that information for us and we will be able to query it at any time. On the contrary, if we are creating a game and we create an in-app product to get some in-game coins, we will consume the product as soon as we add the in-game coins. This way, we enable the user to purchase it again. Subscriptions, on the other hand, set a recurring billing to the user. In addition to the price, we can configure the billing period, a free trial, and even a grace period if there is an issue with the payment. This might be a more suitable way of billing our users if we are creating an app that allows them to access all of our content, for example magazines, comics, movies, and so on, as long as they are subscribed.

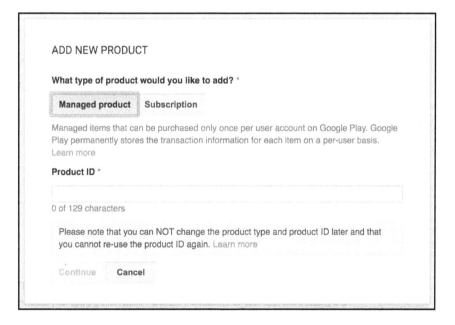

Something we have to pay attention to is the **Product ID** field. A **Product ID** field cannot be changed once it is defined and cannot be reused later on. It is also called SKU or Stock Keeping Unit.

Application code setup

Once we add in-app products to Google Play, we can begin to add the code to our application to allow the user to purchase them. We have to be aware that it takes some time for those in-app products to be available in the store. If we upload a new build to Google Play immediately and we test the in-app purchases straightaway, it might fail, as the in-app products are still not propagated. In addition to this, if we want to test the real thing, we can create, for example, a beta version and only invite ourselves to the distribution list. This way, we can install the app straight from Google Play and test the whole in-app purchases process.

By including `IInAppBillingService.aidl` in our application, Android Studio automatically generates an interface for us to connect to Google Play. If we carefully look at the generated documentation inside `IInAppBillingService.java`, we will see what we can use this service for:

```
/**
 * InAppBillingService is the service that provides in-app billing version 3 and beyond.
 * This service provides the following features:
 * 1. Provides a new API to get details of in-app items published for the app including
 *    price, type, title and description.
 * 2. The purchase flow is synchronous and purchase information is available immediately
 *    after it completes.
 * 3. Purchase information of in-app purchases is maintained within the Google Play system
 *    till the purchase is consumed.
 * 4. An API to consume a purchase of an inapp item. All purchases of one-time
 *    in-app items are consumable and thereafter can be purchased again.
 * 5. An API to get current purchases of the user immediately. This will not contain any
 *    consumed purchases.
 *
 * All calls will give a response code with the following possible values
 * RESULT_OK = 0 - success
 * RESULT_USER_CANCELED = 1 - user pressed back or canceled a dialog
 * RESULT_BILLING_UNAVAILABLE = 3 - this billing API version is not supported for the type requested
 * RESULT_ITEM_UNAVAILABLE = 4 - requested SKU is not available for purchase
 * RESULT_DEVELOPER_ERROR = 5 - invalid arguments provided to the API
 * RESULT_ERROR = 6 - Fatal error during the API action
 * RESULT_ITEM_ALREADY_OWNED = 7 - Failure to purchase since item is already owned
 * RESULT_ITEM_NOT_OWNED = 8 - Failure to consume since item is not owned
 */
```

As this file is automatically generated, it should not be edited, as the changes will be lost when the file is regenerated.

To use this service, we need to declare an instance variable,
`private IInAppBillingService billingService;`, to hold the instance and bind it to
the Google Play service:

```
@Override
protected void onCreate(Bundle savedInstanceState) {
    super.onCreate(savedInstanceState);
    setContentView(R.layout.activity_calculator);

    Intent serviceIntent = new Intent("com.android.vending.billing.InAppBillingService.BIND");
    serviceIntent.setPackage("com.android.vending");
    bindService(serviceIntent, billingServiceConn, Context.BIND_AUTO_CREATE);

    // ...
```

It is important to set the full package `com.android.vending` as, by doing so, we only
allow Google Play to handle billing requests.

Additionally, we will have to create a `ServiceConnection` class to monitor the connection
and disconnection aspects in the service. Inside `ServiceConnection`, we should get the
instance of our interface by calling `IInAppBillingService.Stub.asInterface()` and
also clear the instance by making it null whenever the service is disconnected:

```
private final ServiceConnection billingServiceConn = new ServiceConnection() {
    @Override
    public void onServiceConnected(ComponentName name, IBinder service) {
        Log.d(TAG, "Billing service connected");
        billingService = IInAppBillingService.Stub.asInterface(service);

    }

    @Override
    public void onServiceDisconnected(ComponentName name) {
        Log.d(TAG, "Billing service disconnected");
        billingService = null;
    }
};
```

More information about `ServiceConnection` is available at `https://developer.android.com/reference/android/content/Servic eConnection.html`.

We should not forget to unbind our service if the activity is destroyed:

```java
@Override
protected void onDestroy() {
    super.onDestroy();
    if(billingService != null) {
        unbindService(billingServiceConn);
    }
}
```

Binding to the service is not an immediate action and it is executed asynchronously. We should not assume it will be available just after calling the bind method, so it is our responsibility to verify that the billing service is not null and to track which state we are in inside our application.

Before making any billing request, we should check whether billing is supported. Users might be in a country where Google Play is not supported or in-app purchases, or even paid apps, are not accepted for legal reasons. To check whether billing is supported, we can use the automatically generated method called `isBillingSupported` on the `IInAppBillingService.java` interface:

```java
private boolean isBillingSupported() {
    int billingSupported = -1;
    try {

        billingSupported = billingService.isBillingSupported(BILLING_VERSION, getPackageName(),
                IAP_TYPE);

    } catch(RemoteException e) {
        Log.e(TAG, "Error checking billing support", e);
    }

    return billingSupported == BILLING_RESPONSE_RESULT_OK;
}
```

As parameters, we need to specify the billing API version, 3 in our case, and set it to the `BILLING_VERSION` constant. Also, we need to specify the package name and the type of purchase, which can be either `inapp` for in-app purchases or `subs` for subscriptions:

```
private static final int BILLING_VERSION = 3;
private static final String IAP_TYPE = "inapp";
private static final String SUB_TYPE = "subs";
```

Once you start the application, it is a good practice to check with Google Play which items are already purchased by the user. Doing so, we do not need to keep specific track of purchased items, and the user can use a different device and have the same items or advantages he purchased on another device. Like the previous case, we can use another automatically generated method called `getPurchases` to get the user's previous purchases.

The `getPurchases` method and other methods we will see below return data in a bundle and one of the key-values is the response code. There is a known bug that sometimes returns it as `Integer` and sometimes as `Long`. To work around this issue, we can use the following helper method:

```
private static int getResponseCodeFromBundle(Bundle b) {
    Object o = b.get(RESPONSE_CODE);
    if (o == null) {
        Log.d(TAG, "Bundle with null response code, assuming OK (known issue)");
        return BILLING_RESPONSE_RESULT_OK;
    }

    else if (o instanceof Integer) return (Integer) o;
    else if (o instanceof Long) return (int)((Long)o).longValue();
    else {
        Log.e(TAG, "Unexpected type for bundle response code:");
        Log.e(TAG, o.getClass().getName());
        throw new RuntimeException("Unexpected type for bundle response code: " +
                o.getClass().getName());
    }
}
```

 For more information on in-app purchase examples and workarounds such as this one, check the Google examples in GitHub, at `https://github.com/googlesamples/android-play-billing/blob/master/TrivialDrive/app/src/main/java/com/example/android/trivialdrivesample/util/IabHelper.java`.

Using this helper method, we can now call the `getPurchases` method and, in this example, print the already purchased items:

```
private String getPurchases(String continuationToken) {
    Bundle ownedItems = null;
    try {
        ownedItems = billingService.getPurchases(3, getPackageName(), "inapp", continuationToken);
    } catch (RemoteException e) {
        Log.e(TAG, "Error getting previous purchases", e);
        return null;
    }

    if (ownedItems == null) {
        Log.w(TAG, "Owned items is null getting previous purchases");
        return null;
    }

    int responseCode = getResponseCodeFromBundle(ownedItems);
    if (responseCode != BILLING_RESPONSE_RESULT_OK) {
        Log.e(TAG, "Error " + responseCode + " getting previous purchases");
        return null;
    }

    ArrayList<String> ownedSkus = ownedItems.getStringArrayList("INAPP_PURCHASE_ITEM_LIST");
    ArrayList<String> purchaseDataList = ownedItems.getStringArrayList("INAPP_PURCHASE_DATA_LIST");
    ArrayList<String> signatureList = ownedItems.getStringArrayList("INAPP_DATA_SIGNATURE_LIST");
    continuationToken = ownedItems.getString("INAPP_CONTINUATION_TOKEN");

    for (int i = 0; purchaseDataList != null && i < purchaseDataList.size(); ++i) {
        String purchaseData = purchaseDataList.get(i);
        String signature = signatureList.get(i);
        String sku = ownedSkus.get(i);

        Log.i(TAG, sku + " - " + purchaseData + " - " + signature);
    }

    return continuationToken;
}
```

In the response bundle, we will get lists of purchased SKUs, purchased data in JSON format, and the signature of those purchases on the following keys, respectively: INAPP_PURCHASE_ITEM_LIST, INAPP_PURCHASE_DATA_LIST, and INAPP_DATA_SIGNATURE_LIST.

> Further details on the information returned by `getPurchases` can be found in the Android documentation at https://developer.android.co m/google/play/billing/billing_reference.html#getPurchases.

SKUs will be the product ID of the products the user purchased, purchase data will be JSON-formatted as we see in the following code, and the signature list will contain the signatures of the purchases from this application.

If we parse the purchase data, we can get the purchase time and the payload we added at the time of performing the purchase:

```
{
    "orderId":"GPA.1234-5678-9012-34567",
    "packageName":"com.packt.rrafols.calculatortestexample",
    "productId":"prod_1",
    "purchaseTime":1465861252311,
    "purchaseState":0,
    "developerPayload":"payload",
    "purchaseToken":"token"
}
```

If there are more purchases, there will be a continuation token in `Bundle`, which will be accessible by the `INAPP_CONTINUATION_TOKEN` key. If we want to get more purchases, we should call the `getPurchases` method again with this continuation token. If the continuation token is null, it means there are no more purchases. We can implement a similar loop to the following one to iterate through all the user's purchases:

```
private void getPurchasedItems() {
    String continuationToken = null;

    do {
        continuationToken = getPurchases(continuationToken);
    } while(continuationToken != null);
}
```

One last step before the actual purchase is to get the updated data from the product IDs or SKUs we would like the user to purchase via Google Play. We can get the price, title, and full description, which can be, for example, shown to the user before making the purchase. This can be done by just calling the getSkuDetails method:

```
private void getSkuDetails(ArrayList<String> skuList) {
    Bundle querySkus = new Bundle();
    querySkus.putStringArrayList("ITEM_ID_LIST", skuList);

    try {
        Bundle skuDetails = billingService.getSkuDetails(BILLING_VERSION, getPackageName(),
                IAP_TYPE, querySkus);

        int response = getResponseCodeFromBundle(skuDetails);
        if (response == BILLING_RESPONSE_RESULT_OK) {
            ArrayList<String> responseList = skuDetails.getStringArrayList(DETAILS_LIST);
            if(responseList == null) {
                Log.e(TAG, "Empty response getting SKU details");
                return;
            }

            for(String responseStr : responseList) {
                Log.i(TAG, responseStr);
            }
        } else {
            Log.e(TAG, getResponseDesc(response));
        }
    } catch (RemoteException e) {
        Log.e(TAG, "Exception getting SKU details", e);
    }
}
```

Each string will contain JSON-formatted data about one single SKU. If, for example, we query for two SKUs, prod_1 and prod_2, the format will be similar to what is illustrated in the following JSON example. Note that each product will be in a different string; it will not be a single JSON object:

```
{
    "productId":"prod_1",
    "type":"inapp",
    "price":"€1.19",
    "price_amount_micros":1190000,
    "price_currency_code":"EUR",
    "title":"Product 1 (Application Name)",
    "description":"prod1"
}
{
    "productId":"prod_2",
    "type":"inapp",
```

```
"price":"€2.39",
"price_amount_micros":2390000,
"price_currency_code":"EUR",
"title":"Product 2 (Application Name)",
"description":"Prod 2"
}
```

We also used another method from the previous Google example repository on GitHub. The `getResponseDesc` method prints a human-readable string of the error code.

Now that we have all the details from the SKUs and we know which items the user already owns, we can proceed to purchase one product.

 More information on the in-app product purchase flow is available at `https://developer.android.com/google/play/billing/api.html`.

Purchasing in-app products from our application

Purchasing an in-app product is a two-step process. First, we need to get a buy `Intent` and then we can start the purchase flow with that intent:

```java
private void purchaseProduct(String sku, String purchaseType, String payload) {
    try {
        Bundle buyIntentBundle = billingService.getBuyIntent(BILLING_VERSION, getPackageName(),
                sku, purchaseType, payload);

        int responseCode = getResponseCodeFromBundle(buyIntentBundle);
        if(responseCode != BILLING_RESPONSE_RESULT_OK) {
            Log.e(TAG, "Error " + getResponseDesc(responseCode) + " getting buy intent");
            return;
        }

        PendingIntent pendingIntent = buyIntentBundle.getParcelable(BUY_INTENT);
        if (pendingIntent != null) {
            startIntentSenderForResult(pendingIntent.getIntentSender(),
                    PURCHASE_REQUEST_CODE, new Intent(), 0, 0, 0);
        } else {
            Log.e(TAG, "No pending intent from getBuyIntent");
        }

    } catch (RemoteException | IntentSender.SendIntentException e) {
        Log.e(TAG, "Error purchasing " + sku, e);
    }
}
```

We can get `buyIntent` by calling the `getBuyIntent` method and using these as parameters: the SKU we would like to purchase, the type of purchase (either `inapp` or `subs`), and a developer payload we would like to put. As the developer payload, we can put, for example, a randomly generated string that uniquely identifies this purchase. If the request succeeds, it will return `PendingIntent`. We can use it to start the purchase flow by calling `startIntentSenderForResult`.

We will receive the response asynchronously in activity `onActivityResult`, so we have to check that the request code is the same we used when doing the request, `PURCHASE_REQUEST_CODE` in our specific case:

```java
@Override
protected void onActivityResult(int requestCode, int resultCode, Intent data) {
    if (requestCode == PURCHASE_REQUEST_CODE) {
        int responseCode = data.getIntExtra(RESPONSE_CODE, BILLING_RESPONSE_RESULT_OK);
        String purchaseData = data.getStringExtra("INAPP_PURCHASE_DATA");
        String dataSignature = data.getStringExtra("INAPP_DATA_SIGNATURE");

        if (resultCode == RESULT_OK) {
            if(responseCode == BILLING_RESPONSE_RESULT_OK) {
                try {
                    JSONObject jo = new JSONObject(purchaseData);
                    String sku = jo.getString("productId");
                    Log.i(TAG, sku + " purchased!");
                } catch (JSONException e) {
                    Log.e(TAG, "Failed to parse purchase data.", e);
                }
            } else {
                Log.e(TAG, "Billing error on purchase " + getResponseDesc(responseCode));
            }
        } else if(resultCode == RESULT_CANCELED) {
            Log.w(TAG, "Purchase cancelled");
        } else {
            Log.e(TAG, "Unknown result code " + resultCode);
        }
    } else {
        Log.e(TAG, "Uknown requestCode " + requestCode);
    }
}
```

More information about `startIntentSenderForResult` is available at https://developer.android.com/reference/android/app/Activity.html#startIntentSenderForResult(android.content.IntentSender,int,android.content.Intent,int,int,int).

Consuming purchases

Some in-app products can be purchased once and others can be purchased multiple times. In order to purchase one product more than one time, we need to consume the previous purchase or Google Play will not allow us to purchase it again.

In the JSON data we will receive either when purchasing an item or getting previous purchases, we will get a purchase token as well. We can use this purchase token in the `consumePurchase` method to actually consume a purchase:

```java
private void consumePurchase(String purchaseToken) {
    int response = -1;
    try {
        response = billingService.consumePurchase(BILLING_VERSION, getPackageName(), purchaseToken);
    } catch(RemoteException e) {
        Log.e(TAG, "Exception consuming purchase", e);
        return;
    }

    if(response != BILLING_RESPONSE_RESULT_OK) {
        Log.e(TAG, "Error consuming purchase " + getResponseDesc(response));
    }
}
```

It is recommended that we do not take any action inside the application, for instance increase in-app currency, until the purchase has been consumed successfully.

 More generic information about in-app purchases and how to integrate them in your application is available at https://developer.android.com/google/play/billing/billing_inte grate.html.

In-app advertising

We have seen how to directly monetize our application by either setting a price, making it a paid application, or by adding in-app purchases to unlock new features, remove advertisements, or add some benefits in exchange for a microtransaction. Now we will see how to add a more indirect monetizing mechanism, such as adding advertisements. By adding advertisements to our application, we will not charge our end user, but we will get money by the amount of advertisements shown and clicked by the users of our application.

If we are able to generate a lot of advertisement impressions or make our advertisements non-intrusive and useful to the targeted users, it can be a good way to earn some money, even more than by paid apps or in-app purchases.

In this section, we will see how to add advertisements to our app. We will focus on Google Admob although there are many other advertisement providers. At the end of the day, the approach will be quite similar, and most probably, we will have to integrate with their SDK and follow some simple steps.

Integrating with the Google Mobile Ads SDK

Integrating the Google Mobile Ads SDK into our application is quite straightforward. We have to follow a few steps and a test advertisement will show up in no time.

We have to add a new Gradle dependency to `build.gradle` at the root of our project:

```
classpath 'com.google.gms:google-services:3.0.0'
```

Add one dependency to the `build.gradle` file inside the `app` directory:

```
compile 'com.google.firebase:firebase-ads:9.0.2'
```

And add one at the end of the same file:

```
apply plugin: 'com.google.gms.google-services'
```

After adding all these lines to the `build.gradle` files, we have to synchronize so that Gradle can refresh all the libraries and include the dependencies we have just added.

We would need an Ad Unit ID identifier for each place we would like to show an advertisement. Later, we will show how to create one, but for the moment, we will use the one provided by Firebase for testing purposes:
`ca-app-pub-3940256099942544/6300978111`.

To easily access it, we will create it inside the `Strings.xml` file of our application:

```xml
strings.xml ×

<resources>
    <string name="app_name">CalculatorTestExample</string>
    <string name="not_a_number">NaN</string>
    <string name="invalid_username">Invalid username</string>
    <string name="invalid_password">Invalid password</string>
    <string name="incorrect_credentials">Incorrect username/password</string>

    <string name="banner_ad_unit_id">ca-app-pub-3940256099942544/6300978111</string>
</resources>
```

We will need a `google-services.json` file as well. We can create it from the Firebase developer console; refer to `https://console.firebase.google.com/`.

From the Firebase console, we have to create an Android application; set our application package and this will trigger the download of the `google-services.json` file:

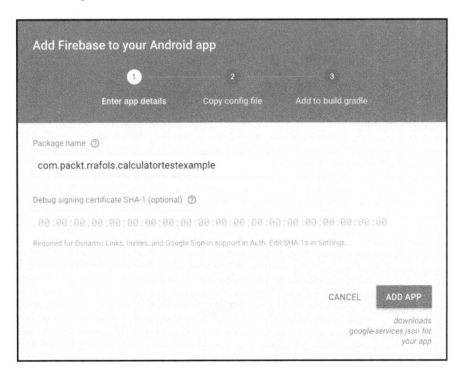

Once we have the file, we have to simply copy it to the `app` folder of our application:

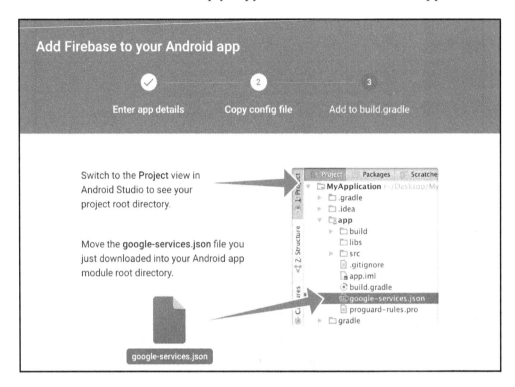

Now we can proceed to add one advertisement to our layout file. We would need to add a new namespace to the layout XML, namely
`xmlns:ads="http://schemas.android.com/apk/res-auto"`, and then add
a `com.google.android.gms.ads.AdView` view as if it was another view:

```
<com.google.android.gms.ads.AdView
    android:id="@+id/adView"
    android:layout_width="wrap_content"
    android:layout_height="wrap_content"
    android:layout_centerHorizontal="true"
    android:layout_alignParentBottom="true"
    ads:adSize="BANNER"
    ads:adUnitId="@string/banner_ad_unit_id">
</com.google.android.gms.ads.AdView>
```

In our main `Activity` field, we will have to initialize the SDK on the `onCreate` method by calling `MobileAds.initialize` and using our application ID. In this example, we used the test application ID, but in our final application, we'll change it to show real advertisements. During development, we have to use test advertisements as it is against the Admob policy to click on our own advertisements using our account.

In addition to this, in this demo, we will load an advertisement as soon as the application starts and show it on the `AdView` we have just added in the previous step:

```
MobileAds.initialize(getApplicationContext(), "ca-app-pub-3940256099942544~3347511713");

AdView mAdView = (AdView) findViewById(R.id.adView);
if(mAdView != null) {
    AdRequest adRequest = new AdRequest.Builder().build();
    mAdView.loadAd(adRequest);
}
```

There are many other ways to show advertisements, for example interstitial, fullscreen ads, or native advertisements that allow some degree of configuration and can be more easily integrated into our application and feel less intrusive.

 More information about different types of advertisements can be found at `https://firebase.google.com/docs/admob/android/native` and `https://firebase.google.com/docs/admob/android/interstitial`.

We can create a valid application ID and Ad Unit ID from our Admob account (`https://ap ps.admob.com`):

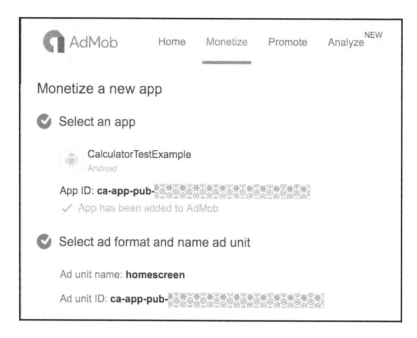

Here, we can see the **App ID** and the **Ad Unit ID**. We just need to replace the test values with the real ones to start monetizing our application. Please remember that it goes against the Admob policy to click on your own advertisements, so it is recommended that you use a test account for development and testing and the real production IDs when publishing the application to Google Play.

Google published a step-by-step tutorial inside their Firebase documentation, available at `h ttps://firebase.google.com/docs/admob/android/quick-start`.

Summary

In this chapter, we learned different mechanisms to monetize our application, from setting a price to downloading it, adding in-app purchases, or using advertisements. Depending on the application type, the targeted users, and the business model we would like to use, we can decide how to use all the different mechanisms to make the app. Sometimes, the best approach is to combine them in a smart way; just be careful not to saturate the user with advertisements or make the game too difficult, or just impossible, unless some purchases are made.

Combining monetizing mechanisms with good analytics will allow us to clearly see what is working and what is not so that we can focus our efforts on fixing or changing that part.

In this book, we started by installing the development environment and went all the way to publishing and monetizing our application. Through this journey, you have learned to create application screens, views, and UI elements. You also learned how to retrieve data from the Internet and store it locally on the device. And finally, you learned how to create some automated tests to make sure the application is working or, at least, verify that the latest changes did not break anything.

The development of mobile applications in Android is in constant evolution. There are many ways in which we can keep up-to-date with it: check official documentation regularly, read development blogs, and even test new libraries and study their source code. One of the most interesting ways, however, is to attend conferences or local meetups. In these events, there is always a lot of interesting content and, even more important, a lot of interesting people. You can meet other Android developers with whom you can discuss difficulties, solutions, and best of all, build the Android community.

Index

www.ingramcontent.com/pod-product-compliance
Lightning Source LLC
Chambersburg PA
CBHW062106050326

40690CB00016B/3218